THURSDAY NIGHT
AT THE MALL

OTHER BOOKS BY THE AUTHOR

Amado Muro and Me: A Tale of Honesty and Deception

THURSDAY NIGHT AT THE MALL

MOVIES, BOOKS, MUSIC, & ASPERGER'S SYNDROME

ROBERT L. SELTZER

TCU Press

FORT WORTH, TEXAS

Library of Congress Cataloging-in-Publication Data

Names: Seltzer, Robert, author.
Title: Thursday night at the mall : movies, books, music, and Asperger's syndrome /
    Robert L. Seltzer.
Description: Fort Worth, Texas : TCU Press, [2022] | Summary: "Author
    Robert L. Seltzer's second memoir examines a complicated father-son relationship
    as Seltzer learns how to be a father to a son with Asperger's. The text presents two
    different timelines: the first captures a year in the life of father Robert and adult son
    Chris as they navigate their relationship and find ways to connect through movies,
    books, and music; the second timeline follows father and son from Chris's birth
    through the trial of diagnosis until the timelines meet up in the present day. Seltzer
    describes himself as "a man fleeing his demons" and his son as "a boy still wrestling
    his." This beautifully written memoir is a raw and honest look at a struggle many
    families will relate to."—Provided by publisher.
Identifiers: LCCN 2022028759 (print) | LCCN 2022028760 (ebook) | ISBN
    9780875658247 (paperback) | ISBN 9780875658285 (ebook)
Subjects: LCSH: Seltzer, Robert--Family. | Fathers of children with disabilities—
    United States—Biography. | Asperger's syndrome—United States—Biography. |
    Fathers and sons—United State—Biography. | Parent and adult child—United
    States—Biography. | BISAC: BIOGRAPHY & AUTOBIOGRAPHY / Personal
    Memoirs | FAMILY & RELATIONSHIPS / Parenting / General | LCGFT:
    Autobiographies.
Classification: LCC HQ773.8 .S45 2022 (print) | LCC HQ773.8 (ebook) |
    DDC 181/.119—dc24/eng/20220724
LC record available at https://lccn.loc.gov/2022028759
LC ebook record available at https://lccn.loc.gov/2022028760

TCU Box 298300
Fort Worth, Texas 76129
To order books: 1.800.826.8911

Design by Preston Thomas

"Life

must

be

lived

forwards

but

can

only

be

understood

backwards."

—KIERKEGAARD

A NOTE ON THE TEXT

Memory is a trickster, and when mine was not as acute as it should have been, I remained deliberately vague about time lines. I did this in service of the facts, not in an effort to blur them. I also used different names to protect the identities of various figures in the story. These decisions, executed sparingly, did not alter the essential truth of the story.

INTRODUCTION
The Search for Identity

A RESTLESS SPIRIT, my father was one of those rare individuals who could wander while sitting still.

The old man was always searching, always exploring. One of the things he yearned to find was his identity. He discovered it when he met my mother, Amada Muro, whose family fled Chihuahua during the Mexican Revolution in 1916.

Meeting each other in El Paso, they got married in 1950, and soon afterwards my father, a short story writer, adapted her maiden name as his pseudonym. An Anglo born in Cleveland, Ohio, Chester Seltzer bypassed immigration authorities to become a Mexican, if only in his heart. He became Amado Muro.

My son, Chris, is like the grandfather he never knew. A restless spirit, he, too, is always searching, always exploring. His search is more problematic, however, and I wonder if he will ever enjoy the success his grandfather did.

In his brilliant work *The Labyrinth of Solitude*, Octavio Paz offers an insight which, for those who think writers have all the answers, may seem startling. "There is no meaning," he states. "There is search for meaning."

I agree—who am I to disagree with Octavio Paz?—but I would amend the statement, if only slightly. The search *is* the meaning, for it is in the journey, the quest—whether it is to become a better society or a better person—that we realize ourselves. Yet that odyssey, as Paz demonstrated, is often more difficult for minorities because of the confusing labels society imposes upon us. We may not know who we are, much less who we want to be.

In her lovely short story "Eleven," Sandra Cisneros depicts this lurch toward self-identity. She describes a girl whose birthday is ruined by an experience which, for the reader, is both heartbreaking and infuriating. The girl sits at her desk, focusing on her studies, when another child discovers a sweater one of the other youngsters must have lost. It is an old, raggedy sweater, a glorified dust cloth, and the teacher assumes it belongs to the eleven-year-old. Why, it *must* belong to her. After all, she is a Latina, and only a Latina would wear such a dreary garment. The teacher never says that, not in those words, but her message is clear: The eleven-year-old is not worthy of wearing anything but a rag.

The girl insists the sweater does not belong to her; the teacher insists it does. Guess who wins? The child finally accepts a sweater she does not want. So, while the teacher has given her something, she has also taken something away—her pride.

In this display of authority, we see a subtle form of racism, subtle because the teacher never calls the student a "wetback" or a "greaser" or a "beaner." She does not have to, because the bigotry is no less pernicious for being subtle. By forcing her to accept the garment, the teacher is imposing an identity on her. *You are not who you think you are*, the teacher is saying. *You are who I think you are.* You are someone who wears a ratty old sweater, someone who is not fit to wear anything finer. Happy Birthday.

In "The Last Time I Saw Junior," the tough, gritty short story by Dagoberto Gilb, we see a kind of bias that is even more insidious because it comes from within. In the story, the narrator helps a buddy who is threatened by a thug. The narrator intimidates the intimidator, and his buddy marvels at his courage.

"You were great!" he tells the narrator. "You were one scary Mexican."

And he *was*. He *was* one scary Mexican. And he feels terrible about it; he feels terrible about it, because it means he has lived up to the stereotype. Or *down* to the stereotype. He has confirmed the image.

It is the same in the classic memoir *Down These Mean Streets* by Piri Thomas. The young Piri wonders why he had to be born Puerto Rican, why he had to have dark skin and "thick, spiky" hair. And he wonders why people have to stare at him, burning holes into his soul, whenever he ventures from Spanish Harlem.

"I don't care what you say, Piri," Jose, his brother, tells him. "We're Puerto Ricans, and that makes us different from Black people."

"Jose, that's what the man's been telling the Negro all along, that 'cause he's white he's different from the Negro, that he's better'n the Negro or anyone that's not white."

In "Guero," an insightful short story by my friend Rafael Castillo, one of the characters tries to deny his heritage. A friend spots him at a mall, but Guero, who is light-skinned and green-eyed, pretends not to see him, afraid he will be "outed" as a Latino. The ploy is both astonishing and understandable. Anticipating the scorn of the majority, Guero leads a false life, his light skin providing him shelter. He becomes a faux Anglo.

In all these books or stories, the marginalized seek acceptance. And yet, as Paz stated, there is no meaning; there is only *search* for meaning. The journey toward acceptance is so powerful—in some cases, so all-consuming, that minorities—Latinos, African Americans, Native Americans, Asian Americans—sometimes see scorn as acceptance. For when the larger group derides you, it often provides you with cachet in the smaller group.

We saw this dynamic play out with the "pachucos" in post-World War II Los Angeles. With their zoot suits and slicked-back hair, the pachucos invited condemnation from polite society, but the condemnation felt like praise to these young Mexican Americans, for it gave them an identity, something they could be proud of.

In the case of my father, the search for identity took a twist. Chester Seltzer was an Anglo scorned by other Anglos. He loved Mexico, and he took solace in joining another group of marginalized people, Mexicans and Mexican Americans. They were outsiders, as he was, but by becoming "one of them," the outsider became an insider.

My father wrote short stories, and when he married my mother in 1950, he adapted her maiden name as his pen name—Amado Muro. But when he changed his name, he also changed the subjects of his stories, writing about Mexicans and Mexican Americans throughout the Southwest, including my hometown of El Paso. The stories were lyrical and passionate, and the man who wrote them, you would swear, was as Mexican as *pulque* or *champurrado*.

My beloved grandmother, the original Amada Muro, always said that my father was born an American—she used the politically incorrect term "gringo"—but would die a Mexican. And when he *did* die, in 1971, his ruse died with him. Literary critics discovered he was not a Mexican at all, but an American, born and reared in Cleveland, Ohio, the son of a powerful journalist. Whether he died an American or a Mexican, as my grandmother said he would, my father found his true identity when he changed his name to Amado Muro. Cultural appropriation? Perhaps. But I prefer to call it cultural *appreciation*. Chester Seltzer became who he wanted to be. He wanted to be Amado Muro.

Will my son, Christopher, become who *he* wants to be? Will he become the latest iteration of Chester Seltzer/Amado Muro in the Seltzer family? Not that he will reinvent himself, create a pseudonym, and become another individual. I do not mean that. But he feels just as marginalized as his grandfather did, and I wonder if he will ever find himself. This book explores his journey. Our journey.

CHAPTER 1

It's a Wonderful Life

DECEMBER 10, 2015

A MISSILE WITH feathers, the bird swooped into the mall through an automatic door, turning the food court into a giant birdcage.

It must have been a common occurrence. The other mall denizens —the *human* mall denizens—ignored the bird, despite the threat of airborne condiments plopping onto their hamburgers, cheesesteaks, and falafels. If the diners, about twenty of them, were unperturbed, so was I. Then, again, I was not dining. I was waiting.

It was 4:00 p.m. Five minutes passed. Ten. Fifteen. Still no Chris. Numbed by boredom, I returned to my car in the parking lot, retrieving the latest book I was reading, *The Mare* by Mary Gaitskill, a tough but poignant novel about a Dominican Republic girl exploring a new world in upstate New York. The book was better company than the random thoughts that invaded my mind as I sat in the food court, loitering under the feathered dive-bomber.

I read for pleasure, but more than that, I read for therapy. When I grew weary of my world, I sought refuge in another world, a world which, while sometimes sadder and harsher, had one advantage over mine. It was *different*. But that year, the more I read, the more I saw Chris in each character and plot. He dominated my thoughts so much that I linked every book to him, whether it was a noir, a tragedy, or a dark comedy. I saw him, for example, in the Dominican Republic girl of *Mare*. Chris was troubled, and he lived in a world as alien to him as upstate New York was to the girl in the novel.

The irony was inescapable: the books forcing me to confront the reality I had sought to flee. It was a strange dynamic, one that meant reading was no longer an escape for me. But I kept reading, escape or no escape, and Chris kept reappearing in page after page. And so, far from liberating me, transporting me to another world, the books rooted me to my own reality.

Sometimes, it seemed as if I picked the books *because* of their connection to Chris. But, no, I picked them for other reasons, based on reviews, articles, or my own whims. The connections with Chris were coincidental. Still . . . those connections were real.

Asperger's syndrome. Chris was thirty before I even heard the term. He was thirty-three now, but in some ways, he remained a child, brilliant but immature, unable to cope with the harsh realities of life. "It sucks being an adult," he often complained. It sucked because people expected him to act his age, handling the responsibilities that increase with each birthday. But his chronological age did not match his emotional age, and so, as his body grew, his psyche remained stagnant. The thirty-three-year-old sometimes acted like a thirteen-year-old, easily hurt and embittered. A perpetual adolescent, he was distant and confused. It was no consolation that he was so bright and articulate, able to expound on subjects ranging from opera to mythology to comic books. The knowledge masked the adolescent inside.

If he was a child at thirty-three, it represented a reversal of what he experienced as a *real* youngster, when he displayed interests in subjects, including literature, beyond his age group. He was a mature child, an immature adult. The contradiction seems baffling, but only in the context of our foggy perspective at the time.

Asperger's syndrome is part of the autism spectrum, but having never heard of the syndrome, we were ill equipped to deal with it. The condition might as well have been part of the rainbow spectrum. We were ignorant, clueless—soldiers without weapons. We had no cohesive plan to confront the condition because we did not recognize the condition we were confronting. All we knew was that Chris was . . . different. (Years later, we would discover that Asperger's syndrome was no longer considered a separate condition; it was merely part of the spectrum, but we did not know that back then, and it remained, whether or not it was recognized by the scientific community, a major force in our lives.)

We felt helpless, Antonia and I. But my wife was less frustrated and, thus, less gloomy. She saw a brighter future for Chris, her empathy and sensitivity overpowering her dread and negativity. *Chris will be all right*, she would say. *Chris will be all right.* That was her mantra, and it was not mindless optimism; it was remarkable fortitude, the unshakable belief that, with love and compassion, she could *make* it all right.

I was different. Reality assaulted my faith, my confidence. I failed to see the bright future Antonia saw; I tried, but my crystal ball clouded with a future filled with defeat and agony. Was I overreacting? Probably. I tried to be optimistic, but a fear gnawed at me, a fear that nothing would change, that the future was just the present with more aches, wrinkles, and gray hair. . . . It was hard to look at this cute little boy without seeing a life he did not deserve, a life of hardship and loneliness.

The older he got, the more concerned we became. He would find friends with common interests—opera, mythology, comic books—and, well, opera, mythology, and comic books. But friendships demand broader connections, broader footholds, and Chris could not find them. They were flimsy linchpins, these three obsessions, and as soon as the topics were exhausted, so were the relationships. He became a loner, engulfed by his quirks and eccentricities.

It was hard to connect with Chris, hard to talk to him. If you made a comment that failed to resonate with him, he would stay quiet, staring straight ahead. And if you asked him how he was doing, he might answer "fine," and leave it at that; if you wanted him to ask how *you* were doing, you might be waiting 'til you got your first Social Security check.

I covered sports for eleven years at the *Philadelphia Inquirer*, and when colleagues took their kids to the games, they reacted with the joy and excitement usually reserved for Christmas—screw the calendar. Not Chris. I took him to a fight in Atlantic City one Saturday afternoon, and he was miserable throughout the card, fidgeting until the final bell sounded. We would have left early if I had not had to cover the match. So much for Christmas on demand.

We had three loves in common—books, music, and films—and that year, in that crummy mall, those three interests gave us hope. Gave *me* hope. We could discuss all three subjects for hours, one thought leapfrogging to another, the kind of spontaneous joy that should animate all conversations. The talks were so engaging, so delightful, that whenever the discussions shifted to topics that triggered his verbosity—yes, opera, mythology, and comic books—I did not mind.

I always regarded myself as shallow (I am sure many of my friends would concur). Which is why, I think, I never—or rarely—suffered from depression, at least not for prolonged periods. I could be pessimistic, but never to the point where it debilitated me, leaving me unable to plow ahead. I could go hours, even days, without a single substantial thought invading my head. . . . Then I would pick up a book, and the words would trigger a chain reaction, one thought leading to another and another. I welcomed this phenomenon, but it was nothing dramatic; I just went from shallow to not *as* shallow.

Chris was different. He was always thinking, his ruminations often dark and negative. He would dwell on slights he had suffered, hurts he had endured decades before, his past coloring his present—and future. He saw no relief from the pain he had experienced as a child. The result was inevitable: Chris was dark and morose—not always, but often enough to brand him, in the eyes of his family, as a kind of misanthrope.

Still, we had those common interests—books, movies, and music —and the connection was encouraging. We always had those connections, but they never spanned the gulf between us. What changed? Maybe we experienced an epiphany, as inexplicable as it was welcome. Maybe time had cleansed us, removing the toxins from our dysfunctional relationship. Maybe we grew.

Whatever the cause, the breakthrough was long overdue, thirty-three years in the making. I could have pounded my head over the lost time, but like Antonia, I started to focus on the positive. The connection was always there, buried in the complexity of our relationship, but we failed, out of stubbornness, lethargy, or confusion, to unearth it. It may sound crazy, but for perhaps the first time in thirty-three years, I felt like a dad, not a detached observer trying to figure out a lonely little boy. Maybe we were both lonely, all along, and maybe we needed each other. Maybe we *found* each other.

Regardless of the dynamic involved, we rediscovered each other that year. The mall gave us a forum to explore our wants and needs, our likes and dislikes, something we had never done before, not in this manner, anyway, with an easy, almost carefree determination. We became friends again. No, not *again*. We became friends, period, as if we were meeting each other for the first time, focusing on the positive instead of the negative. The best part of a friendship is the beginning, the forging of a bond, the exploration of a character and personality you did not know before. I did not know Chris, not really. Was I starting to?

If I was optimistic, it was a cautious optimism, tempered by the history of stops and starts in our relationship. Who knew where this "breakthrough" would lead? Who knew if the turbulence of the past would lead to the serenity of the future? Hopeful but realistic, I continued to experience rough patches, even in these good times, sparked by the frustration and agony of dealing with a human being who lived in his own dark world. But the positive moments were outweighing the negative. Who would have thought?

As a kid, I preferred sunsets to sunrises. They seemed, despite the looming darkness, warmer and brighter—an irony I could not explain. Maybe it was because, as the shadows lengthened, the western horizon exploded with a spectacular array of colors—reds and oranges and purples—and I focused on the fading light, not the emerging darkness. As the sun dipped, draining the sky of light, I would keep staring, fascinated by the phenomenon, as if nothing could extinguish the streams of color in the heavens. It was like watching the fading embers of a campfire. They would die eventually, I knew, but they were more interesting, more substantial, than the darkness around them, and so I kept watching. . . . And then one day, in my middle years, I think, I started to view sunsets differently. It was a gradual change, but I was beginning to see the darkness they presaged, not the light they ignited. Maybe the change in attitude reflected my own darkness. . . . Maybe . . . But that year, slowly but inexorably, I resurrected a piece of my youth, and I began to see what I had seen as a child—sunsets as a heralding, not a farewell.

I was uncertain of what the future might hold. What I *did* know—and what I am sure Chris knew as well—was that something had changed, something vague but real. It started that evening in the mall. We did not realize it at the time, but that evening would launch a series of similar evenings, moments when we talked to each other with a simple grace. There were none of the defensive postures, the guarded attitudes, which had darkened most of our discussions in the past. We were open and spontaneous. It was refreshing, and it happened in the unlikeliest of places. A mall, a crummy mall.

Except for the bird, the food court was dull and sterile, but it offered something the office never could—sanctuary. I was the public editor at the *San Antonio Express-News*. Public editor, a title that was loftier than the job it described. I dealt with readers, via phone and email, eight hours a day. Readers who, in the days before the Trump White House, were already storming the gates of civility that kept the barbarians at bay. A gross exaggeration? Yes, but the hostility that would bubble to the surface during the Trump campaign, like the tar at the pits in La Brea, was beginning to ooze across America.

People exploit the barriers provided by phone and email. There is no face-to-face contact, so they abandon the courtesy proximity demands. The readers were no different; they did not hold back. Compounding the agony was the fact that I had arrived at the newspaper, ten years earlier, as the associate editorial page editor, a position that offered me more distance from the readers; now, I was the public editor, and that distance evaporated.

I found that out in 2013. The San Antonio City Council was considering an antidiscrimination ordinance, aimed mainly at mis-treatment of the LGBT community. We endorsed it on our Editorial Page, and many of our readers were incensed.

"Do you think this ordinance is a good thing?" one reader asked me.

"Yes."

"Then you must be queer."

"I know you mean that as an insult," I told the reader. "But I don't take it as an insult because I see nothing wrong with being gay."

"Fucking fag," he said, hanging up.

I had a colonoscopy that year, and the anesthesiologist asked me what I did for a living. I told her. She smiled, exclaiming that it sounded like a great job.

"It's not," I said. "I'd rather be here."

So, yes, the food court was a haven. Returning from my car, book in hand, I noticed the bird was gone, exiting, perhaps, through the same automatic door that had served as its entrance. Or maybe it was gliding through other sections of the mall? I shrugged, sitting at an empty table. Still no Chris. No matter. I had my book. The words, gritty but lyrical, captivated me, taking me to a world far beyond the food court. I read two pages, and then . . .

"Hi, Dad."

"Hey, Chris, how are you?"

Chris groaned—a deep, guttural noise that reminded me of "Young Frankenstein," the comical monster in the Mel Brooks movie of the same name. It triggered a series of sounds conveying anger and disgust—ugh, grrr, argh. Chris was delivering an impromptu seminar on on·o·mat·o·poe·ia.

"Well, I was fine until I was taking a shower, and then the water got cut off," he said, frowning. "They didn't give us any notice at the apartment. . . . They never do."

Chris had walked from the apartment to the mall, about a fifteen-minute stroll, and the anger he felt at the start of the walk was still there at the end of the walk, seething in his breast. My heart sank. It was not often, but whenever Chris got mad, his wrath could turn a nursery school into a gloomy dungeon. A wild exaggeration? Yes. But there were times when I would have picked the dungeon over the pall he cast on his immediate surroundings.

"That's why I'm late—the damned water problem," he continued. "Sorry."

"That's OK . . . I had my book."

I asked him if he wanted to grab a bite, and he said "sure," but he kept frowning, his face clenched like a fist. I bought him a falafel, and I got a cheesesteak, and we met back at the table where I had been waiting for him earlier. He was still frowning and, for a moment, just a moment, I thought about moving to another table. . . . Then he took a bite of the falafel, and he smiled, and I felt small for wanting to abandon him.

"Sorry, Dad," he said. "I just hate it when they pull things like that at the apartment."

"No problem," I said.

Finishing our meals, we strolled to the line forming in front of The Bijou Theater, which was showing *It's a Wonderful Life* as part of a "free movie night" promotion at the Wonderland of the Americas Mall in San Antonio. It was first-come, first-serve, with a supply of two hundred tickets available. We waited for an hour, the line growing behind us, until an usher waved us forward for our free passes.

Like shoppers on Black Friday, we rushed toward the lobby. There was one more hour to go, this time inside the theater, before the movie started—the price you pay for free tickets to a wonderful life. We welcomed the respite—me from a long day at the *San Antonio Express-News*, Chris from a longer day at Jack in the Box.

"Hey, Dad," Chris had called me about two evenings before, "I saw a poster for *It's a Wonderful Life* at The Bijou. I know how much you've always loved that movie. . . . And it's free. Wanna go?"

I said "sure," so there we were, waiting for the movie to start. The sponsors staged a trivia contest to ease the boredom before the film started, and I whispered to Chris, "I know . . . I just *know* I am going to win."

"What is the name of the town in *It's a Wonderful Life?*" a young woman asked.

My hand shot up, but refusing to take any chances, I dispensed with civility.

"Bedford Falls!" I blurted out before anyone else could challenge me.

"Yesssss," the woman replied, walking toward me with a free DVD of the movie—a special, remastered edition.

"Way to go Dad," Chris said, beaming. "That's cool."

Then the movie started, and we were captivated in a way that contemporary movies could never captivate us. This was not a slice of life; this was a giant helping of it, with all the joy and heartbreak the world throws your way. All the characters, no matter how "minor," were real, leaping from the script to the screen as though they were part of a creative birthing process. And towering above them all was George Bailey, the head of the "Bailey Building & Loan," a man whose decency almost proved his undoing. It was stunning. I appreciated the prize, but I knew the DVD could never approach the majesty of what we were watching on the big screen.

Two hours later, a bell tinkled on a Christmas tree, signaling that Clarence, the apprentice angel, had earned his wings. Chris and I walked out of the theater. We passed the food court. The bird had returned, hovering above the tables. We smiled.

"Well?" I said.

"I loved it, Dad. Thanks."

"Thank *you*."

We got in the car.

"You know, Chris, what I liked about the movie is that George has earned his burst of joy and optimism at the end," I said. "There's nothing Pollyannish about it. George deserves his happiness because of what he's gone through."

"It's not all sunshine," Chris said, agreeing. "There's so much darkness in the movie. George tries to kill himself, after all. . . . It's so dark that I don't even see it as a Christmas movie."

"That's right," I said. "Neither do I."

"And every character makes his point so forcefully—*without any cussing*," he said. "Of course, they couldn't very well cuss back then."

And then he called Mr. Potter, the malevolent banker, an "asshole" without any hint of irony. I started laughing. Chris laughed, too.

"Speaking of Mr. Potter, the movie's not polemical—at least not *overtly* polemical—but it *is* political," I said. "And it should resonate with us today, because of the issue of income equality."

"I agree," he said. "People just want a chance. And they deserve it."

We reached his apartment, and as Chris stepped out of the car, he repeated what he had told me as we walked out of the theater a few minutes earlier.

"Thanks, Dad."

He was so sincere, so sweet and innocent, that I almost sighed.

"You're very welcome."

It was our first "free movie night" together—a date that would seem pivotal only in retrospect. As I drove off, I wondered if Chris would ever be like that bird in the food court, flying freely within an enclosed space. Soaring above his limitations. Being happy.

CHAPTER 2
Unearthing the Past

WHEN I WAS a child, the calendar was my darkest enemy. Time stumbled, and I wanted it to gallop—gallop ever faster—toward my next birthday. Patience was not my strong suit.

"So how old are you now, Beto?" friends of the family would ask.

I never responded with a solid number—ten, eleven, or twelve. I always added a fraction. I was ten and a half, or eleven and two-thirds, or *almost* thirteen. I wanted to be more than I was—not just older but more substantial and, thus, more deserving of respect.

Now that I *am* older, I answer the same question with a solid number. Not sixty and a half. . . or sixty and two-thirds . . . or *almost* sixty-one. Just sixty, period. I want to be less than I am—at least in terms of years. But there is no denying the truth; my youth is gone. The past is not in the rearview mirror; it is buried under a mound of dirt, never to be unearthed, except through memories. Is this why older people seem to love children? Because they excavate the past for us, allowing us to glimpse our buried selves?

Chris never did that for me. Never transported me backwards. Poor Chris. He always seemed older than he was, more sober, more morose, than kids his own age. Oh, there were times when he could be carefree, eager to snatch fun out of the air. Snatch it and hug it, as if he wanted to hold onto it forever and ever. But those days were rare.

When we lived in Cherry Hill, New Jersey, he marveled at the bright colors of autumn. We all did—me, Chris, my wife, Antonia, Texas transplants all. I used to rake the leaves into big piles, spacing them a few feet apart in our backyard, as tall as bales of hay. Then I would toss Chris onto each pile, watching him land on the red, yellow, and orange cushions, the leaves crunching under his little body. He would grimace, bracing himself for each fall, and then he would giggle. It was 1990, and Chris was eight.

Those times stand out because they now seem, through the gauze of memory, few and far between. Much more representative of this skinny little boy was the winter morning I drove him to school, Angel of Mercy Elementary. He usually took the bus, but the bus was late because of icy roads that day, so I decided to drive him.

"Dad, what's the meaning of life?" he asked me during the short trip.

"What?!?" I responded, shocked by the question.

"What's the meaning of life?" he repeated.

I hesitated, unsure of what my response should be.

"Why do you ask?"

"Well, I read *The Strange Case of Dr. Jekyll and Mr. Hyde* by Robert Louis Stevenson last night . . ." he said, pausing.

"Wait a minute," I blurted out. "You read *Dr. Jekyll and Mr. Hyde* last night?"

"Yes," he answered simply.

I had thumbed through a paperback edition of the book the night before, leaving it on the coffee table in the living room. Chris must have picked it up and read it—all ninety-six pages of it. My first literary companions were Dick and Jane; his were Dr. Jekyll and Mr. Hyde. If there was a chasm between Chris and my younger self, there was an even deeper chasm between Chris and his peers. Chris was in the second grade.

Boy reads novel beyond his grade level; father is shocked that boy reads novel beyond his grade level. It was déjà vu all over again, as that great linguist Yogi Berra once said. I had experienced this incident before, through a story about another boy and another father. They lived in Cleveland, Ohio, the boy and his father. It was 1920. The father left a book on the coffee table one night, face down, bent open to the last page he had skimmed. He went to bed, and the next morning, the book was closed, face up, its cover staring at him—*The Adventures of Tom Sawyer*. The boy was sitting on the couch, and the father glared at him, ready to scold him for making him lose his place.

"Injun Joe was scary," the boy said.

"What?" the father asked.

"Injun Joe was scary," the boy repeated.

"You read the book . . . in one night?"

"Yes."

"But . . . but . . ."

The boy was my father. He was five, just three years younger than Chris was when he read *Dr. Jekyll and Mr. Hyde*. The literary legacy stared me in the face. Chris was the reincarnation of the grandfather he never knew—my old man.

As we crossed Route 70 to Angel of Mercy, Chris looked up at me, waiting for an answer. The meaning of life. What was it?

"Well," I stammered, trying to collect my thoughts.

There is a scene in *Billy Elliot*, a charming movie that would come out about twelve years later, in which the young dancer asks his older brother, "Do you ever think about death?" The older sibling answers, "Fuck off." I could not take the easy—and profane—route with Chris, so I said there *was* no meaning of life, not really. I said life was complicated, sometimes ugly, sometimes beautiful, and you had to accept both the beauty and the ugliness with dignity, and one way of doing that was by connecting with those around you—friends, relatives, strangers even, strangers who might someday become friends. You had to reach out to them, and let them reach out to *you*. And if you did that—if you connected with others—life, no matter how hard, could be a little easier, both for you and your loved ones . . . I stopped, afraid I was babbling, afraid my son would realize I was speaking on the fly, with no coherent philosophy to buttress my sentimental speech. . . . But, no, Chris smiled. . . . He seemed to understand.

I drove up to the school, grateful the ride was over. Chris got out, maneuvering his way through the boys and girls playing in the yard before the bell rang. He walked toward the red brick building, resting his back against the wall, alone. I knew he would stay there, alone in a crowd, till the bell rang—despite my ramblings about human connections. And, as I watched him standing there, the gratitude I felt upon approaching the school disappeared.

Decades later, we would find out what troubled Chris. He had Asperger's syndrome. It was not something that was immediately apparent, like epilepsy or blindness; the condition had to be *discovered*. And the mere fact that it was named after someone—Hans Asperger—indicates how inscrutable it is, how complicated and hard to diagnose. It is part of the autism spectrum, and those who have it, like Chris, know there is something . . . *different* . . . about them. But they do not know what, and that is the problem. Kids with the condition—and adults, too—are intelligent, often exceptional, but they are a tick off socially, and the awkwardness, for many, overshadows the brilliance. They do things that are not done in social settings; they belch, they yell, they laugh at inappropriate times. And because these are not hallmarks of most conditions or diseases, people stamp their own labels on those who exhibit the traits. They are weird, different, bizarre. That was Chris. Weird, different, bizarre. Not to us, but to others. . . . Well, sometimes to us, too . . . sadly. . . .

Once we discovered he had Asperger's, we no longer regarded him as any of those things. He was just Chris, different but whole. But it took us years—no, decades—to reach that stage. And, in the meantime, we struggled in the darkness. We were ignorant and confused, and when we heard an explanation, a diagnosis, we were not sure we heard what the experts were telling us. It was like hearing an echo . . . or an echo of an echo . . . uncertain of the original sound that *created* the echo.

CHAPTER 3

Star Wars: The Force Awakens

AFTER CLARENCE, THE kind but befuddled angel, earned his wings in *It's a Wonderful Life*, the young woman who had presented me with the DVD made an announcement: "Free movie night will be on hiatus for the next four weeks. We'll have to open up some of our screens, including our free movie night screen, for *Star Wars: The Force Awakens*. We're expecting a crush. See you in four weeks."

Star Wars was not on our moviegoing agenda. Chris, his integrity as solid as the Millennium Falcon, started boycotting Disney because it had instituted a massive layoff the year before. Not only did the company banish hundreds of workers, according to news reports; it replaced them with immigrants, here on H-1B visas, who would receive lower wages than their dismissed predecessors. Chris was incensed at the layoffs, and he refused to budge, even for *Star Wars*. Yes, he was just one person, but he had seen *The Mouse That Roared* as a child, and he figured that every

20

creature, no matter how tiny, has lungs. He would use his to shout, "Disney, go to hell!" So no *Star Wars* for Chris or, by extension, me.

After the four-week hiatus imposed by a higher galactic power, the next showing on free movie night would be *Monty Python and the Holy Grail*. Chris had seen it before through those primitive formats known as VHS tapes. And I had seen it during its first showing in 1975, not on a big screen but on a *huge* screen. I saw it with Antonia, then my girlfriend, at the Bronco Drive-In in the Lower Valley of El Paso, one of the last outdoor theaters in the area. We sat on the hood of my 1970 Dodge Coronet, and we almost slid off with every belly laugh the film inspired. Would Chris and I enjoy it as much the next time around?

CHAPTER 4

Monty Python and the Holy Grail

JANUARY 7, 2016

THE SUN WAS up there, beyond the skylights, bathing the food court in a dingy yellow glow. Another Thursday afternoon. The usual hum of mall activity. Mothers and fathers ate their dinners. Shoppers strolled past, staring at the mischievous kids. Children scuttled under tables. One child emerged from underneath a folding chair at the next table, a rope of snot hanging from his nose. He giggled.

It was 4:00 p.m. No bird. And no Chris. Anticipating his tardy arrival, I brought the current book I was reading, *Mystic River* by Dennis Lehane, a contemporary noir. *Mystic River* is a hard book that pulls no punches—Chandler meets Dostoevsky. It reminded me of the speech I gave Chris on our way to Angel of Mercy that long-ago morning, without the stammering anxiety that gripped my heart and throat. Lehane explores human connections, between husband

22

and wife, father and daughter, friend and friend. Those relationships are the foundations that keep us grounded, keep us from slipping into the abyss.

Relationships are slender, fragile things, however, often undermined by doubt and insecurity. And when connections are severed, the bedrock crumbles, and your stability crumbles with it. *Mystic River* is about connections—what happens when they form and what happens when they collapse. The book was tough going, brimming with a terrible beauty that propelled me from page to page.

Then, like a kid emerging from beneath one of the tables, Chris appeared out of nowhere. He was wearing a Bob Dylan-style cap— the Dutch boy he favored as a young man in New York—his curly brown hair poking under the bill. Chris sat down, keeping his cap on, as if the sunlight streaming from the skylights were fierce and unyielding. I closed my book.

"Hey, Dad."

"Hey, Chris. How are you?"

"Good," he said, pausing.

"Don't Stop Believin'" by Journey was blaring from a hidden loud speaker in the food court, as shrill as the kids shrieking underneath the tables.

"Hey, Dad, that song reminds me of that big fat book you gave me a while back, the one filled with comic strips," Chris said.

"Oh?"

"Yeah," he said. "There was this one comic that featured Lester Bangs . . ."

"Wait a minute," I said, interrupting Chris. "You mean Lester Bangs, the rock critic?"

"Yeah."

"What was he doing in a comic book?"

Christ glared at me, his eyes threatening to rip out of their sockets. They got bigger and bigger, hotter and hotter, as if his skull were a furnace and his eyes the grates. A few seconds passed—a brief eternity. It would have been intimidating if I did not know him, but I *did* know him, so I stared back, wondering how this food court standoff would end. Chris could contain his anger, but that was the problem; you could sense it bubbling inside him, and you wondered how long it would churn before exploding.

"Uh, because the author *wanted* him in the comic strip?" Chris said, framing the statement in the form of a question.

"You don't have to get mad," I said, my voice edged with the same kind of anger Chris had just flashed. "It was a simple question."

It *was* a simple question, perhaps unanswerable, but a question I had meant to be rhetorical. Lester Bangs? In a comic? What was Lester Bangs—the acerbic rock critic with a fierce devotion to *authentic* rock 'n' roll, whether the pounding rhythms of Little Richard or the heavenly melodies of The Beatles—doing in a comic strip?

"Well, you know I have trouble processing questions like that," Chris answered. "They don't make sense to me. Why would someone ask me a question I can't answer?"

I felt churlish and petty, just as I had during our first movie night together, when I thought about moving to another table to let him stew in his anger. Here I was, reading *Mystic River*, a novel about connections, and I could not connect with my own son. Chris was in a bunker, warring with himself, while I was at home, safe and smug, an ignorant civilian. And, like a civilian in wartime, I had no idea what he was experiencing on the battlefront. I could try, though, *dammit.* I could try to view life through the eyes of a young man who struggled to see a life without obstacles, real or imagined, darkening the landscape, making what is clear murky and what is murky clear.

"You're right," I said, raising both hands in surrender. "I'm sorry."

"Anyway, back to Lester Bangs," he said. "You remember how much he liked punk—genuine, hard-rocking punk. Well, he's watching this punk band in an Arizona bar. And, after the set, he talks to the band members, and they go out for a drive.

"They come across an outdoor concert arena where Journey happens to be playing. He hates their music. You remember—that pathetic, mewling sound."

Dramatizing his distaste for the music, Chris grimaced.

"As they drive through the parking lot, they see the tour bus. Lester Bangs gets an ice pick. I'm not sure what an ice pick was doing in the car. Anyway, he takes the ice pick, and he punctures every tire on the bus. Then he yells out, 'I HATE Journey!'"

Vandalism is an ugly crime—even in the service of rock 'n' roll. And slashing the tires was an atrocity. Then, again, Journey was an even greater atrocity—against the human ear. I laughed so hard I almost tipped my folding chair backwards.

"Thanks for sharing that story, Chris."

"Sure!"

I thought about apologizing, again, but I thought an apology might spoil the moment, so I let it pass. It was time to stand in line for our free passes. After the rough start to the evening, I looked forward to *Monty Python and the Holy Grail.* The opening credits rolled, with non sequitur after non sequitur. . . . And then this, an apology:

> We apologize for the fault in the subtitles. Those responsible have been sacked. . . . We apologize again for the fault in the subtitles. Those responsible for sacking the people who have just been sacked have been sacked. . . . The directors of the firm hired to continue the credits after the other people had been sacked, wish it to be known that they have just been sacked.

What happened between the opening credits and the closing credits, however, was lost within my slumbering cranial cavity. The film ended, and I woke up, shaking my head. I turned to Chris.

"Did I fall asleep?" I asked Chris.

"Yes."

"Did I snore"?

"A little bit. But I was too busy laughing to really hear anything except the dialogue."

"Damn. I must have been more tired than I thought. It was a rough day at the office."

Chris smiled as we headed out the theater.

"Well?" I said, a single word framed as a question, a question I would come to ask after every movie. "Did you like it?"

"I did," Chris said. "Thanks, Dad."

Maybe I was going crazy, but after I dropped Chris off at his apartment, I thought I heard a sound, a chuckle, followed by another and another. Then it hit me: The laughter must have resurfaced from the netherworld of my slumber during the movie. It was Chris laughing . . . Laughing at the Trojan Bunny. Laughing at the Knights who say Ni. Laughing at the Black Knight, reduced to a tin torso after his arms and legs are lopped off.

"Come back, you yellow bastard!" the Black Knight yells at King Arthur. "Come back here and take what's coming to you! I'll bite your legs off!"

I missed it in real time, missed the hilarity and laughter, but I heard it now, in my little Chevy Sonic, a sound as sweet and pure as a heartbeat. And then I heard another sound:

"Thanks, Dad."

CHAPTER 5

Diagnosis: Mentally Retarded

1987

CHRIS WAS DIFFERENT.

It was not just his shyness or his sensibility, both of which made him seem more adult than child. No, it went deeper than that. How much deeper, I was not sure. But one thing was certain: I had never met anyone like Chris, child *or* adult. He was so bright that, at eight, he would use the word "therefore" when he wanted to hammer a point into your frontal lobe.

There were other quirks. Chris loved to play Monopoly, and I bought him a set for Christmas one year, a special edition in which the board and the figures came in a tin box. He opened it on Christmas morning, and there it was, the imperfection—a dent in the box. He started crying, bereft and inconsolable. I took the set back to Toys "R" Us, hoping it was open on this special day. It was. I exchanged the set, thus rescuing Christmas for Chris and his family.

About three years before he read *The Strange Case of Dr. Jekyll and Mr. Hyde*, there were signs of trouble ahead, mostly in the form of his keen intelligence. We enrolled him in a private preschool, hoping the administrators could figure out what emotional malady, if any, plagued Chris. One of the instructors told us, after a few days, that he kept talking to himself in Spanish. Antonia told her he did not speak Spanish; they did not respond. They also said he kept brandishing a stick during recess. Antonia suspected a racist attitude among the administrators.

They invited us to the school one day, so we could witness his behavior ourselves. We viewed Chris through a large window that looked out onto the playground, filled with swings, slides, and merry-go-rounds. Chris, frolicking from play set to play set, settled on the merry-go-round. He started playing with a stick, and while he never struck any of the other kids, one of the teachers scolded him for it. We pulled him out because we never saw the behavior that seemed to trouble them so much.

Next, we enrolled Chris in pre-kindergarten at Billings Elementary in 1987. He was five. It was a crisp fall morning, the kind that fills you with a sense of hope. But hope is not always organic; sometimes, weather conditions are just weather conditions. Antonia felt the same foreboding I did. The bus arrived to pick up Chris, and we hugged him as the bus door opened for him. It would be his first day at the new school.

Antonia, acting on her misgivings, followed the bus to the school. The vehicle arrived, and the kids filed out, one by one. The bus kept disgorging the kids, who skipped to the school building, one after another. When the school bell rang, all the other kids got in line to enter the school, but not Chris. He remained outside, alone, at the back of the building. No one escorted him inside.

"I was so mad," she told me afterwards. "They just left him there."

A year passed. The teachers addressed the misgivings that had arisen long before. They noticed "something different" about him, a vague "something" that disturbed them. Billings administrators, concerned that Chris was not interacting with the teachers or kids at school, referred him to a series of psychiatrists. The conclusion was short and clinical and vague. But, vague or not, it was the first real diagnosis we had received, and we acted on it, albeit apprehensively.

They recommended the Malfred School, a school for "special needs" students. It was part of the Cherry Hill Independent School District. I could not help focusing on the first syllable—"mal," which means "bad" in both English and Spanish. I had no reason for my sense of foreboding. It was just . . . a feeling.

"Maybe this is what he needs," Antonia said uncertainly.

He was not alone; his condition was "unique," but all the youngsters had "something." We navigated through these "afflictions" timidly, even stupidly. But our feelings were no less distressing for our inability to discuss them cogently.

Chris said one of the kids would start screaming for no reason, bucking in his seat as if he were riding a wild mustang. The teachers would try to restrain him, usually without success. This was one condition we could identify. Epilepsy. It was heartbreaking, but the compassion for the other kids did not supersede the concern for our own. We worried that Chris would grow up viewing the world as dark and ominous—darker than it already was for him.

The administrators, concerned about his behavior, suggested Chris undergo a psychiatric evaluation. They wanted to mainstream Chris into grade school, but to get the help he needed, they said, he would need to be labeled "mentally retarded." We knew he needed help, but was this the proper course to follow? And, if we followed their recommendation, how would the label impact his future?

They did not say he *was* "mentally retarded"; they said that, to get help, he would have to be *labeled* "mentally retarded." I started viewing Chris differently. Maybe it was my imagination, but he seemed to withdraw into his body, hugging himself, his arms wrapped around his chest. Shoulders hunched, he receded into himself, becoming smaller and scrawnier with each question from the psychiatrist.

When the psychiatrist uttered the term "mentally retarded," I thought of two things—the condition and the stigma the condition triggers. Chris was "different," and his difference isolated him. He created his own world, a world in which *he* was "normal" and everyone else was "weird."

Chris entered this world through the portal of literature, literature that should have been beyond the grasp of a grade-schooler. Books like *The Strange Case of Dr. Jekyll and Mr. Hyde*. And the short stories of Edgar Allen Poe. The novels and stories should have been beyond his intellect. But no. If anything, they were beyond *my* intellect to explain them to him. We thought about shielding him from such works, but is it a good idea to protect a curious mind, no matter how old, from the wonders of the world—and the questions those wonders provoke? "Dad, what's the meaning of life?" Chris was a little adult. That was his problem, not "mental retardation."

When they told us about the label they would have to hang on them, I thought about children with Down syndrome—children with lovely, innocent faces, so open and giving, embracing a world that, in many instances, did not embrace them. It must be heartbreaking, I thought, for the parents of these children, advanced in ways that some members of society might never understand. Advanced emotionally, if not intellectually. Would it be just as heartbreaking for the parents of children who are labeled "mentally retarded" when they are not? The psychiatrist said he would be "happy" to provide a diagnosis that would help our son. We told him we would think about it. But we did not think about it. Not for a second. We drove home, wondering what kind of rabbit hole had led us to a doctor who could pronounce Chris "mentally retarded," an offensive term that sickened me.

I would call Chris "retarded" years later, a term uttered behind his back, out of anger and frustration. I had forgotten the comment, buried in that part of my brain that conceals guilt and shame, but our daughter Katy, who was born in 1989, would remind me years later, and when she did, it was no less offensive for the emotions that triggered it. I regretted it—regret it to this day—and it took me back to our meeting with the doctor.

The world had turned into a landscape where down was up, where doctors, far from comforting you, made you feel worse. Chris *was* different, but his uniqueness was manifested, in large part, by his intellect, not his lack of intellect. Would we ever find a doctor who understood this? Ever?

A few days later, we were driving along a South Jersey highway, a road fringed by farmland on either side. It was a desolate road, and the car—a 1986 Honda Civic—entombed us in silence. It was dusk. I glanced at Antonia; I could see tears seep out of her eyes. She sniffled, checking the rearview mirror to see if Chris, snuggled in his seat belt, was all right. He was. Pressing his face against the window, he surveyed the farmland stretched in front of him, alert for the cows that dotted the landscape during the day.

Later that evening, Chris was in his bedroom, lounging sideways, his elbow propped on his bed, his cheek cupped in his palm. It was about 5:00 p.m. The light was off, but the sun filtered through the blinds in the fading hours of late afternoon—enough of a reading lamp for this ten-year-old boy. I entered quietly, hesitant to disturb him. He was thumbing through the pictures in *The Lion, the Witch and the Wardrobe* by C. S. Lewis. I cleared my throat, and he said, "Hi, Dad," without taking his eyes off the book.

"Hi, Chris."

He kept thumbing.

"How are you doing?" I asked him.

"Good," he said.

"Sure?"

"Yes," he said, his eyes still focused on the book.

I stood there, wondering which passage of the book was intriguing him at that moment.

"You know we love you, and you know you'll be fine," I said.

"I know," he said, distracted, the lion, the witch, and the cupboard more compelling than the conversation he was having with his father.

Thank God. The book distracted him from school—from psychiatrists—and it also distracted him from the outside world, a world that tried to smother him, marginalize him, reduce him to a label that made it easier for adults to deal with him. The psychiatrist pronounced his diagnosis as if the condition were no more severe than a sore throat. But to recognize a problem is not to solve it. And to recognize a problem that is not there in the first place—is that worse? How do you deal with an inaccurate diagnosis? What happens if you order chemotherapy for a patient who is cancer-free? We were not about to find out. Chris had a condition, we knew that, but we were not ready to accept a treatment that was worse than the problem we were struggling to cure.

Afraid that labeling him would pigeonhole our son for life—and still unaware of what the "problem" was—we settled on a Catholic school about two blocks from our home in Cherry Hill, New Jersey. Angel of Mercy. We worried, however, that he would be too "smart" for his peers, too advanced to connect with them in a normal, healthy manner. *Normal.* What did that mean? We talked to the principal about the troubles he had encountered, and she said the teachers would be sensitive to his needs. He was in the second grade, an eight-year-old with hefty baggage behind him. Would it stay behind him? Or would it pursue him into the future?

One day, his teacher called us in for a conference at Angel of Mercy. We met in her classroom. She sat at her desk, and we squeezed into two of the tiny desks where the kids sat during class time, our bodies scrunched, our knees scraping the bottom of the desk tops. We felt marginalized; we felt like kids.

The teacher said Chris isolated himself from the rest of the kids. *Isolated.* That was the word she used, as if a yellow caution tape separated Chris from the rest of the world. Then the principal walked into the room. She was more personal—albeit not more personable—than the teacher. She said Chris would look at her with a "blank stare," as if he were "autistic." She uttered the word with contempt, as if autism were a crime, not a condition. Autistic? We sat there, unable to respond.

We took Chris to a child psychiatrist. He was bald, middle-aged, and he wore a red vest, his white shirt rolled up to his elbows. His office was filled with hammers, mallets, and baseball bats, all made of foam. The psychiatrist lowered his head, and he invited Chris to whack him with one of the foam objects. Chris picked up a baseball bat, and he whaled away, a little Harmon Killebrew taking his cuts. Batting practice lasted about three minutes, long enough for the psychiatrist to second-guess his strategy. He said Chris seemed "fine," not to worry.

The diagnosis offered little comfort. How could it? It was hard to find comfort in a psychiatric evaluation that boasted all the elegance of a Three Stooges short. There was only one consolation: Throughout the exercise, Chris giggled like the little boy he was but rarely showed the world.

We tried to find solace in what would become our mantra: *Chris is going through a phase. He will come into his own.* He was so smart, after all, so damned smart. The more his behavior countered our mantra, the more we repeated it. It was our life raft. I tried, but Antonia clung more tightly to the mantra than I did. It was her nature.

CHAPTER 6
The Rejects

AFTER EMBRACING THE shrill lunacy of *Monty Python and the Holy Grail*, we rejected the shrill lunacy of *The Goonies*, the next movie on the schedule. When it came to our capacity to endure lunacy, we were selective—very selective. Maybe we thought *Monty Python* was not lunacy for its own sake, but lunacy in the service of satire, which often provides the most trenchant social commentary. Or maybe we just thought the Monty Python troupe was hilarious, especially John Cleese, whose brand of deadpan humor made Buster Keaton seem wildly emotive. Whatever the reason, we welcomed *Monty Python* and shunned *Goonies*.

The Goonies was not the only film we nixed. The other was the next film on the schedule, *The Crimson Pirate*. We—or, rather, I—rejected it because, while I admired Burt Lancaster, I was sometimes put off by his penchant for histrionic melodrama. A swashbuckling adventure would, I was certain, ignite the tinderbox of his worst tendencies—stagy, overwrought theatrics. *Elmer Gantry* meets *Captain Blood*. So sorry, *Goonies*. Sorry, Burt. The shows would have to go on without us in the audience.

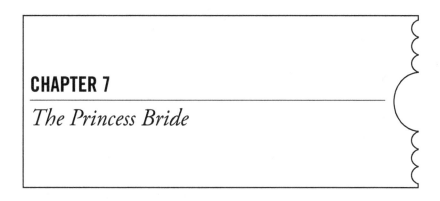

CHAPTER 7

The Princess Bride

THE FOOD COURT was becoming familiar—a hangout, a haven even. It was like a small-town plaza, an indoor space with an outdoor quality. Maybe it was the skylights. Maybe it was the bird. Maybe it was the fast-food outlets, one of which called itself "The Side Wok Café."

Whatever the reason, it was like being outdoors, enclosed but airy, bustling but serene. Malls get a bad rap, I thought. They are not all boiling receptacles of capitalism, a mad jumble of Spencer's this and Victoria's Secret that. Some malls are cool. The workers in the shops and fast-food outlets turn their surroundings into a community.

One evening at the Wonderland Mall, when the cashier at The Side Wok Café forgot the egg roll with my dinner, I went back to let her know. She apologized and gave me two. "Here you go," she said, her voice as soft as a dumpling. I gave the extra egg roll to Chris.

When dusk poured through the skylights, an oily darkness descended on the food court, making the print in my book harder to read. Then, somewhere within the bowels of the mall, a staffer must have hit a switch, because the lights brightened, and dusk did not seem so dusky. I could read again. My current book was *My Happy Life* by Lydia Millet. I needed something uplifting after *Mystic River*, which was a punch to the gut, a blow to your understanding of how the world works. No matter how cynical your outlook, no matter how bitter your worldview, *Mystic River* could darken the gloomiest corners of your soul, making them seem childishly optimistic. It was a great book, each passage jarring you with its gritty lyricism. But I needed an antidote to this dark masterpiece.

I thought *My Happy Life* would be that antidote. I was right and wrong. *My Happy Life* was just as hard as *Mystic River*, its journey into the dark side just as unrelenting. But every horror was mitigated by a young woman with a spirit that battled ugliness with love. It was a slender book, but it packed as many horrors into 150 pages as *Mystic River* did into 428. The nameless translator is naïve, even dim, although it seems cruel to pin a label like "dim" on someone so kind and giving. She is calm and gentle, but she is almost ferociously strong, seeing beauty where others see depravity. And, like Chris, she is almost obsessed about connecting with others. . . . And, again like Chris, she fails; time after time, she fails.

"Feeling seemed to me without bounds and vast, formless and not taking up space. I never liked thinking of wasted hands that reach and find no object. Trembling and suspended."

It was a clear day, not dark, not sunny, but Chris was wearing his Bob Dylan cap, the cap Dylan wears on the cover of his eponymous first album; Chris seemed to wear a cap or a hoodie rain or shine that year, a fashion accessory that came to define him. It was a quirk that would inspire his high school principal to call him—affectionately, believe it or not—the "Unabomber." I forgot gloves. Chris also wore gloves, again rain or shine, although only during the winter months, winter in San Antonio being a relative term, as the lows during January and February were often in the high sixties.

"What are you reading?" he asked.

I held up the book.

"Is it good?" he asked.

"It is," I said. "It's kind of the literary equivalent of *It's a Wonderful Life*. The main character goes through hell—a hell most of us could never imagine—but she never allows hell to go through her. She survives. . . . She earns whatever optimism remains in her heart."

"That sounds great," he said. "Maybe I'll read it one of these days."

"Let me know. I'll lend it to you."

"Cool."

We started talking about literature.

"I took a great American literature course at A&M," said Chris, who had earned an English degree at Texas A&M in 2006. "I loved the professor."

"What did you read?"

"Let's see," he said, taking a mental inventory. "We read *My Ántonia* by Willa Cather . . ."

"I haven't read it, but Mom has, of course," I said, interrupting him.

He said one of the female students had an interesting take on the book.

"The professor asked us what we felt the dominant theme of the book was," Chris said. "This girl said it was that Nebraska turns strong women into strong men."

"A budding literary critic," I said, and Chris laughed.

"What else did you read?"

He started listing the books: *The Great Gatsby, The Adventures of Huckleberry Finn* . . .

"That's my favorite book, *The Adventures of Huckleberry Finn*," I said, interrupting him again. "I reread it every two years or so."

Whenever I read it, I never ceased to be amazed by the language or uplifted by the spirit. And every time I read it, I wanted to read it again and again, savoring the chapters I had just finished.

Especially Chapter 19, the chapter in which Huck describes the night and the dawn and everything in between—the sights and sounds of the river, the smells even, some fresh and lovely, others rank and sickening, but all of them *real*, described by a boy, thirteen or thereabouts, who sees the world with a vision that is both naïve and wise, a wisdom that comes when the world is your classroom. To read *The Adventures of Huckleberry Finn* is to experience the Big Muddy—the world—in your den or living room or wherever you are reading the book.

"I know," Chris said. "I remember you telling me that. It was my favorite, too, at least among the books we read in class."

The professor, Chris said, described Mark Twain as a "misanthrope." I blanched. A *misanthrope*? I understood why the professor branded him with that term, but I challenged the notion. Mark Twain could be childish, selfish, petulant, and egotistical, and he could be cruel, even hateful, toward his older brother, Orion, who possessed none of his fiery genius. And then there was the legendary vitriol toward his fellow travelers on Earth; in one of his missives about the luxury cruise that would turn into a chapter in *The Innocents Abroad*, he was so contemptuous of the passengers that he referred to the voyage as "a funeral excursion without a corpse." And yet . . .

. . . Mark Twain loved the world, loved its wonders and mysteries, its magic and possibilities. He also loved children, a constant source of pleasure—and plotlines. And he loved adults who were unloved by society, men and women oppressed by a brutal institution, slavery, although it was years after the Civil War that he developed his philosophy that all men were equal. . . . Oh, he hated, too, but he hated that which deserved to be hated—especially evil and the hypocrisy that undergirded evil. I told Chris about a nonfiction book I had read, *Huck Finn's America*. In one segment, it described a mob that lynched a Black man after the Civil War, only to discover later that he was innocent of the crime that had led to his death. The mob shrugged it off. Twain wrote a bitter, ironic essay about the incident, "Only a N****r." . . . I paused, sensing that I had transitioned from speaking to speechifying. Chris smiled.

"Dad, that doesn't sound like a misanthrope to me," Chris said. "This whole situation reminds me of a line in the movie we're going to see tonight."

The movie was *The Princess Bride*.

"Oh," I said. "How so?"

"Remember the Sicilian?" Chris asked.

The Sicilian was played by Wallace Shawn, a smarmy little villain whose ego was as large as Fezzik, the character portrayed by Andre the Giant.

"I do," I said.

"Well," Chris said, "the Sicilian keeps saying, 'Inconceivable.' Right? That's what I thought when the professor said Mark Twain was a misanthrope. 'Inconceivable.'"

Now here was a budding literary critic.

"Inconceivable," he repeated.

"Absolutely," I said, laughing.

We needed a respite from our enjoyable but heavy conversation, and we got it. It is impossible to imagine a movie that is more fun than *The Princess Bride*, a movie we had seen dozens of times on DVD. It boasts more cliffhangers than *Raiders of the Lost Ark*—with even more wit and charm. Every scene is perfect, with just the right blend of comedy, romance, and adventure. And, for every sword fight or wrestling match, there is a scene so pure and tender that it could warm the coldest heart, despite the clear satirical intent. And best of all are the scenes in which the grandfather, played by Peter Falk, narrates the story to his hooky-playing grandson, portrayed by Fred Savage. The grandfather is wry and wise, a character as rich and outsized as those in the tale he reads to the boy. The role is virtually a cameo, but it makes you wish the Oscars would anoint actors who flit on and off the screen quicker than you can say, "My name is Inigo Montoya."

"Well?" I asked Chris after the movie.

"I loved it," he said. "It was just as good as I remembered. Better."

I dropped Chris off at his apartment, and on my way home, I popped in a CD of old blues and country songs. The first selection was "Keep on the Sunny Side" by the Carter Family. It reminded me of the organic nature of happiness. If joy is a flower, torment and agony are the seeds that make it blossom. There are philosophers, much smarter than me, who might disagree with that notion, but the great blues artists understood the dynamic: You cannot have happiness without misery. A startling paradox, but there is no music more joyous than the blues, its rhythms imported from Africa.

Without slavery, we would not have the blues—or the rock 'n' roll from which it evolved. Was it worth it? Rock 'n' roll is a blessing, a form of salvation that enters our ears and penetrates our hearts. It gave us great poets like Chuck Berry, the Walt Whitman of rock, who coined the term "motorvating" and referred to the Venus de Milo as the *Milo de Venus*. It gave us Bob Dylan, who would win the Nobel Prize in literature. And it gave us The Beatles, perhaps the greatest artists of the twentieth century. But was it worth it? Was it worth the centuries of cruelty and degradation imposed by slavery and its aftermath? Any reasonable human being, no matter how much he or she may love the blues or rock 'n' roll, would have to say no, no, it was *not* worth it. But slavery did exist, and out of the horror came the blues, an art form that enriches us all.

I wished Chris had been with me, so I could share my musings with him. But I was alone in my crummy little Chevy, so I conversed with myself. . . . When a blues artist starts a song with, "Well, I woke up in the morning," you know that was his or her first mistake. Waking up. Because, just as surely as the sun ignites the morning, the morning ignites the misery. Misery—and plenty of it. An empty bottle. A good woman gone bad. A bad man gone worse. When it comes to pain and suffering, nobody tops a blues singer. Not even a Greek chorus. Right? Well, yes and no. Yes, they sing about tough times, the tunes so baleful that they could wipe the smile off a beauty contestant. But there is not one ounce of whine in the great blues singers, not one ounce.

Most blues artists specialize in irony, but the ultimate irony is inherent in the art form itself. How can a genre focused on pain, a genre steeped in sorrow, be so joyous and uplifting? In song after song, the artists rise above heartache, their dignity belying the sadness they depict. It is one of the most stunning alchemies in music, sorrow distilled into triumph. Therapy with a backbeat.

"The blues is a chair," John Lennon once said, talking about the musical form that led to rock 'n' roll. "It is not the design for a chair or a better chair. . . . It is the first chair."

The blues does not rock. It comes close, deliciously, tantalizingly close, but it has a beat all its own. If the music formed a volcano, the soup—the boiling, churning, gurgling mess beneath the surface—would be the blues. The spew would be rock 'n' roll. Without the blues, there would be no explosion, no rock 'n' roll. It is the tension—the grinding, relentless beat—that gives the blues its power. And the artists realize it. The music is fierce, pulsating, but it rarely surrenders to the explosion that is rock 'n' roll. And, through it all, the artists smile. They sing about discrimination, hard times, and love gone sour. But if they dwell on misery, they never wallow in it. They are like George Bailey, the hero of *It's a Wonderful Life*, fierce and determined in the face of sorrow. . . .

There was always the danger of succumbing to the stereotype of the "happy slave," but slaves sang the blues to vanquish the blues. The attitude reminded me of Frederick Douglass, the former slave who explored the value of gospel songs with eloquent wisdom:

> I did not, when a slave, fully understand the deep meaning of those rude and apparently incoherent songs. . . . The remark in the olden time was not infrequently made, that slaves were the most contented and happy laborers in the world, and their dancing and singing were referred to as proof of this alleged fact; but it was a great mistake to suppose them happy because they sometimes made those joyful noises. The songs of the slaves represented their sorrows, rather than their joys. Like tears, they were a relief to aching hearts.

As my CD segued from "Keep on the Sunny Side" to "(Mama) He Treats Your Daughter Mean" by Ruth Brown, I thought about our conversation before the movie. Mark Twain a misanthrope? Inconceivable. And what about Chris and me? Chris and I had known misery, much of it sparked by our relationship with each other. But would we wallow in it? Were *we* misanthropes? And, if we *were*, would that misanthropy spoil our relationship, unhinge our fragile connection? Or was that possibility inconceivable?

CHAPTER 8

A New Arrival

AND THEN KATY came, and everything changed.

Katy was born in 1989, almost seven years to the day after Chris arrived in Fort Worth. We were all born on consecutive days, with me in the middle. I was sandwiched by my kids, a birthday hoagie. Libras, all. Antonia was the lone outlier in the family, a Cancer born in July.

Like Chris, Katy slipped from the birth canal—what a poetic term—into our hearts, seven and a half pounds of joy that brightened our somber household. As a baby, she was like Chris in so many ways, arriving with a full head of hair, a rich chocolate brown that shone in the sun. Lying in her crib, she looked like a turtle on its shell, her arms and legs suspended in the air as if yanked by invisible strings. And then there was her giggle, a sound so delicate and buoyant that it seemed to produce musical notes in the air— Es, Gs, Bs, Ds, and Fs ("Every Good Boy Does Fine," as we were taught in grade school).

But there were differences, some subtle, others jarring. Even as a baby, Katy was more lighthearted than Chris, more enthralling, because she engaged with both the environment and the adults around her, whereas Chris created his *own* environment, in his mind—an ability that reminded me of The Beatles song, "There's a Place," the place being the mind of the singer. That was Chris. Even when he was sitting in front of us, we never knew where he really was.

Disillusioned by the "batting practice" routine with the last doctor, we vowed to avoid any more comedy skits disguised as clinical sessions. But the "problems" with Chris continued, and when Katy arrived, what we had hoped were mere ticks became more pronounced when juxtaposed with the behavior patterns of a happy, healthy child. So we took a deep breath, awaiting the future.

We read to both children from the start. They giggled at the word "soporific" in *The Tale of Peter Rabbit*. Lettuce made the rabbits "soporific," and the kids envisioned the bunnies, hearts content and bellies full, succumbing to a sluggishness brought on by gluttony.

During Christmas, Antonia and I would take turns reading *A Christmas Carol* to them. We would start about a week before Christmas, alternating staves—or chapters—each night. I would read a stave one night, Antonia another the next, until Ebenezer Scrooge reached his epiphany on Christmas Eve. The four of us would sit in the living room, in front of the fireplace, the dancing flames casting ghostly shadows on our faces. It was the perfect setting for the story. Chris and Katy loved the tale of the miser turned benefactor, both of them charmed by the strange blend of the macabre and the heartwarming.

If Chris had his way, however, there would have been more macabre and less heartwarming. The dark side appealed to him. Why? Perhaps because there was a darkness that resided in his own soul, a realization that life could be cruel, creating a wall between himself and his peers. He would tell me, as a young adult, "Do you think I *want* to be this way?" And that angst, that yearning for what others seemed to have, was there from the start, assaulting his sense of self. He never verbalized it as a child, but it was there. I know it.

Was that the appeal of *The Strange Case of Dr. Jekyll and Mr. Hyde*? The book, after all, is about an identity crisis—a violent, perplexing identity crisis, but an identity crisis nonetheless. Whatever his attraction to the book, it concerned us. Chris was too young to be reading it, and too young to be asking questions like "What is the meaning of life?" If we were honest with ourselves, however, the question filled us with both pride and anxiety. But anxiety won out.

Antonia and I hit on what we considered a happy medium. We would read him books with a radiant spirit that overshadowed the darkness. Books like *The BFG, Charlie and the Chocolate Factory*, and *James and the Giant Peach*, all of them written by Roald Dahl. They were ominous, which he loved, but sweet, which *we* loved. But we could not dam the onrushing tide of darker, gloomier works forever.

Chris would take some of the books to school with him, and his teacher was disturbed by his choice of literature. She called it "macabre." Chris said she pronounced it "muh-kah-bray."

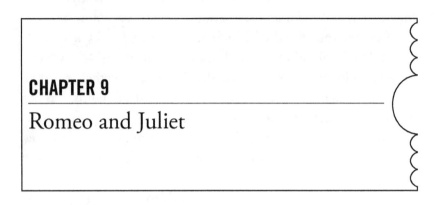

CHAPTER 9
Romeo and Juliet

FEBRUARY 4, 2016

CHRIS WAS BECOMING reliable in his unreliability.

He was late again, which was fine. If he had arrived early—or even on time—I would have been shocked. I looked at the time on my cell phone—does anyone wear wristwatches anymore?—and he was fifteen minutes late. I smiled.

I plopped my book onto the table at the food court, the cover, stark but vivid, transporting me to another time, another place: A thin, gaunt cowboy rides his horse toward the horizon. The land is parched, segmented into cracks of dry earth that look like the countries on a map. The cowboy looks down, his shoulders hunched, as if there is nothing beyond the dry earth, the hopeless terrain. But he is wrong. The hills, lush and green, loom ahead—distant but promising.

Shane. I had read the book in my twenties, and I was struck by its spare prose, its sober portrait of a dark, cruel world that was almost medieval in its brutality and oppression. Here was a society with an updated caste system; decent, hardworking farmers ground into the very earth they were trying to till.

And then one day, Shane rides into town. A man of quiet integrity, he makes peace with his violent past, an irony that is almost heartbreaking in its tragic implications. He yearns to be a good man, and he *is* a good man, but the six-shooter at his hip indicates that the goodness can disappear with the pull of a trigger. Shane is a killer.

The story is told through the eyes of a ten-year-old boy. Bob Starrett learns about evil, but he also learns about goodness, about courage and integrity. And he learns that standing up is hard, but cowering is harder, robbing you of your soul and spirit.

Every two or three years, I reread two books—*The Grapes of Wrath* and *The Adventures of Huckleberry Finn*. The Steinbeck novel is angry and dogmatic, but its power and appeal lie in the very traits that should undermine it. The tragedy is overwhelming for the same reason that all tragedies are overwhelming—the characters do not deserve their fate.

Huckleberry Finn is special. It is a tale that defines America, a tale about the stain we try to remove—slavery. Twain takes an illiterate river rat, Huck Finn, and turns him into a poet, an astonishing alchemy that cements Twain, I believe, as our greatest writer. When Huck recognizes that the slave, Jim, is a valuable human being, with the same feelings as any white man, the scene is beyond poignant, beyond dramatic; it is monumental.

I had never thought of rereading *Shane*, but every time I thought about Chris, I pictured young Bob Starrett, sweet and naïve. I saw Chris as a teen, a preteen, and a baby. I could see him in the delivery room in 1982. It was just after midnight. Chris missed my birthday by a few minutes. *Good.* Chris had his own day. He seemed perfect. His nose was soft, almost rubbery, and his eyes looked like pinpricks of light. And his mouth . . . his mouth was exquisite—a tiny pink bow.

Now, here we were, thirty years later. Time had bulldozed the soft, almost liquid contours of the baby face. The hair, once combed so neatly that it curtained his forehead like a pageboy, turned into a massive swirl, a rebellious mop of curls, coils upon coils that transformed him into a young Jerry Garcia. And the rubbery nose? Also gone, replaced by a long, firm, attractive proboscis—a term I taught Chris when we saw a W. C. Fields movie, *Never Give a Sucker an Even Break*, on television. He was ten. "Proboscis," he said giggling, mouthing the word as if he were chewing a candy bar.

The pinpricks of light were gone, too. His eyes were almond-shaped now, dark brown, with a gleam that emerged when he pontificated, which was often. He loved to speechify.

We were eating in the food court—Chris . . . me—a dinner followed by what we hoped would be a richer, heartier feast—*Romeo and Juliet* starring Claire Danes and Leonardo DiCaprio. . . . Chris loved Shakespeare, loved the pathos and humor, the sorrow and joy. But, most of all, he loved the thunderclaps of drama. Ah, the thunderclaps. Chris loved the grand opera that was Shakespeare, the sweep and power of the language, the crashing cymbals, the booming drums. Oh, Chris appreciated the subtlety and nuance of great literature, but he exhibited an almost Falstaffian appetite for spectacle, for those moments in a movie or play or novel when your psyche is stripped raw. When you have to prove yourself. There were plenty of those moments in Shakespeare, a writer with the courage and ambition to skim the surface of overwrought—without diving in.

"What's your favorite line in Shakespeare?" I asked him.

I should have known how he would answer. Not which line he would utter, but how he would utter it. He pondered the question for a few seconds. Then he stepped into his metaphysical dressing room, rummaging through his wardrobe for a few seconds. He emerged in the garb of Macbeth. . . . And, then, with an air that was both elegant and histrionic, he delivered the lines from *Macbeth*:

Thou hast no marrow in thy bones
Thy blood runs cold

> Thou hast no speculation in those eyes which thou dost
> GLARE WITH!

I smiled, dazzled by his passion—and his memory. How did he remember those lines? He must have read them for the first time in high school. But he did not memorize them. Does anyone *memorize* Shakespeare anymore, unless your high school English teacher is a sadist? No, he loved them so much that he absorbed them. He made them part of his literary DNA. And, yes, he uttered those last two words—*GLARE WITH*—with uppercase emphasis. Why did he like that line above all others? I asked him.

"I like it because it's him (Macbeth) acknowledging that he's going nuts and that the specter of Banquo is just a figment of his imagination, but he says it *REALLY LOUD*, and in front of his whole court, so while it is a powerful statement, it actually winds up being rather comical."

Chris never asked me, but if he had, I would have delivered *my* favorite line from Shakespeare:

> O, that this too too solid flesh would melt
> Thaw and resolve itself into a dew!
> Or that the Everlasting had not fix'd
> His canon 'gainst self-slaughter! O God!
> God!

I loved the language, the use of Everlasting to denote God. And I loved the power and drama of a good man, Hamlet, driven to consider suicide. My second favorite line, also from *Hamlet*, was: *"For there is nothing either good or bad, but thinking makes it so."*

I loved it because it encapsulated the complexity of life, the astounding range of ideas and philosophies that make us one species. There is no *one* path toward enlightenment, despite the enmity that would arise among religions throughout the world. Shakespeare realized that without tolerance—without the willingness to accept, if not embrace, the views of others—we descend into chaos.

But Chris never asked me what my favorite line was. Or my second favorite line. Which was just as well. I could never have matched his delivery, his passion and urgency, both of which, I am sure, would have pleased The Bard.

Finishing our dinner, we started digesting something more satisfying—a discussion on the enduring appeal of Shakespeare. Why did his legacy span five centuries, his poetry continuing to dazzle in an era of social media that devalued elegance of thought and expression? Why? I thought I knew the answer. It was the *frenzy* of life he depicted, the pitch and intensity so profound that the words on the page came to life. They roared with passion, igniting emotions you rarely felt in "real" life. But, then, this *was* real life, because Shakespeare made it so. Even the calm, tender scenes, even the quiet, lyrical asides, made you tremble with emotion. Is that overstating it? Perhaps, but Shakespeare made it easy to overstate.

The universality of The Bard, I told Chris, went beyond his wisdom and poetry. You could pinpoint his appeal on a map, as the wonderful book *Worlds Elsewhere: Journeys around Shakespeare's Globe* documents. There are replicas of the Globe Theater in Cedar City, Utah; Neuss, Germany; Kimberley, South Africa; and Jukkasjärvi, Sweden. And there is a dacha outside Moscow where Boris Pasternak translated *Hamlet* and *King Lear*.

Chris delivered his favorite line with remarkable passion, but if Shakespeare could be compelling and frenetic, it was often the subtlety and nuance, the storm beneath the placid waters, that told you what the characters were feeling. The Bard did not have to shout; his poetry was his bullhorn. *Romeo and Juliet*, the play, epitomized this approach. The lovers, so sweet and tender, yet gripped by despair so profound that they slaughtered themselves. *To be or not to be*, indeed.

The movie was different; it was in-your-face Shakespeare. There was no subtlety. It made a tempest look like a ripple in a backyard pool. The film turned nuance into bombast, bombast into chaos, chaos into . . . well, we know how the play ends.

It was too much, the music, the histrionics, the gyrations of the camera, as if the cinematographers were Rollerblading during the shoots. Would The Bard have frowned on this? Or would he have donned his party hat and dancing shoes, applauding the filmmakers for their daring? Methinks not.

Still, the film was, if not enjoyable, at least engaging and moving. It is hard to ruin Shakespeare. You really have to try (the 1935 version of *A Midsummer Night's Dream* with Jimmy Cagney and Mickey Rooney is a dreary example). And the filmmakers, while provocative in their take on the play, were at least respectful. Respect is the key to interpreting—or reinterpreting—Shakespeare. So the tragedy remained monumental—and heartbreaking. All that loss, all that pain and suffering . . . for what? As in all his dramas, the playwright makes the tragedy more intense, more wrenching and agonizing, by showing us how easily it could have been avoided.

"Thanks, Dad."

CHAPTER 10
Chris at the Altar

1991

CHRIS LOVED CEREMONY, finding comfort in the order and structure, the notion that, yes, life was a journey, but it was a journey with fixed coordinates. You could get from Point A to Point B without wandering from Points A through Points Z. Chris liked his straight lines.

He became an altar boy in the third grade. He was eleven, and he looked like a young Jedi in his robe, his pageboy curtaining his forehead from ear to ear. Chris—the holy warrior. The robe was sometimes white, sometimes black, depending on the season. But it did not matter; whatever the color, Chris seemed to thrive in his Sunday attire. He was more serene, more beatific, more Chris-like, in his spiritual uniform. It was as if the conventions of religion— the rules and strictures—had the opposite effect on him than they did on most children. They did not confine him; they liberated him, allowed him to be who he wanted to be. He wanted to be a boy set apart, not by a condition he could not recognize, but by a desire to be part of something comforting, something noble and pure. Something bigger than himself. He never expressed these ideas, may never have even *thought* them, but he was so bright, so curious and thoughtful, that he *could* have thought them. And I was sure he did; I was sure he gravitated to religion because religion gravitated to *him*, made him feel welcome in a world that was so unwelcoming. The altar was more than a holy place; it was a *safe* place.

Obeying orders in church that he never would in class, Chris followed instructions without scorn or snickering, and when he handled the chalice or tinkled the bell, summoning the celebrants to Holy Communion, he felt important. The robe helped; it was part of a uniform that symbolized his duty, his commitment, and each time he donned it in the sacristy, he donned something else— the persona of a child with focus and resolve. Mentally retarded? No, he was a boy with problems, a boy who *understood* he had problems. And the altar was part of his self-imposed therapy.

We were not militantly Catholic, but we found comfort in the religion, and we wanted Katy and Chris to grow up in the faith. Then, once they grew up, they could make their own decisions, pursuing their own yearnings and answering their own questions. Chris would do just that. Oh my, would he. But that would not come until years later.

One Easter Sunday, years before his detour from Catholicism, he served Mass with his usual enthusiasm, his eyes glowing like candles flickering on the altar. He seemed comfortable, at ease, as if the ceremony were a ballet with every step—every delicate motion—choreographed. If there was any tension, any anxiety, it came when he had to lift the chalice, which was so big that it almost obscured his face. But, no, he handled it deftly, passing it to the priest for the ritual he loved most of all—Holy Communion.

Chris held the bell by his side, tinkling it gently, as the congregants filed to the altar. Then, when the priest passed out the wafers from the paten, a small plate, Chris glided alongside him, mirroring every step as he held the communion tray under the jaw of each congregant to make sure the "body of Christ" did not hit the floor. Not to worry. There were no unexpected freefalls; both Chris and Christ remained where they were supposed to be, one in the paten, the other on his feet.

I loved to watch Chris at the altar, loved to see him tinkle the bell, cradle the chalice. I loved the short, dainty steps he took from one end of the altar to the other, each footfall deliberate but grace-ful. I loved his quiet urgency, the wary eye he kept on the priest, as if awaiting an unexpected directive, a higher command. Chris seemed in his element up there, proud but beatific, his pride never trespassing into smugness. And no wonder. The pride came from a job well done, because after every service, the priest patted him on the head, in full view of the celebrants, as though it were part of the ritual.

Sitting in the pew, Antonia and I gazed at each other, content in the contentment our son felt. We cherished these moments. There were not many of them, but there were enough to sustain us, to keep us going through the hard times. We were not staunch Cath-olics, despite our attendance at church, but it was times like these when we believed that Jesus lived in the church—and in our hearts.

When the Easter service was over, Chris searched us out, smil-ing. We waited in our pew—Antonia, Katy, and me—enjoying the solitude as the church emptied. The priest and Chris ducked into the sacristy, and a few minutes later, Chris emerged in his "civilian" clothes, white shirt and tan slacks. He smiled—again.

It was time for another Easter ritual—an egg hunt. We drove to a park about three blocks from our house. A bright, sunny morning, with thin clouds threading their way across an azure sky. Perfect con-ditions for our two little scavengers, although one of them, Katy, was so small that she would have to enjoy the hunt vicariously, nestled in our arms, lest the other kids trample our three-year-old Easter egg hunter-to-be.

Chris seemed calm, almost nonchalant, his eyes dreamy, his arms still. But his surface tranquility belied an inner intensity. I could sense it. The eggs were almond-shaped sirens, and he heard their bewitching call. He would go from beatific altar boy to rapacious egg hunter, and the transformation would be sublime.

But something happened between beatific and rapacious. Something unexpected. A neighborhood mom yelled, "Ready, set, go!" And, just like that, the siren's song fell flat. Chris, as awkward physically as he was socially, stumbled among the herd of stampeding children. He reached for an egg here, an egg there, but each time he approached the prize, another child intervened, grabbing it in front of his eyes. Befuddled and disheartened, he tried again and again, but the other urchins appeared out of nowhere, turning what looked like sparkling jewels into fool's gold.

Watching the other kids, I was filled with a lucid fury—lucid because I was aware of it . . . and because I did nothing to act on it. I wanted to grab the youngsters by their waistbands, turning them into cartoon characters, their legs churning without going anywhere. I wanted to do a lot of things. . . . But I did nothing, nothing but watch this exercise in futility, until all the eggs were gone. Thank God it was over. My reaction was stupid. I blamed the children, but the children were blameless. They were being kids, and they were better at it than Chris. Much better. Their enthusiasm bordered on greed, but if there is any time when enthusiasm should be boundless, it is in childhood. Right?

In the midst of all the chaos, I started daydreaming. I saw Chris back in the church, safe and secure. If only he could take the altar with him everywhere he went, I thought. If only the Lord, a presence that was ephemeral but palpable, could follow Chris out the church doors. . . . My reverie ended abruptly. The egg hunt was over, and Chris started to cry, and, when he stumbled toward us, Antonia hugged him, holding him so close that they seemed welded to each other, mother and child transformed into a living statue.

CHAPTER 11

Kate and Leopold

FEBRUARY 11, 2016

BACK IN THE MALL.

Was it a home away from home? No, but it was as close as you could get without a coffee table, a television set, and a cold beer in your hand. It was a refuge, as warm and cozy as a den. I was beginning to recognize the regulars, most of them, like me, segueing from middle-aged to elderly. Maybe that is being kind—to me, not to them. I was not segueing so much as rocketing into my senior years. I was sixty-one going on seventy-five. My knees were older than that, shredded from decades of running, including two marathons and countless 10Ks. Forced to choose an alternative to jogging on asphalt streets, I started swimming—at sixty—working my way up to an hour in the pool every day. The water, the source of life, had a dual benefit: It kept me active, and it saved my knees. It also slowed my sprint into old age.

The mall regulars were active, too. One elderly lady walked laps around the mall, pumping her arms like a high school bandleader. She was dressed in black—leotards and sweatshirt—and her demeanor seemed as dark as her apparel, her eyes glowing with laser-like focus.

Less active, but no less engaging, was the giant of a man, also hurtling into his senior years, who ate his supper in the food court every Thursday evening. He chose a different meal every time—a hamburger one week, a pizza the next. The only constant was the intensity—and the joy—with which he chowed. He sported a long, gray beard, and every week, I waited for the crumbs to cascade onto its flowing expanse. I could have waited into old age and beyond; he ate too delicately, too daintily, to litter the vegetation that sprouted from his face.

Chris was late, a circumstance that had evolved from a mild annoyance to an anticipated reprieve. It gave me time to read my books. The latest was *Wittgenstein's Mistress* by David Markson. The author was male, the narrator he created female. Markson pulled off this identity switch adroitly, mainly because the character was so fragile and confused that her gender seemed almost immaterial.

The book was a wild jumble of inquisitions and disquisitions that could be exhilarating one second, exhausting the next. And, yes, once again it reminded me of my son. You never knew what to expect from Chris; he could be quiet one minute, wildly expressive the next, just like the characters in this maddening book I was reading. You could read passages, pages even, without knowing where you were going—or where you had been. It reminded me of the line by Descartes: "I think, therefore, I am." Except that the narrator was not sure what she was thinking, much less who she was. So how could she could be sure of her identity—or anything else? She would express an idea in one sentence, only to contradict it in the next, all the time wondering if the idea she wanted to convey was even worth conveying. And if it was not worth conveying, was it worth contradicting? She was also depressed, so sad and lonely that her only companions were her jumbled thoughts—and the words that gave them life. Or *were* they her only companions? It was hard to tell.

> I believe I have said that I felt depressed at least once before, actually, while writing these pages.
> Although perhaps what I more exactly said I felt once before was a certain undefined anxiety.
> Which in that instance would have only been because of my period coming on, however.
> Or because of hormones.
> And so which would have not really been anxiety at all, but only an illusion.
> Even if one would certainly be hard put to explain the difference between an illusion of anxiety and anxiety itself.

What?!? Does anyone have an aspirin? But, as maddening as the book could be, it was also strangely thrilling, a verbal roller coaster with sudden jolts and dips that made you wonder what lay ahead. I could not put it down, although I knew I would be glad once I did. I would not be able to say that it was a pleasure to meet Wittgenstein's mistress, perhaps, but I could say that it was an education—or was it?

I did not have much time to ponder the question. Chris showed up at 4:30, thirty minutes after our appointed meeting time, delivering me from the linguistic maze that was *Wittgenstein's Mistress*. He was wearing a black jacket and a black cap, which bore the logo of his workplace—Jack in the Box, located half a block from the mall. It was *the* cap, the one that reminded me of the cap Dylan wore on the cover of that eponymous first album, which featured the exquisite homage to Woody Guthrie, "Song to Woody."

"Hey, Chris, good to see you."

"Thanks. You, too."

Chris sat down, removing his cap with a flourish, as if he were presenting me with a bouquet of flowers. He smiled, tossing the cap onto the table. A shabby bouquet. He exhaled.

"What you reading?" he asked.

I held up the book.

"Is it good?" he asked.

"It is, but it's really difficult," I said. "I've never read *Ulysses*, but I can't imagine that it's any more challenging than this."

I would read *Ulysses* a few years later, and it *was* more challenging, but those headaches lay ahead. The novel would shatter my notion of what constitutes a great writer. I always thought an accomplished writer should guide you from sentence to sentence, each one part of a journey leading to an epiphany. Not so with Joyce. His stream of consciousness undermined any sense of continuity, every phrase, every thought, pointing to a dark labyrinth of jumbled thoughts.

"Hey, Dad, that reminds me. . . . Remember when I had to read *Dubliners* in high school, and you went through every short story with me, discussing its meaning?"

"You mean what I *guessed* was its meaning," I said, smiling.

Chris laughed.

"Well, your interpretations made sense to me."

Chris sighed.

"Tired?" I asked.

"A little."

Chris had worked the graveyard shift at Jack in the Box the night before, a schedule he preferred because the rush of drive-through customers eased up at night. But work is work, even in the hush of night. And eight hours at a drive-through window gives you a portal into rudeness, arrogance, and, sometimes, good humor. But he was not complaining.

He had started working at what he called "The Box" in November, the third in a disastrous string of jobs over the last two years. The first was as a door-to-door salesman for a cable TV outfit. He got the job through the Texas Department of Assistive and Rehabilitative Services—DARS—and it seemed like a godsend. At first. He made sales, and the sales grew, and his supervisors were impressed. They promoted him, from salesman to sales manager, but as his responsibilities grew, so did his anxiety, and his anxiety strangled him.

He was living with me at the time, both of us crammed into a one-bedroom apartment. We took turns sleeping in the bedroom. One night I was in the bedroom, and he was on the couch in the living room; the next night, the comforts—and the misery—were reversed.

That was about two years earlier. Chris had come a long way. He was living in his own apartment now. I helped him with the rent, but he was becoming responsible with the money he earned from "The Box."

"That's a cool hat, Chris," I said. "It reminds me of the early Dylan, before he became a mad, inscrutable genius."

Chris smiled, as if wondering whether that was a compliment or an insult.

"You're not mad and inscrutable—at least, I don't think you are, but maybe you are a genius," I said.

The truth is, Chris *was* inscrutable, his nature so guarded, so complex, that it was hard to decipher his feelings. It did not help that he rarely expressed his inner thoughts, and when he did, it was usually in a burst of anger. But beyond his inscrutability, I did think, truly, that he had genius in him.

"Oh, yeah, a genius, huh?" he asked.

Chris had a way of talking that sounded insincere, as if he were reciting lines for an audition for a high school play. He was sincere, but he sounded *fakey*, a term we used as kids, but the façade was built on a foundation of doubt and insecurity. Chris was unsure of himself, of how he came across, so he developed a persona, delivering his lines with the air of a B-movie actor. It was charming if you knew him, off-putting if you did not.

"Oh, yeah, a genius?" he repeated.

I almost regretted saying it. Did he have genius in him? I had no doubt that he did. But how would he mine the ore in his soul? That is the question for all geniuses, but the challenge would be that much harder for Chris, a young man whose sense of alienation was sometimes overwhelming. Was I putting too much pressure on him?

"Yeah," I said.

We changed the subject, and we ordered our dinner—Chris a falafel, me a tuna fish sandwich—and we talked about the movie we were about to see, *Kate and Leopold*. We had never seen it, but it had a time travel theme, so we started talking about science fiction, which led to a discussion about horror.

"What's your favorite horror movie?" I asked.

"*Nosferatu*," he answered immediately.

Nosferatu was the 1922 classic German silent film.

"Why?"

"Because it's true to the old vampire lore," he said. "Dracula was not as elegant or courtly as the Bela Lugosi character would have us believe."

A modest *Dracula* scholar, Chris loved the Bram Stoker novel, a romance that led him to more research.

"I didn't know that," I said.

"Absolutely," he said. "Dracula, according to the lore, looks almost monster-like."

Then, surprising me, he asked me what my favorite horror movie was.

"*Silence of the Lambs*," I said, pausing. "Does it qualify as horror? There are no monsters in it, except of the human variety."

"It qualifies—definitely."

Because of his devotion to the genre, I accepted his confirmation as gospel.

"The greatest horror movies—and books—imply more than they tell," he said. "That's why Edgar Allen Poe is a much better writer than H. P. Lovecraft. Lovecraft bludgeons you. Poe chips away at your sanity."

Later, in the theater, *Kate and Leopold* was chipping away at my sanity. It was a charming movie, in spots, and an engaging movie, again in spots. But those spots could not redeem the whole, mainly because of Kate, portrayed by Meg Ryan.

Kate was a cynical executive for a market research company, but if she broke the glass ceiling, she let the shards fall on the women beneath her. She was rude and insensitive to them, allowing the misery in her personal life to seep into her professional life. Or was it her *perceived* misery? She did not seem to have it that bad, but however bad she had it, she made it worse for her workers.

Leo was different. He was charming and noble, perhaps too charming and noble. The film juxtaposed two personalities and two eras—his and hers. Leo came from the nineteenth century, transported to our age through a complex series of events that created a portal in time. He was a product of his age, out of place in the cauldron of rudeness that was modern-day New York City. Leo was an anachronism, more genteel and sensitive than the louts in this strange town. There must have been depravity in his age, however, just as there is elegance in ours. But reality often gets in the way of tidy plot lines, and the filmmakers would have none of it.

It was disappointing. Chris said his favorite character was Stuart Besser, a secondary figure who loved Kate. They had been lovers years before, but he retained his affection for her after the breakup, an affection that was endearing but unrequited. He was too good for her, Chris said. It was hard to disagree.

"He's a great actor," Chris said.

"He is," I said. "But I've never seen him before."

"He played the executive editor in *Spotlight*," he said.

The actor was Liev Schreiber, and his portrayal in *Spotlight*—a movie we had seen on our own, outside our Thursday night schedule—was intense but nuanced, his integrity simmering throughout the film.

"Really? He's changed so much. I didn't recognize him."

Kate and Leopold was one of the few movies on the summer list we did not like. Maybe we would have better luck the next time. It was *P.S. I Love You.*

"See you next week," I said, dropping Chris off at his apartment.

"Thanks, Dad."

CHAPTER 12

The Accusation

1992

I LOOKED OUT the kitchen window, fascinated by a cloud floating above the tree Chris and his friend, James, were climbing. The cloud drifted through the latticework of branches, a towering mass slashed into white wisps by the tree. Then it stopped, frozen in midflight, like a kite snagged by a tree, the very tree the boys were climbing. The world seemed to stop, too, its rhythms slowed by the unpredictable whims of Nature. Full bore one minute, languid the next.

The boys were not languid. They dangled from a branch with the carefree charm of kids decades away from the crushing responsibility of adulthood. Or were they?

Still hanging from the branch, their legs spinning as if they were on bicycles, the boys laughed maniacally. I could not hear them, but their mouths were agape with joy, and the laughter seemed palpable, if not audible. I smiled.

Then James slipped, plopping onto the grass below, his legs splayed in front of him. His mouth was still open, a wide chasm on a narrow face, but it was not laughter that emanated from his vocal cords. Not this time. He was crying.

I rushed outside, picking him up. James kept crying. He pointed at Chris.

"He did it," he said, pointing at Chris, who had left his perch on the branch. "He knocked me down."

I was stunned.

"Are you sure, James?" I asked.

I set him down, and he said yes, yes, he was sure, the tears still streaming down his face. He glared at Chris, who bowed his head. The cloud, which had been hovering above, drifted away, and Chris shielded his eyes from the sunshine.

"I saw everything from the window, James," I said finally. "You fell. Chris didn't knock you down."

James remained silent, shamed, perhaps, by his false accusation. He looked at me. More silence. Chris stood beside us, but he remained mute, too, and *his* silence was more problematic, more disturbing. I expected him to launch into a spirited defense, but he just stood there, accepting an accusation that was unfair and, worse, untrue. Why? James was the victim of an unfortunate fall, but when he plunged to the grass beneath him, the victim became victimizer, and Chris allowed him to do it. Was Chris accepting all the negative assessments of him—assessments by teachers, principals, psychiatrists? Had they beaten him down, stripped him of so much self-confidence, that he was willing to accept all judgments against him, even false ones?

"Are you OK now, James?" I asked.

"Yes," he said.

"OK, I'll walk you home."

I wanted to shelter Chris from pain, from the barbs life would fling at him. I had my own problems, as we all do, but mine were different, and I wanted to forget mine and absorb his, knowing that I was strong enough to overcome them. I was not sure that *he* could overcome his. And what was worse, I was not sure that he could take it in the future, because the hurt—unlike, perhaps, his capacity to deal with it—would grow and grow. It was an impossible dream on my part, this desire to be a vessel for his agony, but I would have given anything to make it come true.

I told Antonia about the incident later that afternoon, and she pursed her lips, as if suppressing a long and weary sigh. We discussed his *condition*—whatever that condition was. It was almost as if the maturation process had speeded up with Chris. He was like a little teenager, grappling to find his identity in a world that had already found it for him. Retarded. Strange. Weird. All those diagnoses were wrong. And, no, he was not a little teenager; he was a little boy. His condition, whatever it was, did not define him. It was *part* of him.

How big a part? How deep and substantial? Those were the questions. And how could he grow with the labels but without the stultifying limits that labels impose?

We read him *The BFG* that night. Roald Dahl was one of his favorite authors. It is hard to have a favorite author at that age, but Chris was a reader and a listener, and if you stacked each book he had read or heard, the mountain of words would have scraped the ceiling in his room. He loved *Willy Wonka* and *Fantastic Mr. Fox*, and it looked as if he would love *The BFG* as well.

BFG stood for Big Friendly Giant. He was an outsider, his heart as imposing as his stature, and like all noble creatures, he internalized the hopes and dreams of others. The giant takes a girl under his enormous wing. She is an outsider, too, an orphan fascinated by windows because windows represent a portal to the outside world. They find each other, these two outsiders, and they help each other grow. It may seem impossible for a giant to grow, but the girl touches his soul, and he expands in ways that have nothing to do with feet and inches.

When we stopped reading, I told Antonia about my desire to create a force field around Chris. She sighed. I did not know how much he was suffering, not really, and I did not know if I could absorb what he was experiencing. To assume that I could was to diminish what he was going through. I did not want to do that. What I *did* want to do was help him overcome the suffering, help him realize that, no matter what people thought of him, he was still the little boy who read and giggled and broke the hearts of his parents. He was not autistic Chris or retarded Chris or weird Chris. He was just Chris.

CHAPTER 13

P.S. I Love You

FEBRUARY 18, 2016

THE BIRD GLIDED over the tables, its wings as still as the air in the food court.

It was comforting, somehow, to think of him as *the* bird, not *a* bird, as if he were a regular, warm and familiar, another pebble in the mall mosaic. The bird glided from table to table, its feathers a mottled gray and black, dull but vibrant. He pecked at the crumbs on the floor, his beak transformed into a drill, bobbing up and down, up and down, like a figure in a stop-motion film. Did the sanitation department grouse at the bird for these activities? Or did it welcome the scavenging because it helped clean the floor? I asked a janitor that question one day, and he smiled.

"I don't know if he helps clean the floor or not," he said, shrugging. "But I like to see him in there. It makes me feel like I'm outdoors."

It struck me what fragile creatures birds are. I remembered the morning our predator cat—Bulgas, as light-footed as a cat burglar, appropriately enough—disemboweled a bird on our front lawn in El Paso. The heart lay among the scattered feathers, pink, moist, and tiny. How could such a puny organ power such a magnificent flying machine? I wondered. My musings were tempered by a comforting thought: Bird, hundreds of miles from El Paso, was safe from the feline predator.

Chris was late again. Reliably late. But it was a minor transgression. I had another book with me, *Between the World and Me* by Ta-Nehisi Coates, an African American writer—a book of such crystalline majesty that almost every passage represents an epiphany. It won the National Book Award for nonfiction in 2015. Written in the form of a letter to his son, the volume is both searing and poignant, emotional reactions that reflect the complexity of this brilliant work.

I wanted to read it because of the racism that seemed to be strangling the nation, hatred on a level I had not seen since the 1960s, when the nation seemed to teeter on the edge of self-destruction. Assassinations, riots, neighbors turned against neighbors. What we were seeing now was worse than what we saw in the sixties, as if the hostility, unseen and unnoticed for so long, had oozed out of the gutters, where it had resided all along.

Coates recalls that the great American writer Saul Bellow once asked, "Who is the Tolstoy of the Zulus?" He was referring to the author of *War and Peace* and *Anna Karenina*. Coates explores the marginalization that would lead an acclaimed novelist, a Nobel laureate, to ask such a question. Then he responds simply: "Tolstoy is the Tolstoy of the Zulus."

Tolstoy was Russian, but his soul transcended borders. It encompassed something far bigger than nations and continents and territories; it encompassed humanity. Tolstoy did not belong to Russia, Coates said; he belonged to the world—Black and White, rich and poor, Christian and Muslim.

"Hey, Dad."

Chris arrived, garbed in his Box uniform—cap, jacket, and T-shirt.

"Hey, Chris."

"What are you reading?" he asked.

I held up the book, and I mentioned the passage about Tolstoy. It reminded me of a John Fogerty concert we had seen a while back at the Majestic Theater in San Antonio. I had told Chris how saddened I was that there were so few African Americans in the audience.

"He was playing their music," I said.

I told Chris the music was steeped in soul and blues, including covers by great Black artists—Leadbelly, Bo Diddley, Marvin Gaye.

"It's their music," I repeated.

"It's *everybody's* music," he said.

"You're right," I said, chastened by the wisdom of someone almost thirty years younger.

Chris sat down at the table, and the bird swooped at his feet, dive-bombing toward a crumb by his chair.

"We should give the bird a name," I said.

"OK," he replied, shrugging.

I thought he would be more enthusiastic.

"How about Bird?" I asked. "You know, the way some of the animals in *Winnie the Pooh* are known by their species designation. The pig is Piglet, the kangaroo is Roo, and the tiger is Tigger with a double G. So the bird is . . . Bird."

Chris smiled.

"I like that," he said.

Chris loved the *Winnie the Pooh* stories, which we read to him as a child. We loved them, too; we named him Christopher Aaron because it sounded like Christopher Robin, the child who discovers a group of wondrous animals in the Thousand Acre Woods. The years passed, and as his troubles multiplied, we tried to connect him to a happier time in his life—a project that was sometimes difficult. *Winnie the Pooh* represented a happier time. The main character was a befuddled bear, with befuddled friends, but they

confronted their befuddlement as a community, united by a friendship that transcended their confusion over the problems life hurled
at them. Chris had his own community; he had us, his family,
including Katy, who would smile as we read the *Winnie the Pooh*
stories, lulled by words she could not yet understand. But were we
enough?

"I like that," he repeated.

So that was it. We found our companion, befuddled or not, in
the food court. And he had a name—Bird. We were not even sure
if it was the same Bird we saw week after week, swooping into the
food court and into our hearts. Birds are hard to identify, at least
for me, with none of the distinguishing characteristics we notice in
dogs or cats or other animals. But it was comforting to think that
the bird was a constant, greeting us almost every Thursday evening.
So Bird it was.

Bird swooped onto the ledge of the fountain near our table,
pecking at the water that rushed from a deep basin. The rustling
water was soothing, a sonic counterpoint to the traffic beyond the
mall. I sighed.

"Why are fountains so soothing and tranquil, Chris?" I asked.

"I don't know," he said.

I was shocked—and disappointed. I expected a long, involved
explanation. But there was no explanation. Not this time. Just a
shrug—indifference communicated not by language but by body
language. My brain did a double take, and I waited for a response
that never came. It was like waiting for a green light that was stuck
on red. I kept waiting, but his response was as definitive as it was
succinct: "I don't know."

And, yet, Chris did not disappoint. Not really. Yes, I expected
a rambling but articulate dissertation on why the sound of rushing water soothes our souls. That would have been so Chris. But
if Chris could be reliable in some ways, he could be unreliable in
others. I had no right to anticipate one reaction over the other, because either way, explanation or no explanation, Chris was Chris,
as complex as anyone else. Perhaps more so.

"Well," I said, taking a stab at the explanation I had expected from him, "when we're in a natural setting—sitting by a river, walking past a stream in the forest—the water enhances the serenity we would feel, anyway. . . . And when . . ."

Chris interrupted me. There were times when Chris could not focus on what I was saying, much less what I was thinking. But there were other times when he seemed so invested in my thoughts that he could finish my sentences for me. This was one of those times.

"And when we're in an urban setting, far from the forest or the river, the rushing water reminds us of the beauty of nature," he said. "And so, in a setting so remote from nature, we feel this sense of tranquility come over us. It is jarring and soothing at the same time."

. . . *Aaahhh*, Chris . . .

We got in line for the movie—*P.S. I Love You*, released in 2007. I wondered if the title was based on The Beatles song of the same name. It was a Buddy Holly-style ballad, which was appropriate considering that rock critics speculated that the "P.S." in the title stood for Peggy Sue. I asked Chris if he knew if the movie was based on the song, and he said "No, I don't know." A woman in line overheard us.

"No, it has nothing to do with The Beatles," she said. "Although it *is* a love story."

I had figured it was a love story, what with *love* in the title, but her comment was still helpful. I was so Beatles-centric that I assumed their artistic shadow seeped into every corner of our culture. I was wrong—I guess.

The movie, whether or not it was based on a Beatles song, did not disappoint. It was sad but sweet, with a sentiment that toed the pool of schmaltz without diving into it. The characters were believable, men and women who recognized their fragility without succumbing to it—the very definition of bravery. And Hilary Swank showed flashes of the enormous talent that had emerged three years earlier, with her stunning performance in *Million Dollar Baby*. *P.S. I Love You* was not *Citizen Kane*, but it was refreshing, particularly after *Kate and Leopold*.

"They didn't even play the Beatles song," Chris said afterward, smiling.

"I know," I said, feigning disappointment.

We walked to the parking lot, chilled by the winter night.

"Did you like it?" I asked as we got into the car, repeating the question I would ask after every movie.

"I did," he said. "It's always cool to see people portrayed as quiet heroes. We tend to think heroism is possible only on the battlefields. Movies have conditioned us to think that way, I guess. But it's not true."

I wanted to tell him he was proof of that, but we arrived at his apartment, and I let the moment pass.

"Thanks, Dad," he said, stepping out of the car.

CHAPTER 14
The Punishment

OCTOBER 1993

IT WAS AN October afternoon, the sun a burnt orange, shimmering in the autumn sky.

As neighbors raked their lawns and squirrels skittered from tree to tree, a school bus rolled to a stop in our neighborhood. Chris hopped onto the sidewalk, landing in a crouch that made his backpack look like a hump. Then he straightened up, the hump disappeared, and the backpack became a backpack again. He looked like a little soldier, a soldier for God, dressed in his Catholic grade school uniform—navy blue pants, light blue shirt, navy blue tie, a clip-on. I wore the same uniform, in another age, another town, about thirty years earlier.

I hid behind a tree, but he spotted me. Then *he* hid behind a tree, sneaking a peek as if he were a cat burglar. I sidled to another tree, and he sidled to another tree, each of us sneaking peaks at one another. We repeated this ritual every day, sneaking from tree to tree till we reached our house on Cooper Avenue. Then, when we finally reached our house, we emerged from our trees, hugging each other as we took the final steps to the front door.

It was a joyful beginning to what would be a rough afternoon. We rushed into the house, and Chris threw his backpack onto the sofa in the living room, and when it landed on the cushions, an index card slipped out of a sleeve on the side. There was a note on it, bold and black. It was from his fourth-grade teacher, and it looked ominous.

Mr. and Mrs. Seltzer,

Chris seems like a good boy, but he does not pay attention in class. He just sits there, staring ahead. Sometimes, I wonder if he is doing it deliberately. I have to spend too much time and energy on him, and surely he realizes it. It is not fair to the other children. Please talk to him.

Ms. Wilson

Instead of talking to him, I showed him the index card. And then I uttered a word that will haunt me the rest of my life: "Well?" I expected him to answer a question he was incapable of answering—the same question posed by everyone who studied him, diagnosed him, labeled him. Chris looked at me, his eyes empty, his arms dangling as if the sleeves were empty. His response was profound and disquieting—silence.

Frustrated, I pointed to a corner in the living room. Then I told Chris to kneel down and face the wall. He obeyed.

"I want you to think about how you behave in class," I told him. "And I want that behavior to stop."

Sunlight streamed through the cracks in the blinds, creating geometric patterns of light on the wall. Prisms of sunshine. One of them landed above Chris, a golden halo inches from his brown hair. Chris was no angel, but did he deserve the punishment I imposed on him?

I walked to the den, turned on the TV, and starting watching ESPN. I hated the babble of the sportscasters, the mindless devotion to things that did not matter—games. But, as a sportswriter at the *Philadelphia Inquirer*, I felt compelled to keep up with "news" that did not interest me. I loved covering sports—especially boxing, my specialty—but I focused on the competitors, not the sports they played. It was comforting to think I transcended the childish fascination with games and standings and box scores. But it was bullshit. All bullshit. If I was so high-minded, why did I punish Chris? And why did I leave him there for fifteen minutes?

When I finally abandoned ESPN, I found Chris where I had left him—staring at the wall. I told him to get up, and I told him to start paying attention in class. He said he would. I believed him, but I knew, deep down, that curing a symptom would not cure the disease that prompted it. Chris was still Chris.

Later that evening, after dinner, I sat on the porch steps, hunched forward, my arms wrapped around my knees. It was dusk. Our yard was thick with trees—so many that one of the pines grew crooked, bending and twisting in an effort to embrace the sunlight, the life-giving sunlight.

The moon was up there, low and fat, but I could not see it through the canopy of trees. Then, after a few minutes, the moon climbed, and the moonshine filtered through the branches, spraying milky ribbons of light on the grass. I sighed.

Why did I punish Chris the way I did? Whatever transgression he committed, it did not merit the harsh sentence I imposed on him. I knew that, deep down, but I let my frustration overcome my compassion. And that made my transgression worse than his.

As I stared at the lawn, I thought about another evening, in another time and place. I was eight, carefree and mischievous, running across the park near our home in El Paso. It was dusk.

Grabbing a June bug trundling across the grass, I held it in my hand, its tiny, churning legs tickling my palm. *Aaahhh.* What a delicious sensation. I tied a piece of thread around the bug; then, after inspecting my handiwork, I released it, and the insect buzzed through the dry, summer air, the string turned into a leash. The bug led me for hours, it seemed. . . . Childhood was different back then. . . . Was it better?

The front door creaked behind me. It was Antonia. She was short, about five-foot-four, and the first hints of gray were starting to thread through her brown hair. I turned around. The moonlight was hitting her face; like both her children, Antonia had almond eyes, and whenever she expressed concern, they narrowed into slits.

The older I got, the more I recognized my flaws, and the more I recognized my flaws, the more I recognized the virtues of others. That included Antonia. She was the mother her son needed, a woman who smiled when we smiled and grieved when we grieved. Everything was about family. Chris was an individual, worthy of love and respect, but he was part of a unit, and if he was troubled, the unit was troubled.

My arms still wrapped around my ankles, I started rocking gently, my head and torso moving like a rocking horse. Antonia stood above me, and she seemed taller than usual, a strange mixture of fear and resignation on her face. She spoke softly.

"Are you OK?" she asked.

"Yes . . . No."

Was I OK? I was not sure. I felt guilty for punishing Chris, but the guilt, I figured, should have made me feel good. It was a burst of self-awareness, an insight into my action, which indicated I might learn from it. If I did something wrong, that was one thing, but if I did something wrong without realizing it, that was worse. I realized I did something wrong when I punished Chris, and, yet, this self-awareness brought no redemption, no reconciliation. It brought more guilt. Chris was a victim, and I joined his list of tormentors. His *long* list of tormentors. I sighed, as if I could expel the agony in my heart. Again, no dice.

The moon ascended, and the silky ribbons on the grass became thick bands. It was a calm, quiet evening, as if all the trees and bushes, all the shrubs and flowers, were shushing each other. The grass seemed to shimmer.

Was I OK? I did not answer. Antonia sat next to me on the porch steps, draping her arm around my shoulders, her eyes narrowed into slits.

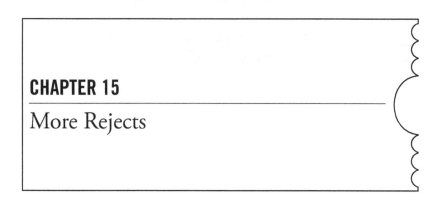

CHAPTER 15
More Rejects

FEBRUARY 25–MARCH 24, 2016

WE DID NOT really reject these movies; circumstances rejected them for us. I went to the food court every week, dutifully but naïvely, waiting for Chris. Waiting and waiting and waiting. I took my books with me, a series of them—*Sideways*, *The Big Sky*, *Ten Thousand Saints*. I would read a few pages, then text Chris. Read a few more pages, then text him again. No answer. I tried to savor the words in the books, but with my focus on Chris, every sentence became a fuzzy, incoherent mess; for perhaps the first time in my life, reading became a chore.

Week after week, Chris was a no-show. He never answered my texts, never explained his absences. So I would leave the food court, slapping my book against my thigh, forlorn and, sometimes, angry. *Dammit, Chris, answer my texts.*

Chris would not respond until a day or two later. His excuses varied, but only slightly. *I was sleeping . . . I was working . . . I was . . . whatever.*

Sometimes, I was so distraught that I would head over to The Box, looking for Chris, hoping he was all right. He was never there, but the manager, cheerful and polite, always reassured me.

"Chris is not working today," she would tell me.

"How is he doing?" I asked.

"He's doing great," she would tell me, smiling. "I love Chris. He's a hard worker."

Chris always spoke well of the manager, Norma, a Latina who seemed to be in her early thirties. She seemed warm and nurturing. And, well, she loved Chris. What was there not to like?

Love or no love, I worried about Chris, worried about his tendency to disappear, to go underground. *Dammit, Chris, answer my texts*. We missed four movies, but I do not even remember the titles, do not even *care* about the titles. I did not miss the movies; I missed Chris. *Dammit*.

CHAPTER 16

Charlie and the Chocolate Factory

MARCH 31, 2016

MY POOR MOTHER.

After my Dad died in 1971, I became obsessed with Bob Dylan. He was the voice I longed to hear, the voice that shouted when everyone else was whispering or whispered when everyone else was shouting. It was not that Dylan knew what to say; it was that he knew how to say it. He could be tender one minute, savage the next, and the helix that bound all these emotions was the fierce intelligence with which he expressed them. The fierce intelligence and the unwavering courage. It takes a brave artist to be honest with himself and his listeners.

I had heard him before, but when my dad died, I stopped hearing and started listening. I was overwhelmed, the first time I had experienced that phenomenon since 1964, when "I Want to Hold Your Hand" exploded from the clunky radio on my night stand. . . . Like The Beatles, Dylan was an original artist, respecting his influences while obliterating them. He was building on the past, but he was doing it in a way that rendered the past irrelevant. Dylan was not *a* folk artist; he was *the* folk artist. And, when he turned electric, he was not *a* folk-rock artist; he was *the* folk-rock artist.

One afternoon in 1971, a few weeks after my dad died, I went from fan to evangelist, asking my mother to hear one of his songs with me—"A Hard Rain's A-Gonna Fall," more than six minutes of apocalyptic images redeemed by the shimmering gifts of the poet who created them. It always gave me chills, and it always left me spent. I think it left my mother spent also, but for a different reason. She was sitting on the bed in my room, quietly awaiting the aural assault, and as soon as the needle hit the vinyl, she started squirming, as if wondering when the screeching would end. Or *if* it would end. It did, and when the song was over, I asked her if she liked it. She said, "Yes," summoning half the sincerity of the poet she had just heard. Oh, well, I thought, I tried.

Now, here I was, about fifty years later, in the food court at the Wonderland Mall. Another Thursday evening. Just me and my book. Chris was late again, but as before, I did not find his tardiness annoying. He was operating on Chris Standard Time, which gave me an opportunity to read my book—*1965: The Most Revolutionary Year in Music*. I just hoped he would show up, late or not.

Andrew Grant Jackson explores the momentous year of the title, momentous for rock 'n' roll and those who love it. The genre seemed moribund, a bloated corpse, and the forensics led to the bloody hands of "artists" like Pat Boone, Frankie Avalon, Paul Anka, and Bobby Rydell. They took what Elvis created, and they punched holes in the music that changed the world. One of the perpetrators, sadly, was Elvis himself, who went from original to self-parody, becoming a sideshow outfitted in spangled jumpsuits about two sizes too small for his expanding girth. If only his music had grown along with his waist.

Then, in 1964, The Beatles did what Elvis had done ten years earlier, shocking the world with music so new and vital that rock 'n' roll did not sound like rock 'n' roll anymore. It was astounding.

Their appearance on *The Ed Sullivan Show* brought an unofficial close to a decade that should have ended four years earlier.

The Beatles did not stop there. They kept yanking the music into foreign territory, each album pushing forward, ever forward, making what Elvis had created a decade earlier seem quaint and charming. The pivotal year was 1965, and it started with "I Feel Fine," a song that started with a strange, whining, echoing guitar riff. George Harrison would say later that The Beatles "invented" Jimi Hendrix.

"I Feel Fine" opened a floodgate for other startlingly original artists, including Dylan, who was inspired by The Beatles to plug in his guitar. The result was stunning: Along with his guitar, he amped up his vision, his imagery, his attempt to comprehend a world that seemed incomprehensible. The "electric" Dylan produced, in this seminal year, two of the greatest albums in rock 'n' roll history— *Bringing It All Back Home* and *Highway 61 Revisited*—followed a year later by *Blonde on Blonde*.

"What are you reading?"

It was Chris. He made it—finally. I showed him the book cover. He read the title slowly, lingering on the words "most revolutionary." He smiled, a grin so broad his mouth looked like a mail slot.

"Is that true?" he asked.

"Pretty much," I said. "Except for, maybe, 1954, when Elvis walked into Sun Records for the first time. Or 1964, when The Beatles appeared on *The Ed Sullivan Show*."

Chris was wearing his Jack in the Box cap, the one that made him look like a young Bob Dylan—sweet and beatific. It struck me that I picked the book because Chris looked like the folk-rock poet; he even had the nasal voice to go with the looks. Then he took off the cap, and his hair, plastered under the fast-food logo, recoiled into a curly brown tuft. Chris was Chris again. I told him about the day I introduced my mother to Bob Dylan, and the grin returned.

"Yeah, that sounds like Grandma," he said, smiling.

And, then he laughed, and it was the sound of every laugh I had ever heard, every bit of joy and wonder and release rolled into one guffaw. He was in a good mood, and I wanted to hold onto that feeling as long as I could. I wanted to hold onto it forever.

My mother died in 1996, the victim of a stroke that had left her paralyzed for a year, marooned in her own body. The kids did not get to know her, not really, but they knew enough. They knew she did not suffer fools easily, and they knew her definition of *fool* was pretty broad, including almost everyone but her.

My dad died in 1971, and three days after the heart attack that killed him, we were on our way to the cemetery following the funeral service. I was seventeen. A neighbor, an elderly woman we barely knew, jumped into the hearse with us, as if she were part of the immediate family. My mother was wearing sunglasses, but I could tell she was glaring behind the shades.

The woman started moaning, asking God why Chester, my father, had to be taken from us. Why, why, why? He was so young, so vibrant; he had so much more to give. My dad was fifty-six, which did not seem young to me, a teenager; but the woman was in her seventies, and she viewed my father as a young man. So she wailed, a Greek chorus compressed into one annoying body.

"*Ya callate, que estas loca?*" my mother, whose family came to El Paso during the Mexican Revolution, finally yelled. "Shut up. Are you crazy?"

The woman complied, her grief muted but no less intense. I could sense my mother glaring at her, behind the shades, and the woman fidgeted. Then she found a new outlet for her sorrow. Adjusting her pillbox hat, its black veil shading her face , she stopped wailing and started sniffling. I was hoping my mother would tell her to shut up again, but she remained silent.

Did the old woman do this with every neighborhood family that suffered a loss? I wondered. Maybe it added drama to her lonely life. Or maybe she was what my mother said she was. Maybe she was crazy.

"Ha!" Chris said, laughing when I finished the story. "That sounds like Grandma."

The smile broadened, then disappeared, the mail slot retracting into a peephole. Why? Chris could be mercurial, but his moods were rarely punctuated by tantrums or rages. No, his swings were more nuanced, although no less intense, usually conveyed by facial expressions. There were times when a darkness seemed to settle on his face, as if he had suddenly sprouted a thick beard. But there were other times, thankfully, when the darkness indicated something more benign—a brain in motion, the gears working to resolve a problem that afflicted his psyche. This was one of those times.

"Uh, Dad, I know you're probably hungry," he said slowly. "But, uh, I just had a burger at The Box . . . and I was wondering if we could skip dinner and head upstairs before the movie starts."

"Sure," I said.

"I want you to meet someone," he said.

Upstairs was the "market," one of his favorite haunts. It was a series of shops, partitioned by black curtains, which led you, maze-like, from one corridor to another—a catacomb for consumers. The vendors sold curios, candles, comic books, and leather goods, items you could never find in the chain stores throughout the rest of the mall.

"This way, Dad," Chris said as I followed him through the maze.

He led me to a place with an earthy odor more pungent than any shoe store. It was a leather goods shop. Everything was made of leather. *Everything.* Even a chess set where every rook and pawn, every knight and queen, could have ended up as a vest or a shoe or a saddle in another store. It smelled heavenly, just this side of overpowering.

"Leonard, this is my Dad," Chris said.

Leonard was the manager, a short, burly man with a thick red beard that obscured his nose and ears—the facial equivalent of kudzu. I could see his blue eyes peeking through the wild brush, but only because they glinted with a keen enthusiasm. He talked . . . and talked . . . and talked, his words punctuated by occasional pauses that served as rhetorical flourishes, not as portals to let others enter the conversation. I did not mind; his verve was refreshing, his vigor inspiring. He was an Iraq War veteran, and he discussed the battles with an urgency that made you hear the blasts and see the blood and smell the corpses, and yet, for all the passion and fervor, all the fire and zeal, he remained strangely calm, as if he were describing the experiences of another soldier, in another time, another war. He spoke for about twenty minutes. I looked at Chris, tilting my head toward the exit.

"Oh, hey, Leonard," Chris said. "We gotta go. We're gonna see a movie."

On our way down the escalator, I asked Chris if he thought Leonard had PTSD—Post Traumatic Stress Disorder.

"Yeah, I do," Chris said. "He's never said so, not directly. But I think he does. That's why he likes to talk about his experiences, I think. If he talks about them, he reduces them to . . . topics, ordinary topics, of conversation. . . . Does that make sense?"

"It does," I said.

Chris was proud of the few friends he had, and he loved introducing them to me. He would spot one somewhere, and he would say, "Oh, there's Mike." Or Bill. Or Susan. And then he would walk up to them and say, "This is my dad."

We got in line. The movie—based on a book by an author Chris loved, Roald Dahl—was *Charlie and the Chocolate Factory*, the remake of the Gene Wilder classic, *Willy Wonka and the Chocolate Factory*. Johnny Depp was Willy Wonka, and he played him with the same blend of creepiness and wholesomeness that Wilder had achieved in 1971. What a tightrope walk. Too much of one and not enough of the other, and the whole movie would plunge into a gooey mess of chocolate sauce. Not to worry, though: Depp, like Wilder before him, maintained the delicate balance.

The real wonder, though, was Charlie, portrayed as a bright but humble child whose spirit burned amid the darkness of poverty. He was the bravest of youngsters, accepting his lot while striving to rise above it. Bravo, Charlie. And his relatives were delightful, nurturing, and compassionate elders with noses and ears so big that they could have sprouted from their vegetable garden. They lived in a tiny house, with the rafters low enough to conk their heads, and yet it was big enough to accommodate the wonderful dreams that fueled both Charlie and his family.

Charlie reminded me of Chris—he lives in squalor, but his internal landscape is rich and splendid, a testament to the power of dreams. He sees beyond the grimy hovel, the raggedy clothes, the bland soups whose sole ingredient seems to be water. Charlie loves his family, and his family loves him. They love him so much that his dream becomes their dream. And what is his dream? To purchase the chocolate bar—the *one* chocolate bar—that will gain him entry to the wondrous candy factory run by the benign but demented Wily Wonka. Charlie gets his wish, but his triumph seems grander than the victories in *Rocky* or *Rudy*, because his dream was not self-fulfillment but a respite from life itself, from the darkness and oppression that can bum-rush you.

Ironically, Freddie Highmore, who played Charlie, would portray Shaun Murphy in the TV series *The Good Doctor*, about a year later. Shaun was autistic, and while his awkwardness alarmed both patients and loved ones—at least, initially—he was calm and professional, his manner as soothing as the sedatives his colleagues prescribed. Watching the show would be an eye-opener, as Chris himself was an eye-opener.

The movie ended, and we walked out of the theater, another Thursday night come to a close. I drove Chris home. He paused before stepping out of the car.

"Thanks, Dad," he said.

And then that mail slot of a smile reappeared.

CHAPTER 17
Leaving Jersey

AUGUST 1995

I WONDERED HOW Antonia and I coped.

The truth is, we did not cope; we got along, moment by moment, day by day. Our coping strategy, such as it was, became less about rescuing our son and more about retaining our sanity. We did not realize it then, but the two strategies complemented each other. It was the same tactic reinforced by flight attendants before takeoff: In case of emergency, put on your face mask before tending to your children.

We started taking the family on weekend trips, usually to places where I had to cover a fight—New York, Atlantic City, Washington, DC. Chris was thirteen, Katy six. The kids loved staying in hotel rooms; they jumped on the beds and stared out the windows—simple activities that provided endless entertainment.

We stayed at a Marriott in Manhattan one weekend. Our room was on the tenth floor, and directly across from our window was a giant billboard of Kelsey Grammer, the star of *Frasier*, and one of his costars, Eddie the dog. The kids stared at the billboard for what seemed like hours, fascinated by a sight foreign to our humdrum neighborhood back home.

On a weekend trip to Washington, DC, we strolled along the grass in front of the Jefferson Memorial. The wind picked up, and trash skittered across the lawn. Chris gave chase, trying to pick up every piece of trash. "Chris!" I yelled. He was trying to clean up the area.

"Chris," I said, mortified. "There's too much trash. You'll never finish. And, besides, it's not your job."

Running and stooping, he stopped to answer me.

"But, Dad, somebody has to do it!"

Antonia and I stared at each other, our eyes clouded with fear and uncertainty. Chris meant well, but the behavior was inappropriate. We wanted to preserve the good intentions while removing the bad consequences. But how?

Back home, on Sundays, I would visit a bakery in Haddon Township, about three miles from our home, returning with an armful of cinnamon muffins and raisin biscuits. I would usually go by myself, but whenever I took Katy, it meant a free cookie or muffin for her. She would eat it on our way back to the car.

"Do you think making Chris happy is the answer?" Antonia asked me.

"Of course," I said. "But don't you think we try to do that, anyway?"

"Yes," she said, her eyes welling with tears.

Despite our travails with Chris, we had some great times in Jersey—moments that were quiet but sublime, telling us that our son was, like Pinocchio, a *real boy*. We would cling to those moments in the hard times. It was all we had.

———

The house was bare, stripped of all its chairs, tables, photographs, and books. Everything but the memories. You can hire a moving company. Haul everything that is not nailed down. Leave the floors and walls naked. But it is almost impossible to evict the ghosts.

We had our memories in this house, our South Jersey home for almost eleven years. Some were good, some bad. But, as with every parting of the way, you cling to both the positive and the negative because, for better or worse, they helped form what you became along the way.

So it was with this house. Antonia and Katy had left two days before, boarding a plane to a town two thousand miles away, the town where we met, Antonia and I. The town where we were married. The town where we lived for the first three years of our married life. Our hometown, El Paso.

Antonia and Katy had left on a Tuesday, and here it was Thursday, two days in an empty house. It was rough seeing them off at the airport; we hugged, and Antonia cried, as if she thought the separation would be permanent. Chris and I made the best of it, sleeping on the pine floor in the den and eating pizza on the front porch. Chris did not mind. It was like camping out.

It was mid-August, the nights cool enough to sit outside, a pizza box on my lap. We grabbed slice after slice. The breeze was refreshing, and the fireflies, dozens of them, turned the air an iridescent green, tiny rays of light marking their gentle flight patterns, up and down, back and forth, up and down again. We stared at them, fascinated. It was like seeing Tinker Bell in our yard. Only better. Tinker Bell was everywhere.

Ghosts. When Chris fell asleep on the den floor that night, he snored gently, his chest a little bellows that emitted sweet puffs of air. I stared at him, and I thought of his years in the house. I thought about the evening he read *The Strange Case of Dr. Jekyll and Mr. Hyde*. I thought about the morning I looked out the kitchen window and saw him climbing the oak tree. And I thought about the afternoon I forced him to kneel in the living room, a punishment that would haunt me for years . . . Damned ghosts.

We decided to stay in our empty house one more night. *Waterworld* was premiering the next day in South Jersey, and Chris asked me if we could watch it. He loved science fiction movies, and he rarely asked for anything. I said yes.

Waterworld was getting dreadful reviews, and I wondered if they were justified. They were. It was a multimillion-dollar monstrosity, its gargantuan budget unable to overcome its pygmy script. And yet . . . and yet . . . it seemed to work . . . somehow, it seemed to work. Dennis Hopper was over-the-top, chewing scenery that did not exist, a futuristic version of Long John Silver, his single eye exuding more malevolence than any other pirate with two eyes. Kevin Costner was Kevin Costner, as noble and earnest as always, an almost impossible trick with a movie so absurd. And Jeanne Tripplehorn was wooden but lovely, the most striking vision in this mad, apocalyptic universe.

And it worked for me because it worked for Chris. He gripped the arm rests during most of the movie, tense and wide-eyed, as if he were playing a game in a video arcade. I saw the movie through the eyes of the twelve-year-old boy sitting next to me and, because of him, I gave the film a glowing review that would have outraged the critics. I did not care.

The movie-house was in Haddon Township, one of those charming towns that dotted the South Jersey landscape. It was a real community, an urban setting with a country feel. Houses lined the main street, sharing the environment with bakeries, bars, and hardware stores. It was a densely populated area, but the traffic was manageable, a stream, not a deluge, flowing through a street so narrow that it seemed to be part of the sidewalk.

In other towns, people stayed in cubicles they called homes, segmented from their communities. Not in South Jersey. People sat on their stoops at night, and neighbors greeted each other as they strolled by. You could hear a hum when you stepped outside— friends talking to each other. *Imagine that.* A Norman Rockwell tableau? Hardly, but it was as close as you could get in a world hijacked by computers, malls, and video games.

When we stepped out of the theater, I felt like a kid again. It had been years since I had been in a theater that was not in a mall. What a refreshing experience. The night air felt like a kiss, soft and sweet. We hesitated in front of the box office, a father and his son illuminated by the marquees above them.

"Do you hear that?" I asked Chris.

"Hear what?"

"Everything."

Night sounds are different from day sounds. They are the same noises, but there are fewer of them, so the ones that survive, the ones that embrace the darkness, seem more vibrant, more sonorous, more alive. The white noise disappears, and the other sounds emerge, deep and resonant. Everyday sounds—humming engines, laughing youngsters, rustling leaves. They are like the lead guitars that pierce the rare interludes in rock 'n' roll songs, thriving in the shattered silence.

It reminded me of that wonderful scene in *The Seven Year Itch*, where Tom Ewell and Marilyn Monroe step out of the theater in Manhattan. They have just seen the *Creature from the Black Lagoon*, and the gritty street is just as vivid, albeit not as menacing, as the marsh they saw on the screen. It is so vibrant and unpredictable that Marilyn delights in the world beneath her feet, a world that enchants both her and her audience. She stands over a grate on the sidewalk, and as a subway rumbles past, a swoosh of air lifts her dress toward the skyscrapers, revealing the most sublime sight a tourist can imagine—her legs.

Haddon Township was not *that* enchanting, but when we stepped out of the theater, we heard all the sounds, each one magnified by the calm of the night. They became part of the rich, warm symphony of life in South Jersey. I repeated my question to Chris.

"Hear that?"

"I do, Dad."

We stood under the marquees for a minute, enjoying the night music.

"Now where did I park the car?" I asked.

Chris pointed to a side road across the main street.

"Over there," he said.

I took his hand, and we crossed the street.

"Thanks, Dad," he said as we drove away.

I was saying good-bye to the *Philadelphia Inquirer*. And we were all saying good-bye to Cherry Hill, Angel of Mercy, and The Malfred School. Saying good-bye to one world and greeting another. We hoped the change would be good for Chris—and the family.

Chris had started to develop friendships at school, nothing solid or profound, but friendships nonetheless. The kids would have each other for sleepovers, staying up late—later than usual—playing video games. The kids seemed to speak in code—*level* this and *portal* that—but it was a form of *communication*, however foreign to my ears, and I was grateful for it. The kids giggled, spotting silliness in everything; we wondered if this was the right time to leave South Jersey, but the decision seemed irrevocable.

Chris and I headed out the next morning. The first leg of a journey is always the most memorable—or the most mundane. I was not sure which category our first leg fit into. Maybe both.

It was 9:00 a.m. I was usually an early riser, but we were two thousand miles from El Paso, and the best course for such a journey, I thought, was slow and steady. So we got a late start. It was a bright, clear morning, the kind in which every cloud, no matter how thin and vaporous, looks like an intruder. We crossed the Benjamin Franklin Bridge, and as we passed the Philadelphia city limits, I extended my middle finger. "F U, Philly." I was sheepish about cussing in front of Chris—even if it was a truncated curse—but he giggled.

I had nothing against Philly, not really, but the last year had been the roughest I had ever endured—at least professionally—and it felt good to turn my back on the town and the job. The trouble started about a year earlier. Walking into the Sports Department at the *Philadelphia Inquirer* one morning, I dropped my notebook onto my desk, and the sports editor poked his head out of his office. He called out to me.

"Hey, you fucking wetback."

I walked out the door without answering him. He followed me. I took the stairs—the office was on the fourth floor—and I could hear him behind me, breathing heavily as he clomped down the stairs. He caught up to me on the street, panting and sweating.

"Robert, what's wrong?" he asked.

"I don't like being called a fucking wetback," I said simply.

I forget his answer—I think he said he was joking—but I never considered filing a complaint with Human Resources, and several months later, still distraught over the incident, I resigned from the *Inquirer*. It was a tough decision. The *Inquirer* was a great newspaper, and I had a dream job, covering boxing in perhaps the best fight town in America. But the "fucking wetback" comment changed everything. Ringside lost its allure, and I never looked back.

The worst thing about the incident was not the epithet itself. It was my reaction to it. I thought I handled it with dignity, but I should have been more forceful, more aggressive. My father would have been.

The old man, Chester Seltzer, was born in Cleveland, Ohio, the son of the most powerful journalist in the state—Louis B. Seltzer, the editor of the *Cleveland Press*. My father pursued the same calling, following his father into journalism, but his real love was literature. It liberated him from the staccato style of the gritty, hard-bitten journalist, and it liberated him from the facts.

As it turned out, the old man invented more than characters and plotlines. He also invented—or reinvented—himself. A wanderer who traveled throughout the world, he met my mother in El Paso, and when they got married in 1950, he adapted her maiden name as his pseudonym—Amado Muro. The Cleveland native became what blood and geography had denied him. He became a Mexican.

I was born four years later, and in 1964, we moved from El Paso to Bakersfield. I was ten, the only Latino in the fifth-grade class at St. Francis Elementary. The other kids picked on me for being a "Mex." I was a brown kid who wanted to be white, and I sought help from a white man who wanted to be brown—my father. He obliged, his gentle wisdom guiding me through a rough time.

As we left Philadelphia, I thought about the old man, about his compassion and courage. He would have handled the sports editor differently, but there was nothing I could do about it now. We were heading home, Chris and I, journeying to El Paso—a man fleeing his demons, a boy still wrestling with his.

CHAPTER 18
The Usual Suspects

APRIL 7, 2016

OUR FRIEND BIRD marched across the food court, a feathered version of Chuck Berry, his head bobbing in duck-walk style, sans guitar and pompadour. He was doing what birds do. Searching for scraps, pecking at scraps, searching for more scraps. His movements were deliberate, almost robotic, and I found comfort in the monotony; nothing deterred Bird from what he had to do, no matter how boring or mindless it may have seemed to the humans around him. Bird was a grinder.

Chris and I *tried* to be grinders. We tried to hang in there. So, like Bird, I hung out at the food court, waiting for Chris to arrive for our weekly liaison.

He was late, again, but I had a trusty companion, a book—*A Childhood: The Biography of a Place* by Harry Crews. The ultimate grinder, the kind Chris and I wanted to be, the author was an unusual child, one who seemed born with scars, and those scars, it seemed, grew more scars, scabs upon scabs, creating a crocodile skin that would protect him from the buckshot life fired his way. Good thing, because life would unload on him.

Crews grew up in Georgia, near the Okefenokee Swamp, and one day he was playing "crack the whip" with the other kids. They were cavorting near a smokehouse, and as they sprinted across the yard, their sweaty hands linked, one of the kids flew loose, landing in a vat of boiling water used to scald the pigs. It was Harry. The metaphorical scars became real scars. He was five.

"I reached over and touched my right hand with my left, and the whole thing came off like a wet glove. I mean, the skin on the top of the wrist and the back of my hand, along with the fingernails, all just turned loose and slid on down to the ground."

The boy found solace in the only book his parents owned, the Sears Roebuck & Co. Catalogue. Crews loved the photos—photos of products but, mostly, photos of people. Every model was perfect, face unmarked, body straight, shoulders square. Unlike little Harry. He began writing stories about them, conjuring pasts, presents, and futures for people he had never seen or met, except in the pages of this big, strange, wonderful book. Harry made them come alive. Thus began the career of a great American writer.

"Hey, Dad."

It was Chris. His voice was low and raspy, the aural equivalent of sandpaper. The tone said more than the words. "Hey, Dad." Two words that were benign, maybe even reassuring. But the tone undermined the language, and whenever I heard it, my shoulders stiffened, as if bracing myself for the storm ahead.

"Hey, Chris," I responded.

My words were just as benign as his, at least on the surface. But did he view them as I viewed his, words carrying more meaning, more freight, than the definitions the dictionary assigned them? I did not intend them to, but he may not have intended them to, either. Sometimes, we get gun-shy even when no guns have been brandished.

"How are you?" I asked, plowing ahead.

"OK," he responded.

No, I was right the first time. The tone, cold and surly, was unmistakable. He was upset. Chris was usually professorial, his words full of sweeping declarations, often fortified by asides so rich and thoughtful that you could almost see the footnotes and parentheses floating in the air. These soliloquies could be trying—and exhausting—but their absences were worse. The speeches could be fun but, more importantly, they let you know Chris was in his safe place, pontificating from an invisible lectern in front of him.

When Chris was upset or angry, he spoke in bursts, turning two-syllable phrases into one-syllable phrases. "OK." He seemed to reach the "K" before he had uttered the "O," so halfway through "OK," the term bumped into a dark wall, and there was nowhere to go. "OK" turned into "K." He pronounced the letter so abruptly and sharply that the "O" ended up battered and bruised, ready for the linguistic equivalent of an emergency room, huddled among the other pile-up victims whose journeys were cut short by an unwilling orator.

As an orator, Chris was usually willing, relishing every word he uttered, every pause he allowed himself, although, once he got going, the pauses were few and far between. Chris, the master of monologue. But not today. . . . Today, he took his wire cutter, and he clipped "OK." I let the word hang there. The worst thing you could do was talk when Chris did not want to talk. It was like extending a visit to the dentist.

We sat in silence, staring at the floor, the diners, and the bird, which provided a semblance of escape. Bird pecked away at the floor, finding scraps of food that were invisible to the humans above. There was a buffet down there, somewhere, and Bird found it. We were eating, too—Chris and I—but we were not enjoying our meal as much as Bird was.

Chris was feeling bad, but he did not seek solace or comfort. It was not like him to open up. He looked down, and I stole glances at him. Chris was so handsome, his curly brown hair forming a turban of soft coils on his head. It was good to be with him, despite the tension. I kept staring at him, more boldly this time, unafraid that he would catch me. What if he did not have a "condition," whatever it might be? I wondered. Would he be reciting his monologues in a university English class? Would his students hang on every word, infected by his enthusiasm, his joy in self-expression? It was easy to fantasize about another path for Chris. Easy to fantasize, but hard for him to realize. He seemed trapped, boxed in by an opponent he could barely recognize.

The movie was starting—*The Usual Suspects* with Kevin Spacey. As with a few giants, like Marlon Brando and Meryl Streep, you know Spacey is acting, every gesture, every tic calculated to provide a glimpse into the psyche of his character. But it does not matter if the methods are transparent. It is the result that counts, and the result is that he is one of those breathtaking talents who leave you captivated long after you have left the theater. As Roger "Verbal" Kint in *The Usual Suspects*, he is bizarre but believable. (His character is as creepy as Spacey himself would prove to be, after the sexual harassment allegations against him emerged in 2017; the charges were dropped two years later, when his accuser died, but the stigma remained.) You can almost smell his hot, stale breath, see the vapor as it issues from his mouth when he speaks. He must have inspired the cast around him, because the other actors embody the same trait, at least in this movie. Gabriel Byrne is a corrupt ex-cop who finds a new career as a jewel smuggler. Kevin Pollak is devious but befuddled. And Benecio Del Toro speaks in a strange, garbled monotone.

As compelling as Spacey was, though, the movie was too complex, too convoluted. I struggled to keep up, my head all but exploding. I felt a nudge in my ribs. It was Chris, trying to keep me awake. Fatigued by the effort to comprehend the crazy plotline, I had drifted off.

Two hours later, we walked out of the theater. I was awake, but my consciousness did nothing to help me understand what had happened on the screen. It was enjoyable nonetheless, and I was glad Chris poked me in the ribs.

"Thanks for waking me up," I told him as we walked to the car.

"Well, the movie was so complicated that I was afraid you'd lose the thread if you fell asleep," he said. "You know how much trouble you have understanding some of these mysteries."

It was true. I would get lost in the twists and turns of movies like *The Maltese Falcon*, confounded by characters and situations that seemed to emerge without rhyme or reason. I loved the eerie atmosphere of the movie, the moral ambiguity, but I would have to see it several times before I realized what was going on. It became a family joke. *The Maltese Falcon* was a mystery, but the real mystery, it seemed, was why it flummoxed Dad.

"Yeah," I said sheepishly. "Well, to be honest, I had no idea what was going on."

Chris laughed.

"I enjoyed it, anyway, though," I said.

"Good," he said.

We reached the apartment, and Chris got out, still laughing.

"Thanks, Dad."

What a relief. Chris was in better spirits than he had been when the evening started. But I wondered what had been bothering him—and might be bothering him still. I had more trouble understanding him than I did *The Maltese Falcon*.

CHAPTER 19

Heading Home

AUGUST 1995

AFTER MY PARTING shot to Philadelphia—my middle finger—I thought about the region that had been our home for almost eleven years.

Philly entombed you, choked you, smothered you, the trees and buildings blocking your view of the sky. But the trees and buildings were not the only culprits. The *real* perpetrator, I thought, was the bend of the Earth, which seemed askew on the East Coast, unless you were in Asbury Park or Atlantic City or Virginia Beach, and you were staring eastward, the sky unencumbered by skyscrapers. I do not remember seeing a single sunset in all the time we lived there. . . . No, that is not true. I was covering a boxing press conference one evening at the Plaza Hotel in Manhattan. I happened to look out the window, and there was the sun sinking in the west, a big orange ball in a cloudless sky. That was the only sunset I remember.

For a West Texan, a *far* West Texan, it was like living in a storm cellar—dank, dark, and depressing. Spring brought no relief; summer brought no relief. It was a yearlong ordeal. A storm cellar is a storm cellar. The sun might be shining, a hellacious ball of fire, but it makes no difference when you are stuck in a basement. Philadelphia was a basement.

We sped past Philly, past the city and suburbs, the road markers blurring into flashes of white and green—tiny signposts that skirted our peripheral vision. Mile 56 . . . Mile 66 . . . Mile 76. . . . We reached the Amish countryside—a welcome sight for two travelers eager to hit rural Pennsylvania. And then, *voila*, the tomb disappeared, replaced by alfalfa fields shimmering in the morning light.

As we drove through Amish country, we marveled at the land. Snow would carpet it soon, burying all the flowers and trees under a thick, white glaze—a blanket that would create a striking paradox, for, if you concentrated hard enough, the hush that ensued would be dense enough to hear. *Shhh, listen,* I imagined myself telling a three-year-old Chris as the snow fell, *do you hear them? The little angels falling from the sky?* But it was hard to picture that scene now, the farmland so lush and green that it could stave off winter forever—or so it seemed.

This highway reverie had a real-life parallel. It occurred almost eleven years earlier. We had just moved to South Jersey and, before finding an apartment, we stayed in a motel for two nights. We were cozy in our dull, dingy room, the three of us, safe from the wintry blast. It was a new phenomenon for the transplanted Texans in the motel—an arctic winter, the snow falling so hard that it slashed sideways, as if automatic rifles were spraying the area with white pellets.

It snowed for hours, and the room, once a sanctuary, grew oppressive. The weather imprisoned us. We were tired of it. And then, finally, the sky smiled on us; it stopped dumping the snow that shackled us to the motel.

Chris was sitting on the bed, legs crossed Native American-style, his elbows propped on his knees, his chin resting in his palms. He was watching TV, but the programs were dull and leaden, a mind-numbing series of childish game shows and sappy sitcoms. Only three years old, he was already acquiring the critical faculties that would lead him to classic literature. But Dr. Jekyll and Mr. Hyde were a few years away, lurking in the distance, and right now, in this dingy motel room, the weather turned our son into a frowning, frustrated inmate. Some winter wonderland.

Bored and restless watching my bored and restless son, I peeked through the blinds. And then, as if sensing the exasperation of the little boy in the motel room, Mother Nature relented. The snow faded, then stopped, that dump truck in the sky having disgorged all its contents—at least for now. I acted quickly.

"Put your coat on, Chris," I said.

He smiled, jumping from the bed as if it were a trampoline.

"Where are we going, Daddy?"

"You'll see."

Antonia got up from her chair.

"Are you sure it's safe?" she asked.

"Of course," I said.

We walked out, and the landscape looked like a picture postcard, the blue sky framed by white buildings, white cars, white roads. Everything but White people. No one was out and about. No one but the two of us.

Chris took one step, hip-deep in snow, his legs churning without going anywhere. I picked him up, cradled him in my arms. And then I started walking, heading toward a drugstore two blocks away—a two-minute walk that took us almost ten minutes.

"Pick one out," I said, pointing to a row of coloring books inside the store.

Chris picked a coloring book about polar bears, an appropriate choice. I got some crayons, and we headed back out. We had been in the store for less than five minutes.

The snow resumed, falling gently, each flake a tender kiss on our cheeks. Chris giggled. It was the first time he had experienced falling snow.

"Shhh, listen," I told Chris. "Do you hear them? The little angels falling from the sky?"

Chris giggled again, but the giggling stopped almost as soon as
it began. The snow resumed, falling harder and harder, the picture
postcard replaced by a dark mural. The little angels had turned into
big demons.

"Daddy, you're walking too slow! You're walking too slow!"

All the way back to the motel. The word *slow* emerged, appropriately enough, slowly. He stretched it into three syllables—*Slo-o-ow*.

"You're walking too slow!"

Now, here we were in rural Pennsylvania. I stopped for gas.
Chris stayed in the minivan. He was reading a collection of short
stories by Edgar Allen Poe, as engrossed by the tales as he had been
by the countryside just a few moments before. I went in to pay.

The shelves were wooden, and there were gaps between the
items on them, mostly cans. These gaps were about three or four
inches, unlike the spaces in urban supermarkets, where the items
were packed as tight as teeth in a full mouth. Dust settled around
the cans, and I pictured little puffs of dirt rising every time a customer grabbed one.

The cashier was an old man, about seventy-five, his skin so raw
and pitted that it looked as if a flock of birds had been pecking it.
I thanked him, and he smiled, his lips creasing without parting—a
closed smile.

When I returned to the Honda Odyssey, Chris was still reading his book, his nose buried in the paperback. His head moved
back and forth, like the platen on an old-fashioned typewriter; he
turned each page with a sense of urgency. It was a joy to watch. I
asked him if I could play some music on the CD player. No answer.
I shrugged.

I popped in a Beatles CD, with or without permission. "Drive
My Car" erupted from the bowels of the dashboard, its sensuous
bass line the perfect musical accompaniment to our road trip. I
glanced at Chris. Still journeying through the pages of his book,
undisturbed by the music. I smiled, relieved but not surprised.

The next song was "Nowhere Man." John and George played lead guitar—back to back, first one musician, then another, hitting the same notes. Who else would do that, at least back then? Who else would *think* to do that? Other bands *did* do it, including The Stones, but did any group do it as well as The Beatles?

The Fab Four also did it vocally. Influenced by the Everly Brothers, whose two-part harmony was angelic, The Beatles outdid them, with John, Paul, and George melding three voices into one, their singing so precise that the lyrics seemed to emerge from one throat. They could have stopped there, but on "Nowhere Man," John and George did with their instruments what they did with their voices; they performed as one, adding depth and resonance to the sound.

They played Stratocasters. *Stratocasters.* I came across the word as a kid, struck by its power and authority. It sounded like a machine. *Stratocaster.* Maybe it *was* a machine. But, in the hands of The Beatles, the instruments were beautiful, even awesome—works of art that produced works of art.

On "Nowhere Man," the opening chords were chunky but ethereal, as if The Beatles were part of a celestial orchestra. And then there were the lyrics. One of the supreme ironies of The Beatles was that they could sing about uncertainty with confidence—confidence and clarity, the sadness tinged with triumph. Who else could do that? Dylan and . . . it was a short list. "Nowhere Man" was one of those songs that you wanted to program to eternal reset. *Nowhere Man, Nowhere Man, Nowhere Man, Nowhere Man, Nowhere Man . . .*

With one arm draped around the wheel, the other resting in my lap, I glanced at Chris. Still reading his book, he was not making much headway. I was puzzled. Chris was usually a fast reader, greedily gulping the prose of his favorite writers. *Hmmm.* Was he having trouble with the language? Were the tales so macabre—*mu-kah-bray*—that he feared moving forward, certain that the next page would unlock even greater horrors? Both reasons seemed inconceivable. Here was a boy, after all, who had devoured *The*

Strange Case of Dr. Jekyll and Mr. Hyde in one night about six years earlier. Then it hit me: He was *re*reading the book, savoring the passages, *mu-kah-bray* or not, that had delighted him moments before.

Whatever his condition, it did not affect his intellect—or the joy he took in the world, *his* world, often encased between two book covers. Chris plunged into his books, swimming in the captivating pool of words they offered. I looked ahead, toward his future. He would be, I was certain, an intelligent, articulate man, condition or no condition.

The minivan swallowed mile after mile, the asphalt disappearing beneath us as we passed corn, tobacco, and sorghum fields. Lancaster, Harrisburg, Pittsburgh, Hershey, Gettysburg. The towns flew by, and as the minivan rolled down the Pennsylvania Turnpike, the sky seemed to expand, huge and sprawling. The windshield splintered the sunshine into prisms of light, red, blue, and orange, each one as bright as tinfoil.

Our first stop was Cleveland. When we reached the Ohio state line, the vista opened, just as it had beyond Philadelphia. But this was different; this was grander; this was the Midwest. Chris and I gazed at the world above us, the sky raw and naked, smudged by thin clouds that feathered the heavens. It made you want to open your mouth, open it wide, a monstrous yawn allowing you to take in the pure, crystalline air, take it in and gulp it. And, then, after you gulped it, the air would enter your bloodstream, circulating through vein after vein until it shot out of your toes and fingertips like shafts of light. Then the process would repeat itself—a constant flow of life-giving oxygen. *Aaahhh*. It was one of those delicious feelings you wanted to last forever.

The vista—and my reaction to the vista—reminded me of a beautiful scene in *It's a Wonderful Life*, the movie Chris and I would see about twenty years later at The Bijou in San Antonio. It was the scene in which Jimmy Stewart, overcome with love for the woman he will marry, looks up at the sky and says, "You want the moon, Mary? Just say the word, and I'll throw a lasso around it and pull it down." He is so pleased with the sentiment—and the turn of phrase—that he repeats it. "I'll give you the moon, Mary."

And, after Jimmy Stewart offers his love the moon in a wonderful movie about a wonderful life, she tells him, "I'll take it. Then what?"

"Well," he says, "then you can swallow it, and it'll all dissolve, see . . . and the moonbeams would shoot out of your fingers and your toes and the ends of your hair . . . am I talking too much?"

Maybe *I* was thinking too much. I laughed, embarrassed by my corny pantheism. I looked at Chris. Putting his book down, he laughed, too. Was he gripped by the same feeling I was, the same exalted sense of oneness with Nature? I figured he was. And, if he was, would he be just as embarrassed? I figured he would be that, too. OK, so we were both corny. At least we were corny together, in our crummy Honda minivan, blazing through the countryside that delivered us from the basement we had inhabited for eleven years. Ohio, beautiful Ohio. I smiled.

My dad was born in Ohio, and while I was born thousands of miles away, in El Paso, I viewed Ohio—"The Heart of it All," the license plates said—as my spiritual birthplace. The old man loved Cleveland, his hometown, and the love reached me through a simple and direct route—my DNA. I was not born in Cleveland, but I was born to *love* Cleveland, love it the way the old man loved it.

We met Joe at a bar. Joe was Joe Maxse, one of my best friends on the boxing beat. He worked for the *Cleveland Plain-Dealer*, his hometown paper. Joe grew up delivering the *Cleveland Press*—the paper my grandfather, Louis B. Seltzer, served as editor for thirty-five years—but the *Press* folded in 1982, and Joe applied for a job at the paper that survived. He covered everything, but his favorite sport was boxing. It was raw and naked and unpredictable, and the men who peopled it—the boxers and trainers, the promoters and managers—made the characters in *Guys and Dolls* seem stiff and proper. Joe fit in.

It was a neighborhood bar, cozy and familiar, a brown brick building with Kelly green awnings slanting from the windows. So nondescript that it blended into the other structures on the street, most of them single-story homes. Oak trees lined the sidewalk, dropping a blanket of acorns that crunched under the customers who marched in and stumbled out. There was even a front lawn, the grass trim and tidy—a green buzz cut. It was one of those places where every pull on the tap was a pat on the back that told the customers, "Hey, relax, stay a little longer." Joe fit in.

Joe fit in everywhere, really—everywhere that was genuine, free of pretense. That included the bar, a welcome sanctuary after our long drive through the Pennsylvania Turnpike. Joe was Cleveland through and through—humble but quirky, with a blue-collar sensibility that trumped his white-collar job. He spotted us striding into the bar.

Whatever hominess it projected outside, the place was all bar inside. Sports posters plastered the walls—Cavs, Browns, Indians. There was Bernie Kosar, the cerebral quarterback, standing on the sideline, tall and gawky, his helmet at his hip; that great tuft of black, bushy hair looked like all the helmet he needed. He towered over the patrons like the savior he was—*almost* was. Kosar led the Browns to three conference championship games, but they lost each one, all to the Denver Broncos, who went on to the Super Bowl—and lost.

As the door closed behind us, Chris looked up, fascinated. You could see the guts of the building up there, the pipes, ducts and air-conditioning units crisscrossing the ceiling like waffle grids. Chris pointed up, smiling.

"Heh, heh, heh, there he is," Joe said, imitating a deep, guttural cackle we knew well.

He was mimicking Don King, the notorious boxing promoter.

"Bob Seltzer, greatest boxing writer in the world, heh, heh, heh."

King had a way of lavishing praise on you, only to lavish the same praise on the next boxing writer he met a few seconds later. In King World, the "greatest" was the guy standing in front of him. Everyone was the late W. C. Heinz, who *was* the greatest boxing writer in the world.

"Heh, heh, heh, who's this?" he asked, looking down at Chris.

"Christopher Aaron Seltzer," Chris said.

It may have been the first time the bar patrons had witnessed such formality.

"Hi, Christopher Aaron Seltzer," Joe said, shaking his hand.

We walked to the bar, where Joe had been sitting. Chris climbed onto the stool, using the bar for leverage. He tried to twirl in his stool, but he remained stationary, his feet dangling about two feet from the floor.

"This is Bob Seltzer," Joe told the bartender. "His mom was from Chihuahua."

Amy was Latina. She had short red hair, but the red in her face was more striking, making her cheeks look as if they had been plucked from an apple orchard. I wondered if Amy was a nickname. My mom could have been nicknamed Amy, but everyone stuck to her given name, Amada. Was Amy an Amada? I never asked.

"Oh, hi, nice to meet you," she said, shaking my hand.

The guy next to me, whom I had noticed before, invaded our conversation.

"So you're a Mex?" the guy asked.

I looked at him. He was short and fleshy, his Indians T-shirt about two sizes too small. His skin was pink, and there was a sheen to it, like the trail a snail leaves on the sidewalk. I tried to think of a response that did not involve the term "jackass."

"What'll you have?" Amy asked, breaking in.

We ordered, and our pink-skinned friend went back to nursing his beer, holding the mug with one hand while drumming the bar with the other.

"What's wrong with that man?" Chris asked, whispering.

"Ignorant," Joe and I answered, not whispering.

I ordered Chris a Coke and fried okra, and he forgot about the UN ambassador next to us. Joe and I drank our beers. And Pink Skin, apparently less obtuse than we thought, left us alone.

We stayed with Joe three nights. He lived in a two-story house, a Dutch colonial that looked like our home in Cherry Hill, white

with burgundy trim. It was in a quiet neighborhood, also remi-
niscent of Cherry Hill. There were no fences between the houses,
just bushes and shrubs. And with good reason. The neighbors did
not *want* to fence each other out. They wanted to embrace each
other, and they did; they would be sitting on their porches, enjoying the cool evening air, and if they spotted you across the street,
they would call out to you, as if you were standing next to them,
eyeball-to-eyeball—*Hey ya, Joe, how ya doing?*

————

It was a cool, pleasant afternoon. Cloudless. The sky yielding to
eternity. The heavens as blue as the water below. Lake Erie. A broad
pond shimmering in the afternoon sun. Even the air around us
seemed blue—blue on blue on blue. It was hard to tell where the
lake ended and the sky began.

Our most pastoral and serene sport, baseball exudes brevity.
Even at its most intense, the action is over within seconds, the
product of split-second timing—choreography in cleats. It is both
awesome and sublime.

We were watching the Indians at Jacobs Field, a gift from Joe. It
was a lovely ballpark, a 1930s-style stadium dropped, smack-dab,
into the middle of the 1990s. This was no cookie-cutter stadium,
a massive piece of junk that looked half-finished. No, this was a
warm, inviting arena, a grandstand on steroids, huge but intimate,
a perfect complement to the game played on the sparkling diamond below.

We climbed the steps, and we heard the soft rumble of fans following us to their seats. Chris was not—*is* not—a sports fan. But
when you go to a ballpark, baseball is not a game; it is a picnic, the
contest transformed into a communal event that has nothing to do
with the numbers on the scoreboard. It is about togetherness, about
strangers becoming friends, if only for three hours, their differences
melting in a desire to smile and laugh and, most of all, share.

Chris understood. He wanted to belong, and as one face among
thousands, he *did* belong, in this stadium by the lake. Who cares
if he did not know an RBI from an RPM? He was happy—and

hungry. I gave him some money for a soda and a hot dog, and as he headed for the concession stands, Joe leaned toward me.

"He doesn't talk much, does he?"

We left the next day. Nine o'clock Saturday morning. Congregating on the sidewalk outside the Dutch colonial, we talked for about twenty minutes, stretching our good-byes—Joe in khaki shorts, bare-chested, ready to mow the lawn; Chris and I in blue jeans and T-shirts, ready to head down Ohio, Kentucky, and Tennessee, then on to Arkansas and, finally, Texas.

The neighbors came out, waving at Joe from across the street. They chatted as if there were no intervening street, as if they were sitting at a table in a patio, close enough to clink beer bottles. Neighbors. Joe fit in everywhere. Would Chris fit in anywhere?

I got sick on the road, hit by a sore throat and dull fever. We stopped at a liquor store near Cincinnati. I bought a fifth of whiskey—70 proof. Potent medicine. We spent the night in Louisville, Kentucky. It was a cheap motel, across from a KFC. I winced as we crossed the threshold—and not just from the aches that wracked my body. It was a crummy room. You know the kind. A naked light bulb hanging from a dingy ceiling. A worn carpet, as thin as wax paper. A bed with no headboard. A door that was too small for its frame, creating gaps that allowed the dust and stink of the outside world inside. Not exactly the Ritz—or even the Holiday Inn Express—but we were grateful for the sanctuary it provided, no matter how modest.

I gave Chris ten dollars for a chicken dinner, and he came back ten minutes later, arranging the food on the table by the window—chicken, fries, biscuit, Coke. The lights were out, but the curtain was drawn open, and the urban light show flashed outside, traffic lights and fast-food signs blinking in the evening sky. Chris ate silently. He wiped his mouth after every bite.

Alone at the table, eating his meal, Chris seemed content, if not happy. Contentment means satisfying an urge, a hunger. It is momentary, because you will feel the hunger again and again, and you will have to satisfy it again and again. Happiness is different; it takes more than fried chicken to achieve it—and more than fried chicken to maintain it. Would Chris ever be happy? Or would his fate be darker, muddier? I could not keep the negative thoughts from invading my soul. I feared that whatever he wanted—*truly* wanted—would lurk in the shadows, forever beyond his grasp. Could he wrest meaning from the meaningless? For that is what happiness is, right? A flame in the darkness?

The next morning, I felt better—better than I had a right to. The aches were gone. The sore throat and dull fever, all gone. And so were my dark thoughts. It was another day. I left the whiskey bottle, almost full, on the dusty dresser—booty for the cleaning lady (if they had one) or her boyfriend. I did not need it any longer. The "medicine" had done its job.

Hitting the road, we passed Fort Knox, a squat, drab, prison-like structure where the bars did not hold men within their cells. Or did they? Could bars of gold—vast amounts of wealth—create their own prisons, prisons of greed and avarice? Hardly an original question, but I thought about posing it to Chris. He probably could have answered with an eloquence beyond his years. But I stayed silent.

Our first stop was the Grand Ol' Opry Amusement Park in Nashville, now defunct. Chris got on the roller coaster. I waited for him, earthbound, afraid that the queasiness I had felt the night before would return with extra force.

The roller coaster looped into the heavens, and Chris flashed by with hypnotic regularity—up and down, back and forth—his smiled broadened by the gusts of air that billowed his cheeks. I could have been up there with him, sharing the sensation of hurtling into the sky, and I regretted my decision to remain below. If I *had* been sitting next to him, I thought, I might have felt the same exhilaration, the same delirious fear, but, caught up in the fun *I* was feeling, I would have been unable to witness the fun *he* was feeling. And that would have been no fun at all. I made the right choice. . . . Besides, I was afraid of roller coasters.

Later, back on the road, it struck me that Chris had the most fun when he was alone. Alone with his books. Alone with his roller coasters. Alone with his thoughts. Solitude was his friend, not his enemy. But it still pained me.

After the roller coaster in Nashville, it was on to a different kind of ride—a wild musical ride that started in a tiny record studio in Memphis, Tennessee. Sun Records Studio. The place where Elvis, the Hillbilly Cat, became royalty—the King of Rock 'n' Roll. He was not just a singer; he was a cultural force, every pelvic thrust a blow to a country that wanted its pop stars more subdued. Elvis was a heathen.

"Hell, these were timid times, an' here's this white kid up there shakin' his ass," Lewis Grizzard, the late humorist, once said. "An' I remember my grandfather sayin' that this was the devil's music, an' anybody who listened to it was surely gonna go straight t' hell, which, y'know, did concern me some. Still, I liked it, an' I figured I'd just take my chances."

The country took its chances, too. When Elvis recorded "That's All Right" in 1954, it distilled everything that came before—blues, country, gospel, boogie-woogie—into an exciting new art form, so raw and visceral that it seemed to blow the roofs off the juke joints where it was performed. Rock 'n' roll.

It was early afternoon when we hit downtown Memphis. We were too early for the next tour at Sun Records, so we dropped into the cafe next door. I ordered without reviewing the menu—a beer for me, a soda for Chris. It was just one beer, but it had the same effect that five beers might have had, making me so emotional that I started to cry.

"What's wrong, Dad?" Chris asked, his eyes widening in alarm.

"This is where it all began, Chris," I said, still crying. "This is where rock 'n' roll began."

Chris rolled his eyes, his alarm turning to bemusement.

"Oh . . . OK," he said.

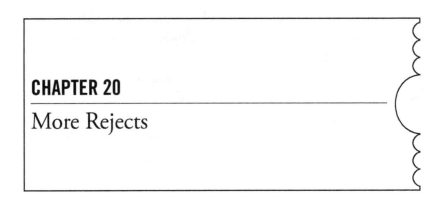

CHAPTER 20

More Rejects

APRIL 14–MAY 12, 2016

FUNNY THING ABOUT rejects. Once you reject something, it becomes easier to reject something else, then something else after that, then. . . . Rejection follows rejection follows rejection. A chain of refuse—in our case, cinematic refuse—that snaked behind two hard-to-please moviegoers. These were our first rejects since March, and we made up for lost time.

We discarded movie after movie. There must have been at least four spurned films, all of them on consecutive weeks, meaning my Thursday nights were lonelier, emptier during that stretch. I almost wished we had gone to see the flotsam on film. But we held firm. We had our standards, and we would live up to them, regardless of the loneliness our purity imposed on us—well, on me, anyway.

What were these rejects? Well, it would be unfair to defile so many films. In some cases, we had seen them before and, thus, did not want to renew our acquaintance with the rubbish. In others, we based our opinions on reviews and critiques we had seen or read. But my reticence is based mainly on kindness, yes, kindness. As Mark Twain states after Tom Sawyer, pressed into answering who the first two Apostles were, blurts out, "David and Goliath": "Let us draw the curtain of charity over the rest of the scene."

CHAPTER 21
The Suicide Kings

BIRD WAS AWOL, an absence I felt with a pang—not because I missed our winged companion, although I did, but because our lofty friend must have heard—and obeyed—the enchanting call of spring, with its blue skies and radiant flowers. Bird was out there, somewhere, taking it all in, an airborne tourist who left his home behind, the food court at the mall. A temporary absence, I hoped.

Then, again, Mother Nature was a shabby presence on Fredericksburg Road, where the mall was located. It was an urban thicket, strewn with laundromats, pawnshops, and tattoo parlors. Not exactly Walden Pond. Besides, I was here, in the mall, to meet Chris, and I would not skip the opportunity for a romp through the Redwood Forest, the Grand Canyon, or the Catskill Mountains.

The mall was not Yellowstone Park, but it had its own allures. This was San Antonio, so the people were friendly, the shoppers as well as the shop owners. Not that San Antonio was unique among

Texas cities. You could say the same about El Paso and Fort Worth and even Houston, which gets a bad rap because of its size and wealth. I lived there for a year, and the people were as cordial as any I had ever known. Good memories.

I also would have good memories of my Thursday nights with Chris. Even the evenings when he was late, as he was now. I had my book with me—*Ruby* by Cynthia Bond, an almost relentlessly horrific and depressing novel. I did not *like* darkness, but I sought it. Friends and relatives often described me as "dark," my love of certain books and films exhibit A in their case against me—*The Plague, The Painted Bird, Crime and Punishment, A Clockwork Orange.*

Ruby was worse, as dark and sordid as any book I had ever read, a journey through the vile and grotesque. Rape, pedophilia, misogyny. But great writers embody a dramatic irony. They dive into the garbage of life, the refuse that would repel most human beings, but they describe it in prose so urgent and compelling that you keep reading and reading. Bond was that kind of writer. The plot grinds your nose into the muck, but the prose elevates you. It is . . . *incantatory*, the rich, pungent sentences so lyrical that they transcend the horrors they describe. An amazing feat. And it is through this feat that Bond conveys the shimmering spirit at the heart of this masterwork. Sometimes, the mere act of survival is a triumph. Ruby, the heroine of this stunning book, is a survivor.

Repulsed by the topic but enchanted by the prose, I looked up from my book. Chris, himself a survivor, was walking toward me, trailing his shadow, his strides long and purposeful. And then, suddenly, there he was, standing in front of me, his shadow fused to his body.

"Hey."

Chris arrived, but his greeting unnerved me. It was just a "Hey," not a "Hey, Dad." The "Dad" conveyed a note of familiarity, of chumminess, that always lifted my spirits. But the "Dad," like Bird, was AWOL today.

"Hey, Chris, how are you?"

"Uuuggghhh," he responded.

There was that groan, that low, inarticulate grumble that re-minded me of *Young Frankenstein*.

"What's wrong?" I asked.

"Well . . ."

It was the job, he said. Ah, so that was the reason he seemed so preoccupied during our last date. Norma, his kindly manager, had left for another franchise, and her replacement was less under-standing and congenial. Chris worked the drive-through window at The Box, and he was coming up short, sometimes by more than ten dollars a day. The manager expected—no, demanded—that he make up the difference. Chris insisted the imbalance was coming from the counter inside, not his window. I believed him.

Norma, the previous manager, would have believed him, too. I remembered the second time I saw her at The Box. It was a sunny afternoon, the sky a piercing blue. I was driving by and, knowing that his shift was about to end, I stopped to see if Chris needed a ride home. The timing was perfect; Chris was taking off his apron and cap, but he asked me to wait while he fetched the manager, whom he wanted me to meet, not knowing that I had already met her. They emerged from the kitchen a few seconds later.

"Thanks for being so nice to Chris," I said, shaking her hand.

"Oh, it's easy," she said. "I love Chris."

And, then, she hugged him, and Chris smiled his boyish, em-barrassed smile. It was heartwarming, but Norma was gone, trans-ferred to another location. And the new manager, it seemed, did not share her affection for my son. Chris was bright and conscien-tious, a young man who craved approval, but . . . There was always a "but" with Chris. He could panic under pressure, his nerves fray-ing as his workload increased. I pictured him at the drive-through window, anxious and isolated, juggling the change as customer after customer zoomed by. He would start out poised, his move-ments slow and measured. But chaos was peeking over his shoul-der, always peeking, and the poise, I suspected, evaporated as the pressure mounted. . . . And, yet, I believed him.

"What are you going to do?" I asked. "Are you going to make

up the difference?"

"No," he said. "I quit."

"Oh. . . How much notice did you give?"

"None. I just quit."

My first impulse was to chastise him—or, at least, question his judgment. But I did neither. Chris was an adult, despite what I sometimes considered his fierce grip on adolescence, and he had a right to make his own decisions, however misguided I thought they might be.

"Don't worry," he said, waving his right hand as if shooing away a fly. "I've already applied at some other fast-food restaurants, and the interviews went really well. I'll be fine."

I was not as optimistic. Chris navigated life like a surfer, always teetering on the edge of disaster, and the more he sensed a wipeout, the more pessimistic he became. He was fine when things were going well, but at the first hint of failure, the optimism vanished, as fleeting as the tide.

"Don't worry," he repeated.

But I did worry. Worry that one impulsive moment—quitting his job—could lead to weeks, if not months, of futility, searching for a job listed in some imaginary want ad. Chris was optimistic, generally a good trait, but sometimes his optimism failed to jibe with reality, and the loftier his grandiose visions, the harder his inevitable falls.

"OK," I said. "I won't worry."

We ate. I had a tuna salad sandwich, Chris a falafel. Bird was still AWOL. I longed for his presence, his energy, his flapping wings. But Bird was still out there, somewhere, soaring over the urban thicket on Fredericksburg Road. We ate quietly; for the first time since our Thursday night dates, we had nothing to say to each other, the silence so vast that the food court seemed like a crypt.

"There are times when I finish the day with more money, not less, than what the receipts should indicate," he said, finally. "But they never offer to give me the surplus back. And, now, they want me to make up the deficit. I just don't think it's fair, Dad."

"I understand," I said simply.

We got in line. The movie was *Suicide Kings* with Christopher Walken and Denis Leary, both known for their biting cynicism. I asked Chris if he had ever seen *Pulp Fiction*, and he said yes. He knew what I was getting at. The bizarre cameo by Walken, who plays Captain Koons, an officer with a mission. Prudence—and an aversion to spoilers (for those who have not seen the movie)—prevents me from revealing the details, but it is Walken at his best, delivering his lines with a solemnity that belies—or amplifies—the absurdity.

"Ha!" Chris laughed, shattering, at least momentarily, the oppressive aura of our conversation during dinner.

Suicide Kings was not *Pulp Fiction*, but it featured Walken, and his role was larger, meatier than his bit in *Pulp Fiction*. It was vintage Walken, his voice moist and smarmy, his delivery slow and laconic. Walken could recite Keats, linger on each golden phrase, each soaring metaphor, and somehow, *somehow*, turn the shimmering beauty into twisted satire. And he could do it with a sly humor that was irresistible. But . . . but . . . I had to enjoy Walken without enjoying the movie he graced. I fell asleep, again, nodding off at several points during *Suicide Kings*, and each time my chin slumped onto my chest, Chris nudged me in the ribs, afraid I would miss the thread of the movie. A fear that was well founded. I lost the thread almost as soon as the opening credits rolled. But it was good to see Walken, if only intermittently.

"Remember that time I slept through the whole movie?" I asked Chris as we walked out of the theater after *Suicide Kings*.

"Dad, what movie are you talking about? You slept through a *lot* of movies."

"Oh," I said, apparently unaware of my own track record. "Well, I'm talking about one in particular, I guess. It was one of the *Lord of the Rings* movies. The third one, I think."

"Oh, yeah," Chris said, smiling. "Only you could sleep through all that mayhem."

I drove Chris home. When he got out of the car, he said, "Thanks, Dad." But all I could hear was, "Dad, it's not fair."

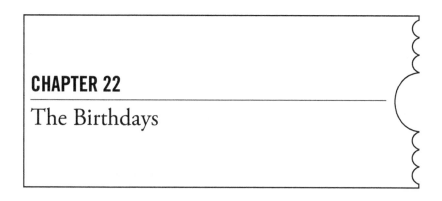

CHAPTER 22

The Birthdays

I REMEMBER THE past—most of it—vividly.

As the past recedes, it becomes more accessible. I embrace the paradox, and I remember. . . . I remember days so wonderful that my heart aches with the joy I felt more than ten, twenty, thirty years before . . . And days so boring that my heart aches for a different reason, days when I sat in the living room, alone, transfixed by the shafts of sunlight streaming through the windows . . . And the bad days. I remember them, too, as sharp and painful as a fresh wound. . . . I remember the crap and the glory and everything in between. And the more time passes, the sharper my memory becomes.

And yet, some things I remember better than others. Some things seem soldered into my brain, bolted into my being, never to be loosened and lost. Other things, well, other things are ephemeral, mere passersby, fleeing as quickly as they arrive.

I remember two days in the fall. Vividly. It was 1982.

The first day was my birthday. I was twenty-eight, two years from the arbitrary age when we are said to lose our "youth" card. Twenty-eight going on thirty. I did not fear the milestone, perhaps because I never felt burdened by adulthood to begin with, despite my advancing age. Oh, I was mature (I think) and responsible (I think), but in my mind, I was still a boy, twelve or fourteen or sixteen, captivated by the things that captivated me years before—books, music, movies, friends, and family, although it was only me and Antonia.

Maybe I *should* have felt burdened by adulthood—or the *approach* of adulthood. Antonia was pregnant with our first child. She was due in two weeks. We purchased books on parenting, and we remodeled one of the bedrooms for the pending arrival, although, not knowing the gender of the child, we left the walls and decorations neutral—no blues or pinks.

On this day, though, we were thinking of my own birth, the one that occurred twenty-eight years before. Antonia was treating me to dinner on my birthday. We went to The Barrel, a steak place in downtown Fort Worth, where I was a feature writer at the *Star-Telegram*.

They had a bountiful salad bar, and we ate what amounted to a full meal before our steaks arrived. I drank wine, and Antonia, mindful of the being burgeoning within her, stuck to water. I convinced her to have a sip, then another, then . . . No, she was steadfast. Just two.

When we got home, feeling no older than I had before, I turned on *Hill Street Blues*, a police drama that was my favorite TV show. And then it happened. The real drama was in our home, not on Hill Street. Antonia felt a twinge in her belly. The twinge became a nudge, and the nudge became a kick. Maybe it was the wine that induced the commotion in her tummy; whatever the cause, we did not have time to explore the possibilities. We raced to the hospital. Antonia was still wearing the dress she wore to The Barrel, a white dress with a broad, navy-blue tie blossoming from her collar.

Christopher Aaron Seltzer was born the next morning, missing my birthday by about two hours. I was glad. Chris deserved his own day, and he would have it.

Born with a full head of brown hair, Chris was pugnacious, his ruddy face frowning. Not a *full* frown. Not really. It was halfway between a scowl and a smile, which made his face hard to read, just as *he* would be hard to read thirteen years later. Imagine a door with a welcome mat *and* a DO NOT DISTURB sign. That was little Christopher Aaron Seltzer. He reminded me of the great Roberto Duran, the former lightweight champion, *Manos de Piedra*, Hands of Stone.

Hard to read or not, it was a joyous arrival. About an hour after the delivery, a nurse carried Chris, wrapped in a blanket, into the room where Antonia was recovering. Antonia held him for the first time, and her eyes lit up like Christmas trees. Both mother and baby were serene. If anyone cried, it was Antonia, and they were quiet tears—tears of joy and gratitude.

About an hour later, two women wheeled a steak dinner into the room—our second steak dinner of the night, although it was the next morning by now. No matter. We indulged in the redundancy, celebrating the meal for its symbolism more than its sustenance. They also brought us some champagne, which helped enhance our celebratory mood; this time, Antonia allowed herself more than a couple of sips.

Now, here we were, thirteen years later, Chris and I, driving across the country. After the tour of Sun Records, my drizzling eyes dry, my Elvis appetite sated, we hit the road again, crossing that great swirling mass of muddy water—the Mississippi River. I savored the view, the gentle waves corrugating under the Memphis & Arkansas Bridge. And I thought about Huck and Jim, rafting down the same river, escaping—or *trying* to escape—the society that oppressed them both. A White boy and a Black man, each wise enough to see beyond skin color. Chris had not read *The Adventures of Huckleberry Finn*, not yet, but if it had been science fiction, he could have recited chunks of the book to me as we engaged in our own adventure. I wish he had.

We departed Arkansas almost as soon as we entered it, and when we reached Texarkana, I felt the same phenomenon I had experienced while driving through the Amish country of Pennsylvania a few days before. The sky seemed to blossom before us, radiant and majestic, embracing every motorist, every pedestrian on the earth below. *Aaahhh, Texas.* Philadelphia was dark and gloomy, and we did not escape the dungeon—*truly* escape the dungeon—until we hit the Lone Star State. Sweet release. It felt good to be back home.

My viewpoint was unfair to Philly, a city of great charm and history. I knew that. The sky, after all, hovered over everyone, from coast to coast. If I looked at it scientifically—something I was not inclined to do—I would realize that the atmosphere in Philly was no different from the atmosphere in Fort Worth or San Angelo or El Paso. . . . But, whatever I lacked in atmospheric or meteorological knowledge, I knew what my heart told me. It told me what all the atmospheric and meteorological data could not. It told me Texas kicked butt. The sky was different there. Cleaner. Purer. Better.

"Look at the sky," I told Chris. "Isn't it beautiful?"

Chris lifted his head from his book.

"It *is*," he said smiling.

Two minutes later, it started raining. It lashed the windshield, coming down in thick silver ropes. Chris, setting his book on his lap, looked at the deluge. Then he looked at me. So much for my big, beautiful Texas sky. We kept driving.

Our last stop before El Paso: Fort Worth. I took Chris to The Barrel. It had changed. There was a bathtub full of iced beer as you entered, and the place was darker, seedier, its elegance having faded along with the years on the calendar.

We reached Fort Worth in midafternoon. The Stock Show & Rodeo must have been in town. You could smell the cow manure, rich and pungent. We parked near the restaurant, the scent wafting in the air, earthy but pleasant.

Chris and I settled into our seats, a booth near the kitchen. I studied the menu, and Chris studied the kitchen doorway, transfixed by the bustle. He gazed at the waiters scurrying from table to table, their legs churning while their palms remained motionless, *eerily* motionless. They were balancing the trays on those palms, a magic act that intrigued Chris. The young waiters looked like mythological creatures, half man, half beast—from the waist down, they were gerbils on an activity wheel; from the waist up, they were mannequins, as static as still-life paintings. *How do they do it?* Chris seemed to be asking.

Curiosity gave way to hunger. Chris and I ordered, and as we waited for our meals to arrive, delivered by these strange creatures known as waiters, I thought about my last dinner at The Barrel. I had not told Chris about the significance of our visit. Why? Maybe because the joy I felt then had turned into wistfulness, the wistfulness a father feels when he sees a child suffering, the hurt brought on by something neither father nor son understands.

I had a steak, just as I had all those years before, and Chris had a hamburger that seemed as large as his head. I watched him eat, his face hidden behind the bun. He ate with a relish—no pun intended—that seems to animate all youth. I remembered my own dad, staring at me while I vacuumed some tacos or burritos, smiling as if he were savoring the food himself.

With our meal coming to an end, I finally told Chris about my last dinner at The Barrel, about how it was a prelude to a wonderful birthday gift a few hours *after* my birthday. He smiled. And now, as the years pass, I remember my dinner with Chris as vividly as I do my dinner with his mom. Sometimes joyfully, sometimes wistfully.

CHAPTER 23
No More Thursday Nights

MAY 25, 2016

THE PHONE CALL came on Wednesday evening, the day before our next Thursday-night movie date. It was Chris. He sounded agitated. Not that I could tell by what he said. It was what he did *not* say that was so revealing.

There was no tone of urgency in his voice, but whenever Chris was disturbed about something, *anything*, he spoke slowly and deliberately—so slowly and deliberately that I wondered if he was still on the line. "Chris? Chris? Are you still there?" I would ask. And then he would answer, "Yeah . . . Dad . . . I'm . . . still . . . here."

This was one of those times. I waited, but the gaps in his delivery were longer than a checkout line on Black Friday. Be patient, I told myself. And then, finally, after enough time had passed to deliver a Shakespearean monologue, he got it out: The Wonderland Mall was ending its free movie nights on Thursday.

"What?!?" I responded.

"Yeah," he said. "I was walking through the mall today, and they had a poster saying that was it, no more free movies."

"Why?" I asked.

"I . . . don't . . . know," he said. "There . . . was . . . no . . . explanation."

"I guess it just wasn't cost-effective."

"Yeah . . . I guess . . ."

The call lasted about four minutes, prolonged by the gaps between words. *Hi . . . Dad . . . how . . . are . . . you?* But, when Chris finally communicated his message, it was succinct and dramatic.

When the conversation ended, I stared at the phone, as if it had been the source of the bad news, not the instrument through which it was delivered. So that was it. Our Thursday nights were gone, relegated to the photo album in our heads. *Damn.*

Movies connect you with the characters in the theater—the George Baileys, the Willy Wonkas, the Romeos and Juliets. But, in our case, they did something equally wondrous: They connected us to ourselves. For a few hours every Thursday night, real life became as bold and impactful as cinematic life, the life we saw on the screen. Chris and I talked and ate and laughed, and then we saw a movie. But I would remember the talking and eating and laughing with greater warmth and fondness than I would the movies.

Our Thursday nights were more than dates, more than get-togethers. They were therapy sessions, allowing us to rebuild a bridge that had crumbled over the years. It provided us a context, a launching point from which to connect—or *re*connect.

We should not have needed it, this context. But human beings are weak, fragile, imperfect, and we seldom see the need to build a bridge, much less execute the construction project. If you are lucky, it just happens. Chris and I were lucky. We went to see *It's a Wonderful Life*, and before we knew it, we started pouring the asphalt for the bridge, movie by movie, dinner by dinner, conversation by conservation. We did not *intend* it to happen; it just did. If we had intended it—who knows?—it might have been a colossal failure.

And now the context, the impetus for the rebirth of our relationship, was gone. Would we find another? Something that connected us as smoothly and naturally as our Thursday nights did? We would try. I knew that. But the beauty of our Thursday nights was that we did not have to try.

CHAPTER 24
Back Home

EL PASO WAS IDYLLIC.

I got a job as a sportswriter at the *El Paso Times*, and we bought a home on the West Side, a home which, nestled in the hills, provided a clear view of the western and southern landscapes. We could see Mexico from our backyard, and we could see the sunsets every evening, waves of color rolling across the sky—reds, oranges, and purples that blazed until darkness subdued the flames. An enchanting experience, considering our years in the storm cellar that was the East Coast.

We lived across from a city park. Katy and I played basketball at the court, although "play" is a lofty term for what we did. We goofed around, mainly, a two-person version of the Harlem Globetrotters—less manic and, yes, less athletic. But no less absurd. We attempted feats beyond our skill set, dribbling between our legs, spinning the ball on our middle fingers. And dunking. Perhaps the most futile undertaking since Sisyphus tried to roll that rock up that hill. I had the vertical leap of a cinder block, and Katy, well, Katy was too short.

Too short? Maybe, but Katy defied the physical evidence. Barely reaching my chest, she boasted that she was taller than me. *Hmmm.* I stood about six-foot-three.

"I'm taller than you, Dad."

I did not argue. Almost seven years old, her growth spurt a few years away, she was Goliath when she crowded me on the court. Attempting to swat a jump shot, she would inch closer, ever closer, her tenacity overcoming her stature. A mini Hakeem Olajuwon. She made me alter shots I did not want to alter.

We played in the mornings, always. The mountain air was fresh and pure, transforming our bodies into molecules that seemed to glide and sway with the morning breeze. Dawn. We could see the lights twinkling across the Rio Grande, the amber glow of electricity from the hillside villages in Juárez. There were no lights there when I was a kid, no electricity. The villagers lived in darkness.

Hoops was fun, the hilarity sometimes making us double over in laughter. But the games were never about fun. They were about being together, Katy and me, bonding on a court in the sweet morning air.

A thunderstorm struck the West Side one Friday night, a burst that aborted our sleep. Dishes rattled. Dogs barked. Clocks blinked—12:00 . . . 12:00 . . . 12:00 . . . The celestial artillery seemed to last hours.

The next morning, with calm restored, Katy and I headed to the court, eager hoopsters ready for fun. Then we saw the tree, a massive oak, about thirty feet from the court. It lay on its side, its branches pressed against the moist grass, its trunk suspended above the ruptured earth, the bark blackened by a lightning bolt. We could see the roots—stalks, once proud and sturdy, now naked and exposed, reduced to tendrils.

Katy and I looked at each other, our eyes wide, but we kept marching to the court, unperturbed. Whatever happened last night would not impede us this morning. We hit the court, now sheathed with a layer of dirt that was thin and delicate, as if sifted from the sky. Katy bounced the ball, and little puffs of brown powder rose in the air. No problem. It was a new day.

Tall and slender, with an erect posture straight out of West Point, she would grow to about five-foot-nine. She walked with short, delicate steps, as if she were wearing ballet slippers. And, like her mom, she had a hearty laugh, her almond eyes squinting whenever she convulsed, which was often.

Chris never joined us, partly because he slept late on the weekends, the crisp dawn air failing to lure him out of bed, the way it did Katy and me. And partly because he was clumsy on the court, his movements mechanical, robotic. But it was more that. Chris was a loner, and the older Katy got, the more apparent his isolation became. Katy craved community, togetherness—things Chris seemed to shun.

We also flew kites at the park, all of us, even Chris. We would run from one end of the park to the other, the string unspooling as the kite bobbed in the sky, sometimes jerked and whipped by the gusts of spring. There were times, though, when the kite seemed to float up there forever, calmly and placidly, obscuring the sun millions of miles above. We looked up, and the kite, framed by the blinding aura of the hidden orb, looked like a second sun, a miniature version of the real sun. Except that, instead of a circle, it was a triangle or rectangle or octagon.

The kids looked up, their rich brown hair shading their eyes. They would run and laugh, stumbling because, well, because when you run and laugh at the same time, it depletes your oxygen supply and expands your hilarity supply. And hilarity, as every kid knows, impairs your balance. Is there a mathematical equation for that dynamic? There should be. (Fun equals Smiles/Giggles Squared.) Einstein missed the boat. Antonia and I stumbled along with the youngsters. It seemed like the most pleasure a person could experience, running across a park with a kite chasing you on a sun-kissed afternoon in El Paso. And we shared it as a family.

It did not last, this idyllic run. How could it? Even joy has a shelf life, I guess. Chris was getting older, and as he grew, his problems seemed to grow with him. I blamed it . . . well . . . I did not know *what* to blame it on. Trying to understand him—much less diagnose him—seemed futile.

Chris got moodier, his beloved books unable to sustain him the way they had a few years earlier. He still read, but the words remained trapped between the covers, drab and dreary, their enchanting call muted by . . . what? A darker siren in his soul, a demon the authors he loved could no longer exorcise?

Even when we were together, he was alone, a boy on an island. We would watch VHS tapes in the den—*Bambi*, *Pinocchio*, and *Dumbo*—but he would remain in his room, lost in darkness. Chris would walk into the den every once in a while, emerging like a bear from his cave, but his sojourns were brief. So brief that he never sat down. He loitered at the doorway, one foot in the kitchen, another in the den, and when he grew weary of the movie, he would return to his room, waving dismissively as he walked away.

"Hey," he would say as he departed.

"Hey" became his mantra. It was as if he could not allow himself a deeper, richer form of communication with his family—an interaction. No. Just a "hey."

He started waking up late on weekends, later than usual, and when we got tired of waiting for him, we would go on weekend outings by ourselves, the three of us. Antonia and I felt guilty about leaving him behind on our weekend jaunts, but we felt less burdened, less constricted without him, and that amplified the guilt. We had to put quotation marks around "fun," because "fun" was more complicated now, with or without Chris. It was a problem without a solution.

Antonia and I enrolled Chris at Morehead Middle School, his first public school since his early years in New Jersey. We felt good about the decision. The principal was Arnold Potranco, a bright, amiable man we knew well. He was a fellow journalism major from our days at the University of Texas, El Paso (UTEP), where Antonia and I met. Arnold attended our wedding, and years later, we would reminisce about his raw energy on the dance floor at the wedding hall, stomping his feet with an enthusiasm that was, well, unbecoming of the principal he would become. We did not hold it against him. Arnold would look after Chris, his sweet, nurturing spirit enveloping him like a shawl.

Or so we thought. About three weeks into the fall semester, Arnold left for another school, a victim of the juggling act that seemed to plague the El Paso Independent School District. They were always pulling principals from one school to another. Did consistency mean nothing to these people? Push-pull. Push-pull. It was maddening.

I saw Arnold as a victim. But, no, he was not a victim; for all we knew, he was off to a better place, an environment more suited to his special talents. It was Antonia and I—and Chris—who were the victims, for we had lost the security blanket we hoped would protect our son.

CHAPTER 25
Limburger Cheese

JUNE 2, 2016

IT SHOULD HAVE been just another Thursday, one in a string of Thursdays that stretched back to the winter of 2015—a day marked by nothing more unusual than a date with my son, dinner and a movie. A routine event, so routine that I had forgotten how much comfort I found in it, how much security and reassurance. And, now, "Free Movie Night" was gone.

I felt lost. It was like moving to another city, with everything alien, unfamiliar. How do you act in this new city? How do you act without movie night? The movies were cool, *more* than cool. They were great fun, something we both loved—real lives unfolding before us, drama on celluloid. I missed Bird, too. But Bird and the movies were secondary to what happened before and after the movies—our conversations. We discussed nothing of great import. We did not solve the great crises of the day. Or even discuss them. But we talked, and the talk seemed to erase the distance between us—distance forged by age, personality, and disposition. The barriers crumbled like centuries-old walls.

We talked about books, movies, music, limburger cheese. Yes, limburger cheese. Chris was one of those individuals who seemed to know a little bit about everything. Correction: A *lot* about everything. He seemed to retain everything he read, saw, or heard. And once he had read, seen, or heard it, he could regurgitate it with all the aplomb of a Harvard professor. So, yes, one day, he expounded on the wonders of limburger cheese.

"Limburger is made from cow's milk," he said.

I thought most cheese came from cows, but I said nothing.

"The name comes from the Duchy of Limburg, near Holland and Belgium," he said. "As you know, it's known for its strong, pungent smell, but what you may not have known is that the odor is caused by bacteria. A few years back, a study showed that the malaria mosquito is attracted as much to the smell of limburger as to the smell of human feet. The study earned the Nobel Prize in biology."

That must be why my childhood friends called it "dirty socks" cheese, I told Chris.

"Anyway," Chris said. "It's now produced mostly in Germany."

I never thought of limburger cheese as a topic worthy of discussion, just as I would never think of my socks as a topic worthy of discussion. How wrong I was. Not about my socks, but about . . . well, you know. Chris pontificated about limburger cheese, and I was transfixed. I could almost taste the cheese as he spoke. I promised to take him to Sprouts one day so we could buy a hunk of it. He approved of the plan.

I picked him up at his apartment the next Saturday morning, and we drove to Sprouts, a high-end grocery store that specialized in organic food. Weird, looking back, but our expectation bordered on the excitement a child feels on Christmas morning. We hurried to the dairy section, our steps quickening as we approached the open refrigerators stocked with cheese. But not just *any* cheese. *Our* cheese. It was our Golden Fleece—a prize for which we would brave any challenge. A gross exaggeration, of course. But we wanted to put into our mouths what Chris had put into words. Limburger cheese. Sweet, glorious limburger cheese.

It was not like me to rhapsodize about something as insignificant as cheese. I was no Christopher Aaron Seltzer when it came to oratory about subjects like cheese . . . and comics . . . and opera. But the more that day receded into the past, the more important it became to me. Chris and I were searching for something together, something exquisite. It happened to be limburger cheese, but it could have been anything. Salsa or salami or spinach. Anything. Whatever it was—or *could* have been—we were searching for it together, a father and son on an expedition that was as far from exotic as you could imagine.

We never found the cheese. The cheese section had cheddar and mozzarella, brie and Havarti, feta and Camembert. Everything, it seemed, but limburger. *Damn.*

No limburger. And, now, no Thursday movie nights, either. I was disoriented, stuck in my crummy, one-bedroom apartment, books everywhere, spilling from closets, tables, and, yes, bookshelves. The place looked like an attic. I would donate, every six months or so, some books to the neighborhood library, but it was always a painful journey, giving up prized possessions because there was no more room for them in my cramped apartment. The books enlivened the same space they swallowed, and every time I dropped them off at the library, I felt as if I were giving them up to an orphanage.

No matter how many books I donated, the apartment remained cramped, another book purchased for every one donated. It was like the scene in *Fantasia*, where Mickey Mouse, the apprentice sorcerer, cannot keep the maniacal brooms from dumping more and more water into the lair of his menacing master.

More than ever, the books became my therapy. I devoted my first *non-movie* Thursday night to reading, the lone holdover from our date nights, when I would read while waiting for Chris in the food court. On my first movie-free Thursday night, I started reading *Bottom of the 33rd: Hope, Redemption, and Baseball's Longest Game*, a book as lyrical as its subject—baseball.

Football is my favorite sport, a fondness that grew out of my devotion to the Cleveland Browns, the team I loved because it was the team my father loved. But football is about sweat and power and brutality. Baseball is different; baseball is about grace and speed and efficiency. It is about focus and intellect, about a batter trying to outsmart a pitcher who can throw a ball faster than a train can thunder down a track. It is this duel, this confrontation worthy of *High Noon*, that makes baseball books almost routinely better than books about any other sport, with all due respect to W. C. Heinz, the greatest boxing writer who ever lived—and one of the greatest writers who ever lived, *period*.

Bottom of the 33rd, by Dan Barry, was worthy of its genre. I was enthralled from the start. The prose was simple but poetic, as all prose should be, and the writer made the underdogs, the minor league grunts toiling in the shadow of giants, as heroic as the stars they aspired to be. But . . . but . . . reading this wonderful book in my apartment was not the same as reading it in the food court, under the skylight, surrounded by diners and shoppers wandering through the indoor plaza that was the mall. And there was no Bird in my apartment. . . . Worst of all, my focus was fragile, broken by thoughts about Chris, about what he might have been doing, at that very moment. Where are you, Chris?

CHAPTER 26

On to High School

JULY 1998

CHRIS SURVIVED MIDDLE school. Survived what I called the three As. The angst. The anxiety. The apprehension. What he could not survive was the graduation ceremony. So he did not even try. His passage through middle school, in his view, did not call for a celebration so much as a sigh of relief. Antonia and I agreed, and we all sighed together. Middle school was in our rearview mirror. High school lay ahead, a road that might prove just as event-filled—and treacherous.

High school. I was lucky. I suffered the usual maladies that afflict all adolescents—anxiety, insecurity, uncertainty about who I was and who I wanted to be—but high school itself was a sanctuary. Maybe it was the era, the explosion of liberal thought that dominated the 1960s—civil rights, nonviolence, artistic expression. Robert Kennedy, Muhammad Ali, Martin Luther King Jr., Bob Dylan, Buffy St. Marie, The Beatles.

Or maybe it was more complicated than that. Small communities sometimes transcend what is happening on a national scale, and I think Cathedral High School would have been warm and inviting no matter what was happening in the world beyond. We did not have anyone with the power or charisma of King, Kennedy, or Ali, but we had men and women who exhibited kindness and grace on a smaller scale, from the teachers to the coaches to the principal.

These men and women defined Cathedral, a Catholic school with a student body of about three hundred, all boys. We learned as much from these individuals as we did from the textbooks we read in class every day. They taught us about kindness and compassion—and about respect for those who were different from us. Not just differences in ethnicity and skin color. But differences that might have been less apparent, less clear. We had nerds back then—they were called "goofballs" or "freaks"—but nobody belittled them. And we had gay kids, but nobody mocked them, and nobody made them feel less than what they were. Oh, the kids hurled insults at each other—they were kids, after all—but the ribbing, usually, was gentle, good-natured, resulting in the most delicate balance you could expect from high school kids—laughter without derision.

Now, thirty years later, I wondered if Cathedral would be just as beneficial for Chris as it was for me. I interviewed the principal, Leo Cancellare, for a story in the *El Paso Times*. Short but massive, with a smile that seemed as broad as his chest, Cancellare was also the swimming coach, a motivator known for fielding teams that were almost a lock to win state titles year after year, and I wanted to explore both the man and the coach.

Cathedral did not have its own swimming pool—or football field—so the kids trained at a pool in Ascarate Park, a county park about ten miles from the school. Practice started at five o'clock every morning, and the water completed what the alarm clock began. It woke the kids up. The young athletes showed up groggy, their eyes still glazed from their aborted sleep, but they swam up and down their lanes, churning across the water with a precision that was almost robotic.

In mid-July, a few weeks before the start of school, I met the coach/principal during practice. The facility was supposed to be indoors, but the county ran out of money, and the project was left incomplete. Pillars lined the pool, four on either side, but there was no ceiling above them, so the pillars supported the sky. The ceiling would have to wait until the construction gods deemed the facility ready for more concrete. Until then, the facility would look like a Roman ruin, although the kids—and the coach—did not care. They had their pool, finished or not.

It was still dark, the soft pinks and oranges that would smudge the eastern sky lurking beyond the horizon. Cancellare embraced the early morning hour. He was vibrant and enthusiastic, as if he had washed down ten cups of coffee. There was no coffee around, none that *I* could see, but it was clear that he ran on something stronger than caffeine. Dedication? The pursuit of excellence? Love for his players? Maybe it was all three.

My newspaper colleagues told me about him, praising his wisdom and toughness, and though I was not assigned to cover him, I wanted to meet this local legend; it was one of the few times I interviewed an athletic figure for personal reasons. Chris accompanied me during my visit with the coach. It was a tradition with us, going back to my days as the boxing writer for the *Philadelphia Inquirer*. He was not a sports fan, but I would take him to resorts in Pennsylvania and New Jersey, where the top boxers trained—resorts in wooded, secluded areas where the biggest temptations were diners with signs that advertised pies "baked on premises." Chris met welterweight champion Meldrick Taylor and heavyweight champion Riddick Bowe in these towns. He asked Bowe if he was a heavyweight. Bowe stood six-foot-five and weighed 250 pounds, big even by heavyweight standards. He looked down at Chris, grim-faced.

"What do you think?" he asked.

Chris shrugged.

"I don't know," he said. "I don't think I've ever seen a heavyweight up close before."

Bowe laughed.

"Well, now you have."

Chris was usually a late-riser, but there he was, standing next to me during the interview with the coach/principal. The pool glistened under the early morning sky, and the kids completed lap after lap, their strokes raising dimples in the water. Chris watched, his brown, liquid eyes following the athletes as they glided by. Then the interview ended.

"How old are you, son?" Cancellare asked him.

"Thirteen," Chris answered.

"Do you like to swim?"

"Yes, sir."

Chris was lean, with broad shoulders that narrowed into a tiny waist. He stood about five-foot-six, but his frame made him seem taller. Chris looked like a V with legs.

"Do you want to swim for me?" the coach asked him.

Chris looked at the coach, then looked at me, unsure of what his answer should be.

"Coach, we haven't registered him for any high school yet," I said. "We were still deciding."

"Still deciding?" he asked, his voice a few decibels shy of a roar. "What's to decide?"

What, indeed?

"Well," I said, "maybe you're right. I'll talk it over with my wife."

The coach and the boy smiled at each other. Antonia and I agreed: Cathedral, it was.

Antonia always thought Chris needed a good role model outside the family, a mentor. Coach Leo seemed to fit the bill. He liked Chris, and Chris liked him, and aside from any coaching skills he possessed, his charm and decency were as palpable as his massive physique. I told Antonia about my interview with the coach, and she was impressed. Maybe the coach, she mused, would be good for Chris; maybe he needed someone outside the family unit, someone without our baggage, to guide him.

Chris may have had the body of a swimmer, but he had the commitment of a land-locked thirteen-year-old. He was dutiful, showing up to practice every morning, but his sense of duty disappeared once he hit the pool. He lacked the urgency and determination of the other kids, so he sat by the edge of the pool during practice, paddling his legs in the water while the other kids churned by, lap after lap. Cancellare did not seem to care. He liked Chris, and he liked having him around, even if he did nothing more strenuous than loiter.

The coach took his athletes on camping trips before the start of school, and when he invited Chris one morning, one of the other swimmers frowned. He was about to say something, but Cancellare cut him off. Chris stepped back, as if he had been punched in the gut. Did he assume the comment, aborted by Coach, would be negative? Coach looked at Chris for a few seconds; then he walked over to him, draping a massive arm around his shoulders.

"You don't know this guy," he told the boy whose words remained trapped in his throat. "He's cool. He's hilarious. And he's going with us. . . . Right, Chris?"

"Right," Chris answered before asking permission from me.

No problem. There was never any doubt that I would let him go, and Chris knew it. Cancellare—I would come to address him as Coach—was one of those people who uplifted you while making you aware of your own failings. That is not a bad thing. He could have been a preacher or a motivational speaker because, while he made the bar seem impossibly high, he made you want to reach for it, made you want to *try*. This is why he was a great coach—and a better man . . .

And yet, every time I saw Chris and Coach interacting, it was bittersweet. Cancellare, I knew, would be good for my son. Chris got along better with adults than he did with kids. Which was good and bad. It was good because one group accepted him; it was bad because the other did not—and it was the latter group whose lack of acceptance and appreciation would mark him, brand him. Chris was a little adult, always wavering between serious and dour, but quirky, always quirky. Traits that endeared him to adults—but marked him as an outlier among his peers. The truth was, Chris had no peers.

If Chris was a disinterested trainee, he was also a disinterested competitor. Coach was known to dive into the pool, fully dressed, to upbraid an athlete for his lack of commitment. The kids always reacted with renewed purpose and dedication. More magic from the soggy motivator.

Coach never did that with Chris, and I always wondered why. Maybe he realized what all the counselors failed to grasp: that Chris had a condition. Or maybe he realized that, whatever talent Chris possessed, it did not include knifing through the water, and there was no use prodding him to do something he did not want to do.

Chris routinely finished last in the meets, straggling like a drunk at closing time. I always congratulated him for finishing, for hanging in there, but it was hard to watch him, alone in the pool, swimming lap after lap by himself. Most of his teammates had left the facility by the time he finished. The natatoriums were always dark, the facility suffused with the dull yellow glow of the overhead lights. It looked like the aftertaste of sunset, a melancholy tinge of fading light.

They found the cancer in 1998. It was ironic. Here was Coach, a massive, seemingly invincible human being, assaulted by a foe he could not even see. You always got the sense, standing at poolside, his arms folded across his chest, that Coach could face any danger head-on. But this foe did not attack him head-on. It swarmed from within, battalions of lethal cells he was powerless to resist. He tried, retaining his grace and humor till the end. But his body was weaker than his mind, and it would finally give in. The only question was when.

He was as jovial as ever one Saturday afternoon, following another successful swimming meet. Successful for everyone but Chris, who emerged from the shower, alone again, his teammates having long since left the facility. Coach stayed. He high fived Chris, told him, "Nice job." There were no speeches, no phony soliloquies about "hanging in there." Just the high five and the "nice job." One gesture, two words, each sweetly eloquent.

Coach died in 1999, a year after the cancer was discovered. He was forty-one. Leo Marketing, one of the most successful advertising

"I'll be right back," Chris said, heading toward the dunes.

"OK," I said. "Don't be long. Lunch will be ready soon."

"OK."

By the time he returned, we had finished our meal. Chris did not care. Keeping his sunglasses on, he started eating what we had left. Then he took off his glasses, and he looked like a raccoon, white moons encircling his eyes. The rest of his face was red. Chris had fallen asleep under the blistering sun, his skin cooked almost as thoroughly as the steaks on the grill. *Oh, Chris, Chris, Chris.* He finished his meal, and we headed home, stopping at a drugstore on the way to buy him some skin ointment.

It was beyond problematic, this self-imposed isolation; it was worrisome. Or should have been. But we were so used to it that the problematic seemed routine. "Well, that's Chris," we would say. It *was* Chris, but did it *have* to be? We grappled with the question, grappled with it throughout his adolescence and, finally, we decided to do what we had done years before. We decided to take him to a counselor, despite our disastrous encounters with therapists in New Jersey, our misgivings vanquished by the notion that something, *something*, had to be wrong.

"The worst part of this is that he's so miserable," Antonia said. "He *knows* something's wrong. So do we, but what?"

We spent most of our time wondering what that *something* was. It is hard to make someone happy when you do not know what is making them *un*happy. We were detectives without clues, and our biggest fear was that the *experts*—the counselors—were equally clueless. But who else could we turn to?

Chris was a junior when he went to see the counselor. There were no Styrofoam baseball bats in his office, which was a plus. It meant he did not belong to the Curly Howard School of Therapy. A huge relief, but the results were the same. He had three visits with Chris, and his assessment was eerily familiar: The boy is fine, he said.

We moved on. Chris still had his plays, but as often happens to actors in the real world, the drama morphed from the stage to everyday life. It happened toward the end of his junior year. Things had changed at Cathedral since my days there. It was still a fine school, with teachers as committed and sensitive as they were in my day, but there were kids who belittled Chris, made him feel smaller than he was, and he accepted it, swallowed it.

The alienation grew. Chris seemed more alone than ever, and if you do not belong in high school, when belonging is synonymous with self-worth, the isolation is crippling. It reminded me of the scene in *The Graduate*, when Benjamin, prodded by fatuous adults, tests one of his graduation gifts in the backyard swimming pool—a scuba diving outfit. He is alone in the water, as still and quiet as an embryo bathed in the amniotic fluid, afraid to venture into the world. Chris wanted to emerge from the pool, wanted to join his classmates in whatever adolescent antics occupied them at the moment, but he did not know how.

Chris was unable to express his resentment, buried under the rubble of his grievances. Everyone needs an outlet, a safety valve. Chris had none. We decided to take him out of the school.

CHAPTER 27

A Different Kind of Movie Night

JUNE 23, 2016

"UGLY" IS A curious adjective, often used as a barb, a poison projectile aimed at unsuspecting innocents.

It was a popular term among my grade school classmates. Tomás was ugly. Carmen was ugly. Everyone was ugly except the kids hurling the epithet.

"Ugly" was on my mind. And in the theater. It was not free, but after one month without movies, we returned to the theater—*the* theater. The Bijou. It felt right, like home. The movie was *The Ugliest Woman in the World*.

Measured by the calendar, one month seems insignificant. But if you measure it by something grander, if you measure it by the human contact that can take place in one month, between May 26 and June 23, the gap becomes more crucial. Chris and I lost something in that month. Something we took for granted. Something we might not have appreciated without the *absence* of that month.

But the absence was there, and we knew what we missed. We missed each other.

We met in the food court, and for the first time since our first movie night back in December, we expanded our customary greetings. "Hey, Dad" . . . "Hey, Chris" . . . We hugged each other.

"Good to see you, Chris."

"You, too, Dad."

It was good to see the food court, too. Our sanctuary, a place where we could leave the outside world outside. It was weird, but the six-week gap seemed so long that I expected to see a *different* food court, a food court that was shockingly unrecognizable. But it was the same, and so was Chris.

Settling into old habits, I was early, and Chris was late. *Perfect.* I found joy in that. Bird was there, too, which completed the picture. He patrolled the floor, searching for scraps, his neck bobbing in that jerky movement that reminded me of a stop-motion film. Bird, an animated creature come to life.

My latest book was *Buffalo Trail* by Jeff Guinn, an old friend from my days at the *Fort Worth Star-Telegram* from 1979 to 1985. I had lost contact with him over the years, which I regretted, but I knew him through his books—books so compelling and powerful that the pages seemed to renew our friendship. The book embodied a curious paradox. It was a *quiet* epic, quiet because, while the writing was lyrical, it did not call attention to itself; it was too smooth for that, too graceful and flowing. Every word compelled you to read the next word . . . and the next word . . . and the next word . . . And, as the writing propelled you, the author unveiled his story, and it was here that the book became epic. Some "epics" are dull and moribund, ships without the oars to carry them across the ocean. Not *Buffalo Trail*. The subject was the Indian Wars of the nineteenth century, viewed through the lens of a few combatants. Guinn handled it without outrage or sanctimony, alternating perspectives from one chapter to another—the Native American in one, the "white man" in the other. The tactic was breathtaking.

The book was violent, sometimes grotesque, but reading it gave me a warm feeling, perhaps because of the connection I felt with Guinn. I *wanted* to connect, wanted to desperately, even if the person I was connecting with was not there. We were keen on connections, my son and I; we may not have been very adept at them, but we were keen on them.

Chris arrived, and we hugged each other. I told Chris about Guinn.

"He was a freelancer when I was at the *Fort Worth Star-Telegram*," I said. "He would probably have been the best writer on the staff. He knew you. . . . You were a baby."

"Really?"

"Yeah."

"Cool."

We ate—Chris a pizza, me a hamburger—but we focused more on talking than eating, so before we knew it, it was time for the movie, and we had to wolf down our meals. The four-week wait was worth it.

Beauty, in the eyes of those who appreciate it, is not skin-deep; it is deep, period. It requires no grand insight to state the following: When people brand others ugly, they are the ones who deserve the label. And *their* ugliness, caustic, corrosive, and degrading, is worse, because their ugliness is not a passive condition, it is a conscious assault against others.

Lizzie Velasquez is "The Ugliest Woman in the World," the title of a YouTube video she discovered when she was seventeen. Imagine. Seventeen. An age when you are grappling to secure your identity. And she finds that a mean and malignant identity has been thrust upon her by people she does not even know. The documentary, also titled *The Ugliest Woman in the World,* focused on her condition and her struggle to overcome something worse than her condition—the derision and hostility of those who, being shallow, had a shallow definition of beauty. It was heartbreaking.

Or *could* have been heartbreaking. Velasquez withstands all the arrows pointed at her heart, arrows that wound her without destroying her. It is tempting to resort to cliché, to say she is beautiful inside. But that is not true, at least not strictly true. When a person is pure and courageous, when a person shimmers on the inside, she glows on the outside, too. You can see that with Lizzie Velasquez—the glint in her eyes, the familiarity with strangers, the courage to tell her story. She is beautiful, inside and out.

Lizzie Velasquez suffers from Marfan Syndrome, a genetic disorder that prevents her from gaining weight. She weighs sixty-three pounds, and she is blind in one eye, her bones so brittle that she walks and speaks haltingly, with an effort that is painful to witness. The hatred shocks her, but does not defeat her.

She is as beautiful as her detractors are ugly. Is she beautiful *because* her detractors are ugly? Perhaps. Sometimes, if not *most* of the time, we judge people by the scorn they face—and overcome. Lizzie Velasquez has triumphed over that scorn, but she has not done it alone, for her family is as beautiful as she is, warm and nurturing and supportive. They love her.

"I always knew I wanted to show those people that they weren't going to define me," she said, discussing bullies during a television interview. "I didn't want the definition of me that they were creating to become my truth. I wanted to make my own truth."

A disquieting moment in the movie comes when Lizzie Velasquez meets Hillary Clinton, then Secretary of State, during an educational convention in Mexico City. Clinton is the consummate politician, cool and glib, oozing sympathy without *feeling* sympathy. It is the creepiest scene in the movie.

"I don't think she was ugly, Dad," Chris said afterwards. "When I saw her on the screen, the first thing I felt was sorrow, not revulsion, because you knew, just *knew*, the attacks she had to endure because of how she looked."

Her parents are lovely people, I told Chris.

"They are," he said. "Thank God she has them."

I dropped Chris off at his apartment.

"Thanks, Dad."

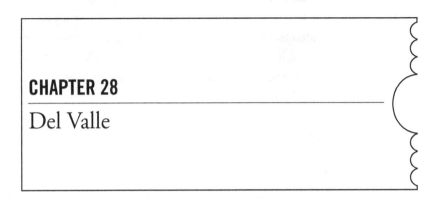

CHAPTER 28
Del Valle

CATHEDRAL WAS A school; Del Valle was a campus, a sprawling complex with a courtyard, a baseball diamond, and a football field. Modest amenities, perhaps, but more than Cathedral featured, much more. With about two thousand fewer students than Del Valle, Cathedral offered warmth and intimacy, and it was a great school. For me. Not for Chris. Del Valle might not prove to be a great school for Chris, either. But we had to try. We *had* to.

Del Valle was located in the Lower Valley, amidst hardscrabble farm land—even farm land is hardscrabble in the desert—acres and acres of crops, mostly cotton. The land was encroached by more acres and acres . . . of concrete. Strip malls were sprouting everywhere, so many that the area started to look like a giant, endless frontage road—convenience stores, muffler shops, stereo outlets, many of them with those floppy, inflatable figures out front, their arms and heads flailing in the desert wind, beckoning you to stop, look, and buy. They paved paradise, and they put up a strip mall, dozens of them.

Most of the kids were Latinos, many of them immigrants from Mexico. Some worked the fields in years past, before and after school. They were smart and diligent, and they saw education as a tool, a tool as effective as the hoes the migrant workers wielded in the fields nearby. But a tool to keep them *out* of those fields, out of the life that forced their families to move from town to town, chasing the crops that assured their survival.

Antonia was a journalism teacher at Del Valle, and her kids were earnest and hardworking. Chris became one of them. An indifferent swimmer at Cathedral, Chris seemed to find his calling in journalism, his apathy morphed into dedication. It was a startling—and welcome—transformation. Maybe, just maybe, it would augur well for his time at Del Valle.

Chris was so committed, so steadfast and unwavering, that Antonia named him managing editor of the school newspaper, the *Conquistador*. He deserved to be editor, and Antonia knew it, but she was sheepish about naming him, afraid her selection might be seen as favoritism. He would deserve it, but the other students might bristle. Antonia would regret her decision years later, well-meaning though it was.

Still shy and quiet, Chris turned the journalism classroom into a sanctuary; except for the other classes he had to attend, he was always there. He ate there, studied there, daydreamed there. You would have thought he was a student-teacher, always hovering over the *real* teacher, his mother. Except that he was not hovering, not really, because, despite the proximity to his mom, he was still isolated, alone in the black velvet world of his imagination.

"I wish he would go down to the cafeteria and eat with the other students," Antonia said. "I wish he would *try* to belong. He's not always going to have my room as a sanctuary."

We all have our safe places, harbors that keep the turbulence at bay. The difference, with Chris, was that he needed a safe place 24-7. His books helped, his music helped, even his family helped, at times. But they were all temporary, transitory. Chris needed a vaccine, and all he got were aspirins.

Antonia asked me to visit her classroom one day. I spoke to the kids about professional journalism, journalism beyond the high school classroom. My talk lasted about thirty minutes, including questions and answers, and afterwards, I edited some of their stories, praising them for what they did well and advising them about what they could do better. They accepted my tips with grace and appreciation. Except for Chris—Chris chafed at my advice. I remembered when I asked my dad to edit one of the sports stories I had written for the *Shamrock*, the Cathedral High School newspaper. He tightened it, eliminating some verbiage, and I thanked him. I never bristled, but I dismissed his edits, retyping it with the original wording. Different situation, different time. At least, Chris was honest with me, I thought.

"I'm sorry," Antonia said that evening. "Chris has a hard time with criticism."

"I know."

Chris never developed strong friendships at Del Valle, but he never got into trouble, either, and whatever turmoil roiled inside him remained inside him. He started wearing his Del Valle T-shirts inside out, his resentment trumping his fashion sense. Grateful that he never got into trouble with the administration, we ignored the warning signs of deeper trouble within.

Things were different at home. The house was not the sanctuary the classroom was. Not for Chris and not for us. He was getting more mercurial, his mood shifting from moment to moment, and friction started to develop between Chris and Katy. Friction is normal for siblings, especially when one is a teen, the other a preteen. But this was not normal. Chris started detecting slights where none was intended, and as a result, Katy started doing the same. The result was volatile. Major blowouts grew out of minor disagreements. We became so concerned that we kept a wary eye on both kids.

Looking back, I remember the arguments, not what sparked them. I remember the explosions, but I forget who—or what—lit the fuse. The trauma overshadows the *cause* of the trauma. A discussion arose one Thanksgiving morning. The discussion escalated into a debate. The debate escalated into an argument. Domino after domino toppled, and there we were, wondering how we had reached this point. Chris stormed out of the house. I followed him, pleading with him to come back. This was Thanksgiving, after all, the day we are supposed to express our appreciation for each other. Chris stopped in mid-stride and, inches from my face, said, "Fuck off." I let him go. When he returned, the turkey was cold; Antonia heated up a plate for him.

Home, always a fortress for me, became a battleground. I hated it, and so I fled. I did not go anywhere, did not escape to another house or another town, but I was gone, nonetheless. Like Chris, I was there, but not there. I started stopping at bars after work. It became a habit. I did not find solace in a bottle; I found it in a bar. It was not the drinks that made me forget; it was the place where drinks were poured, a warm, comfortable environment so foreign to my own home.

My mother had died about four years before. Most people—or many people—die instantly. Not my mother. It took her a year to stop breathing. She had suffered a stroke in 1996, and it left her paralyzed, unable to walk or talk, her once caustic tongue unable to deliver her cherished put-downs, some charming, some not so charming. I visited her at the rehab center every day, and when she died one morning, she looked so skinny, so hauntingly skinny, her flesh as thin as tissue. She was eighty-five.

After she died, I developed an unbearable pain in my right shoulder blade. I tried pain reliever after pain reliever, but nothing helped. Antonia suggested I see a chiropractor. He took X-rays of me. Then he asked me if I had been experiencing stress lately. I said, "Yes." He asked, "For how long?" I said, "For a year." He said the anxiety had thrown my skeletal structure out of whack, causing the bones to pinch a nerve. I thought, *My God, I was hurting myself without realizing it*. He cracked my back, and most of the pain disappeared.

There was no chiropractor for my emotional pain, so I continued heading to a bar almost every day. A friend joked that my most intimate relationships were with bartenders (I *think* he was joking). I did not drink to excess—at least I do not *think* I drank to excess—limiting my beverages, most of the time, to light beer, but it hardly mattered. I was not where I was supposed to be—at home. I was at a bar, a home away from home, leaving Antonia and Katy to face the growing problem that was Chris. Was I ashamed? I was too caught up in my angst and sorrow to detach myself long enough for self-analysis. But I am not too detached now . . .

Dark is dark, but there are gradations among the shadows, shadings that make one street corner more menacing than another. And what if that street corner is your mind? There is dark, and there is the dark I experienced. It is self-indulgent, I know, to assume that your presence is so profound as to impact everyone around you. But it happens; even when you do not want it to—or *intend* it to—it happens.

I felt beaten down; watching someone die will do that to you, especially when you see the life in a once vibrant body exit slowly, day by agonizing day. My mother hung on for a year. There were moments when the joy, bright and shimmering, leaped from her paralyzed body. She loved Bobby Darin, the great pop singer, so I took a CD player to her room in the rehab facility one day. I played *Mack the Knife* for her, and she smiled, trying to shimmy in her bed, her shoulders rocking gently from side to side, the wildest motion she could manage. It was both heartbreaking and encouraging, but the optimism triumphed over the darkness. Those moments, though, were rare. And, when she died, I was too numb to cry; it seemed as if she had passed long before her final breath.

I thought a year would be enough to prepare me for her death; I was wrong. The pain in my shoulder was one manifestation of the trauma I had undergone. But there were others, more subtle but no less painful. I was weary, so I checked out, sleepwalking through work and, worse, sleepwalking through life at home. When I stopped at a bar almost every evening after work, it meant there was one less person to help Antonia and Katy and Chris. The dysfunction would lead to our divorce a few years later, not because I was unhappy with my marriage but because I was unhappy with my life. I would get a job with the *San Antonio Express-News* in 2005, and when I left El Paso, it made the distance between my family and me both metaphorical and physical. Antonia, Chris, and Katy stayed in El Paso. The divorce occurred in 2008.

We remained great friends, because it was the family, not the marriage, that crumbled. I had become disengaged, and we all suffered as a result. I did not divorce Antonia; I divorced the family. The kids took it well, perhaps because the divorce only made official what my distance had already created—a breach. And because Antonia and I remained close, perhaps closer than we had been before.

The tension had been palpable, almost unbearable, and it was unfair to blame Chris. It was not Chris but our reaction to Chris that was so problematic. It affected everyone, mother, father, kids. Katy would ask her mother, years later, if she regretted having kids. Antonia answered immediately. "No!" The worst thing about the hardships we suffered, the thing that caused us the most heartache, was that Katy would feel compelled to ask that question.

There were times when I hated Chris. But if there were times when I hated him, there were times—much more frequent—when I hated myself for hating him. There were also times when I loved him, loved him dearly. But here was my dilemma. I expressed my affection more openly, more outwardly. I hugged him. I tousled his hair. I laughed at his jokes. Not as often as I should have, but, yes, I did all those things.

The hate? It was hidden, buried in my heart, unexpressed, at least for the most part, by words or facial signals—tics, frowns, grimaces. But, buried or open, which was more apparent to him, the love or the hate?

Hate . . . Did I really hate Chris? No, I never hated Chris. Not really. I resented him, frustrated by his inability to communicate with us. What *should* have frustrated me, I would realize later, was my inability to communicate with *him*, to understand him, his quirks, his idiosyncrasies, his capricious habits.

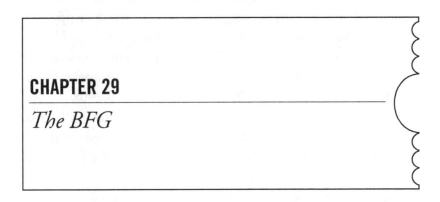

CHAPTER 29
The BFG

JULY 21, 2016

I THOUGHT OUR Thursday nights would never be the same, but I was wrong. *The Ugliest Woman in the World* proved that. Chris and I proceeded without disruption, as if those lost weeks—those weeks without our Thursday nights—had never happened.

True, there was something about a "free" movie, something that liberated both our pocketbooks and our emotions. It felt special, the way I felt when I got a discount coupon from Barnes & Noble, which made the book I purchased seem that much more satisfying. So it was with our free movie nights, which were now gone, "The End" flashing on the movie screen in our minds.

But we moved on. It helped that I picked the right movie for our first "pay movie" night—*The Ugliest Woman in the World*. The film embodied a glorious irony, depicting stupidity and cruelty without succumbing to them. *The Ugliest Woman in the World* was both depressing and uplifting, but it was more uplifting than depressing.

Our date nights, however, were never about the movies—or never about *just* the movies. They were about *us*, about companionship. We were together, Chris and I.

The "free" was gone from our movie nights, but we managed. We ate, we talked, we saw a movie—a trifecta for good times. It would have been petty to complain about the price tag.

Chris had gotten a new job, this one at Cane's, another fast-food restaurant. He was in good spirits, which put *me* in good spirits. Chris had been without a job for two months, but since I was paying for his apartment, he managed to make it through without undue hardship.

The biggest hardship about his new schedule was that we no longer saw each other every week. We had to be scrupulous about picking the *right* movie, just as we had been careful with the free movies; we did not go to *every* movie. It had been weeks since our last date, and it was time for another movie night, and this one would pose a special challenge. I picked what I hoped would be another inspirational film, *The BFG*. It was based on a book by Roald Dahl, whom Chris loved. So that was not the problem; the problem was the venue. The film was showing at the Northwest Theaters, a Cineplex about two miles from our haven, The Bijou.

I took a book, just in case Chris was late. I was hoping he would be, a sign that some things never change. Chris came through. Late again.

It was not as warm and inviting as the food court, but there was an area in the Northwest lobby with tables and chairs. I hunkered down, reading as I waited for Chris. The book was *Carrie* by Stephen King, a book I chose because Chris loved horror stories. I was stunned, pleasantly stunned, having always regarded King as a hack, even though I had never read him. My bias was stupid, based on his best-seller status, as if great writers had to toil in obscurity, appreciated by a discerning few. I was clearly not discerning. King is a beautiful writer, his lyrical sentences belying his horrific tales. The story was passionate but nuanced, and even the characters who flitted off and on the stage quicker than you could say "boo" were rendered fully and artfully. What a joy. I pledged to myself that *Carrie* would not be the last Stephen King book I read.

"Hey, Dad."

"Hey, Chris."

"What you reading?" Chris asked, sitting down.

I raised my paperback copy of *Carrie*, and Chris smiled.

"I've never read him, but I know a lot of people who have," he said.

I had already bought our tickets, and we had a few minutes before the movie started, so Chris sat down. The lobby was not as cozy as the den the food court had become, but we dismissed our surroundings as the conversation heated up. The topic was horror.

"I like to be scared," Chris said. "Life can get so boring, and sometimes, it feels good when that shiver of fear crawls up and down your spine."

"I never thought of it that way," I said. "But you're right."

"Yeah, it breaks the monotony of real life," he said. "Of course, after you've read the book or finished the movie, you're glad to return to real life. Fun—even *scary* fun—has its limits."

The movie was in 3-D, and we donned our glasses as we settled into our seats. The screen seemed fuzzy, as if I were watching through a wet window. The characters looked like ghosts, vague and indistinct.

"Does the screen look fuzzy to you?" I whispered to Chris.

"Well, I don't think the technology is quite where it should be yet," Chris whispered back. "Maybe one of these days, it will be."

"Hmmm, OK," I said, shrugging.

Fuzzy or not, the movie was delightful, especially the scene where the giant emerges for the first time, his shadow elongating as he rounds a street corner—a shadow so big that it looks like an entity unto itself, dark and menacing. Dark and menacing. Appearances are deceiving. "BFG" stands for "Big Friendly Giant," so this Goliath is benign, his heart as big as his body. He also seems scrawny, strangely scrawny, for a creature so massive, his gaunt face highlighting his appealing vulnerability.

Ah, but who, looking at him, would recognize the kindness that resides inside? The answer is a child. Old and wizened, vulnerable despite his massive size, the BFG meets a girl in an orphanage, ten-year-old Sophie. Both are needy, the girl and the giant, scorned by a society that focuses on appearance. They understand each other, *love* each other, and that love helps them overcome the challenges an ignorant world hurls at them.

It was a delightful movie, not a *great* movie. An unfair assessment, perhaps, but we have come to expect greatness from David Spielberg, the director. The film was missing that spark he usually provides, that combination of light and darkness that animates most of his movies. *The BFG* was *too* charming.

When I took off my glasses, I realized they were my *sun* glasses. Damn. No wonder the screen was fuzzy. Not as fuzzy as my brain. But fuzzy nonetheless. Maybe I would have thought it was a great movie if I had seen it clearly. Chris was still chuckling when I dropped him off at his apartment.

"Thanks, Dad," he said.

CHAPTER 30

Chris Makes It; We Make It

MAY 15, 2001

CHRIS SURVIVED DEL Valle, and we survived Chris . . . No, that is too harsh . . . Chris was not something to survive. He was not a tornado or a hurricane or a tsunami. It only felt that way at the time. Still . . .

"Now comes the hard part . . ." Antonia said, pausing. "College. Do you think he should go to UTEP, so he can be close to home?"

How to answer? Would *any* college be ideal? Would Harvard be better than UTEP or LSU or Montana State? The campus would be different, but the freshman would be the same.

"I don't know what to tell you," I said. "Should we wait to see if he gets any offers?"

"OK," she said.

If Chris was not a natural disaster, what was he? He was a boy on the cusp of becoming a man, a "cusp" that seemed elusive because of all the obstacles in front of him. Obstacles that were psychological or emotional or . . . what? We had no clue. What was so frustrating, so vexing and confounding, is that there were moments, lots of them, when Chris seemed more adult than adults. But—again, there was always a "but" with Chris—that was the problem. Adults are OK with other adults. But, sometimes, they have a tough time hanging with kids. Chris had trouble with relationships, period, but he could hang with adults better than he could with kids. He was always on insecure footing with them, every step he took fraught with the risk of embarrassment and humiliation. That was why he was comfortable with Leo Cancellare, but not with the swimmers he coached.

Still, he *did* survive Del Valle. There were no notes from teachers, no meetings with administrators. And there was at least one highlight.

Chris was an average student—with Cs, Bs, and B-minuses dominating his report card—but we always thought he was smarter than his grades indicated. Then, again, he seldom studied, reading his horror stories when he should have been preparing for exams, even in journalism. So the B average was understandable.

Then came the SAT. It was on a Saturday during his senior year. We dropped Chris off at school, then killed a few hours at a mall. We picked him up about three hours later, and he was the same Chris he had been when we dropped him off—quiet, subdued, determined to get one of the most important moments of his adolescent life over with as soon as possible. We wanted to get it over with, too. When Chris was surly, the world turned dark.

Chris crushed the SAT. He did so well that his adviser gushed over him for days. Then she had an idea. Maybe he should take it again, her rationale being that he might do even better the next time. It would increase his chances of attending a great university, maybe even an Ivy League school.

So we scheduled Chris for another go at the exam. He was not pleased, and when we dropped him off at school this time around, his surliness—and our misery—increased. We thought he would sabotage his own efforts; we were wrong. He surpassed his original score, and his adviser, ramping up her earlier gushing, said he could go to any college he wanted.

She was right. The letters kept coming—Dartmouth, Stanford, UT Austin, Texas A&M. Recruiters visited El Paso, inviting kids who had aced the SAT, Chris among them, to informal get-togethers. His early choice was Dartmouth. They had a hockey team, and even though his only experiences on ice were at ice rinks in New Jersey malls, he thought he could compete—the same way he thought he could compete as a swimmer under Coach Leo. But swimming, while demanding, is an elegant activity, whereas hockey may be the toughest sport of all; there is a reason why dentists—and denture makers—love hockey players. If Chris was a hockey player, I was William Shakespeare.

Chris gave up his dream of becoming the next Wayne Gretzky. We narrowed the choices to UT Austin and Texas A&M. He and I drove to each university on successive weekends.

They would be long weekends—one in Austin, the other in College Station, home of Texas A&M. Then back to El Paso. Both trips totaled about 1,400 miles.

As the miles rolled under the van, we marveled at the landscapes, more varied than the areas you would find in five other states combined. Deserts, forests, rolling hills, gentle creeks glistening under the bridges along the freeway.

Then, too, having stayed put in El Paso for years, I had forgotten how vast Texas was. It felt as if we were driving cross-country again, spanning the continent after all those years in Philly. Chris nodded off during a thunderstorm between Ozona and Junction. It was what Texans call a "gully washer," the waters rising so high that dozens of cows must have floated in the swirling water, ending up on top of their barns. They stood there placidly, the water puddling around their legs. I nudged Chris, pointing to the cows on either side of I-10. He looked like a six-year-old again, gaping in wonder.

And, then, the storm stopped. We were in Austin. It was one of those beautiful spring days in Texas, the kind that compel you to look upward, savoring the translucent beauty of the sky. The heavens were one thing, but down on Earth, the beauty was beyond our reach, as elusive as a dream.

The Austin campus was frenetic, with students frowning as they scurried from class to class. Trying to maneuver through the crowd of scholars, I spotted one young female muttering to herself, as if an interior monologue had burst into the open. Then I realized she was not alone; you could see lips moving everywhere, one-sided conversations that seemed inspired by anxiety or anger or both. I asked Chris if he saw what I saw. He said, "I *did*," his eyes open wide. Is that what happens when the equivalent of a small city—the student body population was forty-five thousand—is crammed onto a campus?

The next weekend, Texas A&M was more intimate and inviting. There were just as many students, but the campus was bigger, more sprawling—and, thus, less crowded. A&M looked like a city in both population and area.

The College Station campus was teeming with high school seniors—hundreds of kids from every state in the country, most of them from Texas. The best and the brightest. Chris was one of them. It made me proud. Chris belonged.

But it is not the leaders of the group—in this case, the university administrators—who grant you admission to the club. It is the rank-and-file, the kids. If they embrace you, you are in; if not, you are on the *outside* looking in.

We were walking through campus, on our way to what seemed like an endless series of seminars. Chris spotted two girls up ahead, both of them cute and cheerful. He quickened his pace, sprinting with that peculiar stride of his, running without swinging his arms. Chris caught up to them, so excited that he almost forgot what to say.

"Hi!" he beamed, almost shouting.

Both girls seemed to recoil. Chris stopped in his tracks, the smile wiped off his face. He looked down; the girls kept walking. I could hear them mumbling to each other as they passed.

When we returned home, we discussed the options—UT Austin or Texas A&M. There was that brushback from the young women at A&M, but that could have happened at Texas, too, and Chris seemed to realize that. We talked it over—Chris, Antonia, and I. The discussion did not last long. A&M was friendlier, its students greeting strangers with a "howdy," as if inviting you into their home. Who could resist that warmth? Chris would be an Aggie.

Spring turned to summer, and A&M beckoned. If Chris was gripped by the excitement of launching his new journey, he did not show it. Chris remained Chris—intellectually alert, emotionally laconic.

Holed up in his room for hours—sometimes, it seemed, like days—Chris would read his comic books and horror stories with more urgency and desperation than ever; literature, once again, became his escape. But it was more than that. Literature, for most people, is a portal into worlds they want to *visit*, not inhabit. Chris was different. He did not want to *tour* those worlds; he wanted to *inhabit* them—permanently. We could sense that, Antonia and I, and it was disturbing. It meant that the real world was too oppressive, too stultifying for Chris, so he found comfort in his fictional universes which, except in his imagination, were no more substantial than the pages on which they were written.

The days crept past. Still no excitement from Chris. No hint that his world was about to change. His world? His world was encased between the covers of his books—books which, even at their darkest, were preferable to the reality he faced every day.

In mid-August, we headed to College Station again, this time for freshman orientation. Chris seemed a little livelier, perhaps because he was hoping to see some cows stranded atop their barns, waiting for the sky to stop cascading. If so, he was disappointed. No thunderstorms, no levitating cows.

The orientation lasted three days. We roomed in a dorm. It reminded me of our night in Louisville—not exactly The Ritz. The days were packed with seminars, an exhausting gantlet of speeches, videos and tours. We attended some sessions together, some separately.

We split up one morning, and when we reconnoitered for lunch in the cafeteria, Chris was more animated than he had been in months. The words cascaded from his mouth—a deluge that was both startling and comforting. *Finally*. Some excitement.

Already an Aggie, Chris would become a Cadet, a tradition dating to 1876, when the school was founded. It became voluntary in 1965. Thousands of kids entered the Corps, and now Chris would be one of them. Wearing a uniform. Waking up at 5:00 a.m. Running across the football stadium, Kyle Field, leading the fans in the roars that swept from the seats to the sidelines. And perhaps, one day, taking care of Reveille the Collie, the Corps mascot.

A Cadet. Chris had been quiet that morning, a reticence bordering on dark and dour. We ate breakfast in the cafeteria, and when I tried to make conversation, he kept staring at his bacon and eggs, poking them with his fork, unresponsive. I tried again; same nonresponse. And then I cringed. Was A&M a good idea, after all?

Chris and I had split up after breakfast that morning, heading to different sessions. I dismissed most of the speakers I heard, nodding off the way I often did at the movies. My job was to let Chris know what I had heard, but it is hard to report what you have heard when you have not heard it. I figured Chris would face a similar problem—like father, like son. I was wrong.

Chris attended a seminar on the Cadet program that morning, and it was a joy to hear him expound on his "future" as a Cadet. The running and the push-ups, the strictness and the conformity—all the things that might make most young men bristle. Not Chris. He embraced structure, finding comfort within the confines of a world with rules and regulations, a world that told you how to act. A society with guidelines satisfied his desire to belong, to be one of the guys. To be "normal." It reminded me of his days as an altar boy.

"Dad, I'm excited about this," he said. "It's going to be great. It's going to be special. I can't wait."

The enthusiasm did not last. The push-ups, the running, the constant laundering of his uniform—all of it wore on Chris. Already up for hours, he would nod off during his morning classes, seeing his college career disappear in a haze of snoring and day-dreaming. Chris wanted to quit.

Despite the joy Chris expressed, I had felt misgivings about his decision to join the Corps. My father was a conscientious objector, sentenced to three years in prison during World War II, and I grew up with similar political leanings. But my concern went deeper than that. What if Chris extended his Cadet experience, joining the military after college? The events of 9/11 changed the world; these were perilous times, the enemy emerging without uniforms or flags, an amorphous swarm of menace and hostility that struck without warning. Military or civilian, the terrorists killed indiscriminately. And the US soldiers who survived returned to wage war on a different battlefield—their psyches.

But I changed my mind. No, Chris changed it for me. He was so enthusiastic, so passionate, that my concern vanished like a wisp of fog. I embraced what Chris embraced, and together we envisioned a bright future for this young student. And then he changed his mind, numbed by the crushing daily routine—running, calisthenics, taking orders. Go, go, go. Always on the go. *Enough.* I tried to change his mind, tried to convince him to forge ahead. We exchanged emails for weeks. I even phoned his Corps director, a young man who shared my desire to keep Chris aboard.

"Chris is a great cadet," he said. "He is exactly the kind of young man we want—driven and sincere."

I could tell he was younger, but the director reminded me of Coach. He had the same passion, the same drive and energy, and, more importantly, he seemed to have the same affection for Chris. The director had known Chris for only a few weeks, but he saw what Coach saw—an earnest boy yearning for approval. I could see Chris, responding to every command with a steady and sincere "Yes, sir." But the grind got to Chris. It chipped away at his enthusiasm and commitment, just as it had with the swimming all those months before. And when his commitment faded, something else faded with it—his sense of belonging.

CHAPTER 31

Pete's Dragon

SEPTEMBER 15, 2016

I MISSED BIRD, our winged friend. He was a fixture in the mall, gliding above the food court, as true and pure as an arrow, alert for any morsels left by the diners. *Aaahhh*, Bird.

Bird was gone, a passenger on the same vessel that took our Thursday nights away. Except for our occasional visits back to The Bijou, it would never be the same, although it came close, and we managed. The Northwest Cineplex became our theater of choice.

I waited for Chris at a table in the lobby, just as I had waited for him before we saw *The BFG*. He was late again, but it was comforting to know that some things never changed. Then, again, I had company, my current book, *Running the Books: The Adventures of an Accidental Prison Librarian*. I read it with keen interest, fascinated by all prison books because my father had been imprisoned for three years as a conscientious objector during World War II.

They existed, I am sure, but I had never read a bad prison book. *Borstal Boy, On the Yard, Cool Hand Luke, In the Belly of the Beast.* They were tough, dark, and gritty, with occasional slivers of sunlight entering the souls of the inmates.

Running the Books was different, written by an "outsider," Avi Steinberg, someone who has not been beaten down by "the big house"—yet. A Harvard graduate with a dead-end job as an obit writer, he applies for a job as a librarian at a prison in his home-town, Boston. He gets the job, and he finds patrons he never saw at the Harvard library—pimps, prostitutes, loan sharks, sex offend-ers. Everything but lovers of literature. He discovers a harsh lesson: The most hardened criminal, the one whose rap sheet makes you want to retch, is the one who requires the most compassion, the most understanding.

"You got your work cut out for you," a female coworker tells him.

Steinberg is up to the challenge.

Chris arrived.

"Hey, Dad."

"Hey, Chris. Hungry?"

"No, thanks. I already ate."

He sat down, asked me what I was reading.

"*Running the Books,*" I said, holding up the volume.

"Good?" he asked.

"Yes," I said. "You know I've rarely read a book I didn't like."

"That's interesting," he said. "I wish I could say the same. I've read books that I've regretted cracking open. Even if I stopped reading them almost immediately, I still regret it."

Then the young man who did not want to eat started talking about—what else?—food.

"Dad, eating is cool," he said. "The food fills you, and if you're lucky, it tastes good. But it's even cooler when you eat with some-one, because you can digest the meal along with the humor or wisdom—or both—of the person you're eating with."

"Well, I don't know if I'm wise or funny," I said. "But, maybe, we should eat together the next time."

"Cool," he said, laughing.

One more rhapsodic comment, and we would have missed the movie, *Pete's Dragon*. It was produced by Disney, but Chris had relaxed his self-imposed prohibition against Disney movies. A boy and his dragon. It seems silly, but the film was impossible to resist, full of awe and charm and wonder. The boy sees what others cannot, perhaps because vision is not just about eyesight; it is about what you detect with your heart and soul. Pete sees because he believes. Afterwards, Chris and I agreed on three points:

- The dragon is charming, as cute as a puppy, never mind those talons and that blow-torch of a mouth.
- Robert Redford, who plays the grandfather of the young protagonist, has turned into a cool old man. Who would have thought?
- The movie is heartwarming and inspiring, the corn leavened by heart.

Pete has a hard time convincing his mother and grandfather that there is a dragon out there, appearing and disappearing, often melding into the environment.

"Why do adults have such a hard time believing kids?" Chris asked afterwards.

"Well, do you blame them?" I said. "After all, a dragon?"

Chris, at thirty-four, still saw the world through the eyes of a child, and he felt the bitterness and resentment any youngster feels when adults threaten his sense of self-worth. As the years passed, I detected an irony in Chris, in his development. A youngster with the intellect of an adult, he always seemed older than his peers; but now that he *was* older, he seemed more immature, the demands of adulthood beyond his ability to cope. He kept complaining that "being an adult sucked."

And, so, he viewed the film through the lens of a youngster.

But he detected at least one positive note in *Pete's Dragon*. Once his mother and grandfather realize Pete is telling the truth, they journey back to their own childhood, embracing the awe and wonder they had dismissed earlier.

"That was cool," he said.

We rolled up to the parking lot at his apartment.

"Thanks, Dad."

CHAPTER 32

From Cartoon to Opera

APRIL 16, 2005

CHRIS MAJORED IN English at A&M, and he would call us periodically, usually once a week. He seemed upbeat and confident, a teenager settling into his new life. But we wondered if the physical—and, perhaps, emotional—distance shielded us from the reality he may have been confronting: the isolation and anxiety of his new world. It was impossible to know with Chris.

Geographically, I was closer to Chris than Antonia. I was an older version of Chris, my commitment and dedication fading at the *El Paso Times*. I needed a change, and I made it. The *San Antonio Express-News* offered me a job as the associate editorial page editor, and I took it, hoping that, eventually, Antonia and Katy would follow me . . .

Lonely but settled in San Antonio, I got a call from Chris one day. It was about three o'clock on a Thursday afternoon. He invited me to watch a production of *Aida* that Sunday on campus. About

560 miles closer to College Station than I had been in El Paso, I said "yes."

Poor Chris. He got saddled with a father whose idea of opera was *What's Opera, Doc?* the Looney Toons cartoon in which Bugs Bunny lends melody to mayhem. So much for fine art.

Trying to instill culture in a plebeian is no easy task, but Chris pursued it with the bright-eyed zeal that seems the special province of youth, even a youth as troubled as Chris. What did he have to lose? If he failed, he—and I—would be no worse off than before. His culturally bereft father would remain culturally bereft, the stench of ignorance still clinging to him like a noxious gas.

Ah, but if Chris succeeded, I would rise in stature, ennobled by my passionate embrace of an art form I had previously shunned—opera. Chris had played the opera for me once—on a CD, an experience that reminded me of the time I played "A Hard Rain's A-Gonna Fall" for my mom. Now, I would be hearing it—and seeing it—live.

Not that Chris was a cultural evangelist, forcing me to change despite my misgivings. He merely wanted to share his love of an art form with me. I was willing—no, eager—to let him try. So I drove the 180 miles to College Station that Sunday morning, wondering throughout the trip, *What if I don't like it? What do I tell Chris?* My vision of opera—forged by a sassy rabbit and a demented, bald-headed hunter—would never be the same.

One afternoon, weeks before, Chris texted me about the classical music program on NPR he loved. They were playing a composition he remembered from his childhood. He knew the name of it, but knowing the cultural limitations of his father, he used the title with which I would be familiar.

"The radio is playing 'Kill the Wabbit,'—:p," he texted me.

"Ha!" I replied.

In more cultured circles, the composition was known as *The Ring of the Nibelung* by Richard Wagner.

"Yea," Chris continued. "I always get a belt outta how many of these compositions I recognize because of old cartoons we used to watch."

The gene pool is a mystery. It gave us Frank Sinatra, the greatest pop singer in history, and Frank Sinatra Jr., whose only distinction was being the son of the greatest pop singer in history. DNA is not everything. So it was with me and my son. Somehow, the DNA strands failed to link all our likes and dislikes.

I grew up on music, a love that blossomed on the night of February 9, 1964, when The Beatles appeared on *The Ed Sullivan Show*; each note, each lyric reviving the carcass of the sad old beast that was rock 'n' roll. The Beatles changed the music, just as surely as they would change society. They injected it with an infectious spirit, as wholesome as it was rebellious. Yes, they were charming, even gracious, but all great artists are rebels, leaping on the shoulders of their predecessors to elevate their art forms. About a week after *The Ed Sullivan Show*, a folk group appeared on another TV variety show. It was the Brothers Four. They sang "Rock Island Line."

"Now, really, don't you think they're better than The Beatles?" my father asked me.

Only nine years old, I was struck mute by the question. My mouth stuck on one word—"Uhhhh." No, DNA is not everything.

Chris grew up on The Beatles, too, and he loved them—a love distilled from my own enthusiasm for the group. He even liked Black Sabbath, an affection I did not share. But he went beyond The Beatles and Black Sabbath, going from the visceral appeal of rock to the sublime appeal of opera.

We settled into our seats at Rudder Auditorium, both of us wearing white shirts and blue ties—a sign that we recognized we had gone beyond rock 'n' roll, if only for one afternoon. The maestro waved his wand, and the music began, gentle one moment, portentous the next. It was infectious, compelling, and enthralling.

There was a small, rectangular screen above the stage. The gods—who were among the unseen characters in the opera—were smiling on me. The screen provided a digital translation of the lyrics, without which I would have been lost. Thank God—or gods.

To appreciate the music, rock fans need only a passing acquaintance with the English language. Unless the artists are The Beatles or Bob Dylan or Chuck Berry, poetry is usually a bonus in a rock 'n' roll song. Not so with opera. The poetry is part of the package.

Set in ancient Egypt, *Aida* is about greed, love, and unrequited ardor. Perhaps all great operas—indeed, all great stories—tackle those issues. If so, how many do it with more passion and power than *Aida*?

It was three hours of deceit, honor, and tragedy. And when it was over, Chris looked at me expectantly. I eased his anxiety.

"I loved it," I said simply.

"Thanks for coming, Dad," he said.

He smiled. No, DNA is not everything. But at times like these, it could be pretty cool. And it would provide me with a glimpse of the joy we would share years later on our movie nights.

CHAPTER 33

Beyond Thursday Night

JULY 16, 2016

I MISSED OUR free Thursday night movies, but with those nights in the rearview mirror, we had to get more creative about our get-togethers.

No longer shackled by the calendar, Chris and I could roam beyond Thursdays at The Bijou. Our Thursday nights perished, but something would spawn in their place, perhaps something more exciting, more . . . adventurous. What would it be?

Computers are cold, lifeless machines, with email communications lacking the zest of face-to-face conversations. But sometimes, *sometimes*, the vibrancy twists its way through the digital passageways, the electronic corridors—a burst of warmth that seems all the more appealing considering the route it took to get there. This is what happened with Joseph Rodriguez. Rodriguez was a young professor at UTEP, my alma mater, and when we started emailing each other, his devotion and enthusiasm seemed to light up the computer screen. We had never met, our relationship confined to email discussions, but I felt as if I knew him. He specialized in young adult literature, and his students, I knew, were fortunate to have such a committed educator.

As a high school student in Houston, Joseph read a short story in an English class that astounded him. It seemed simple, even prosaic, in retrospect, but the story was lyrical, and it gladdened his heart: One of the characters was named Rodriguez, and it was an epiphany, a validation. Rodriguez—and others like him—were worthy of literature, worthy of seeing their hopes, dreams, and aspirations chronicled. *Sweet.*

It was the first time he had seen his name in a short story, in *any* kind of literature. But it was not just the name that exhilarated him. It was the person behind the name. A rich, vibrant character. A human being. A *Brown* human being.

The short story was written by my father, Amado Muro, and Joseph felt a kinship with this man, this Anglo who understood the Mexican culture as if he had been born into it, generations of pride and dignity running through his DNA. The connection between the two men would run deeper; years later, when he settled into education as his career choice, Joseph would earn a graduate degree at Kenyon College in Ohio, the same institution my father attended in the 1930s.

In 2015, Joseph discovered that I was the son of the "Pale Chicano," as my father was called after his death. He emailed me, and the cold, lifeless computer did not seem so cold and lifeless any more. We would become friends, first electronically, then personally.

A few months after our initial electronic conversation, Joseph emailed me one morning. He would be in San Antonio to attend a poetry reading by Tino Villanueva, a native of San Marcos. Did I want to go? "Of course," I said.

I invited Chris, and he did not hesitate, either—which surprised me. Not that Chris shunned poetry readings—or any other kind of literary events. He was just so unpredictable, and I never knew what he would endorse and what he would reject.

The poetry reading was at the downtown library, and I picked Chris up at his apartment. He was hungry—it was about 5:00 p.m.—and while I stopped for gas at a convenience store, he scurried inside to buy one of those "delicacies" that dripped with more grease than a corndog at a county fair—tacos or "tornados," those spicy, lard-encrusted sausages. (I remembered the morning I bought a cup of coffee at the neighborhood convenience store, part of the same chain. The java was not greasy. Standing at the coffee bar, I felt a rush of air behind my back, and when I turned around, I saw a rotund body flash by, a beach ball with legs. He was heading to the bathroom, screaming, "Oh, my God! Oh, my God!" I asked the cashier why he was "Oh, my-Godding." She took my $1.75 for the coffee. "Oh," she said matter-of-factly, "he just ate a hot dog.") Chris emerged empty-handed. Thank God.

"What happened?" I asked.

"They were out."

"I'm sorry. I'll take you to dinner after the reading."

"No problem," he said.

Have you ever known someone only through phone or email conversations, and then, when you finally meet him, you are startled because he looks nothing like the individual you conjured in your mind? Joseph was different. He looked like the person I had pictured—about five-foot-ten, with brown hair and brown eyes—but it was his demeanor that struck me the most dramatically. He was soft-spoken, with a calm, gentle manner that put you at ease. We hugged, and I introduced him to Chris.

"Great to meet you, Chris," he said.

And then he looked at me.

"And great to meet you—finally."

Villanueva read from his collection, *Scene from the Movie GIANT*, which won the American Book Award in 1993. The "scene" is one of the most powerful in movie history. Bick Benedict, a wealthy rancher portrayed by Rock Hudson, takes his family to a small, rural diner near Big Bend. The manager/waiter disparages the baby, whose mother is Mexican. Benedict defends his grandson. The

manager-waiter continues the abuse. A fight ensues, punches flying, chairs crashing, faces bleeding. Both men land crushing blows,
but Benedict ends up on the floor, as flat as West Texas roadkill; his
body is battered, but his dignity is intact, for he has stood up to the
brutal bias of the times.

I saw the film on "Saturday Night at the Movies," the weekly
program that featured old movies in the 1960s; I was about eight. It
was the first time I had seen Mexicans—or Mexican Americans—
treated respectfully on film, as valuable and precious as any white
man. I get chills thinking about the scene and, now, the poem
inspired by it.

> A heart you carry in your memory for years. A scene from
> The past has caught me in the act of living; even
> To myself I cannot say except with worried phrases
> Upon a paper, how I withstood arrogance in a gruff
> Voice coming with the deep-dyed colors of the screen.

After the reading, Joseph and I hugged each other again. We
promised to hook up again, somewhere, somehow, and then he
whispered something in my ear. "Your son seems like a fine young
man," he said.

"Thank you!" I said, beaming.

Chris and I headed to the parking lot.

"Now for dinner," I told Chris as we got in the car. "Is Chinese
OK?"

"Sure," he said.

And then, as we drove to the buffet, Chris gave his own poetry
reading, provoked by nothing more than a thought that had invaded his mind. A stray thought that morphed into a full-fledged
lecture. Whenever Chris pontificated, I felt the way I felt after reading a book by Rick Bragg or Edna O'Brien or John Edgar Wideman, my jaw dropping with every sentence, every page. I would
come to the last page, and I would feel like a hack, diminished by
the grandeur of their prose. How could I match this? Chris was my

own personal Rick Bragg or Edna O'Brien or John Edgar Wideman. His language was so rich, so sumptuous. It made me proud.

Chris discussed a local writer, speaking with a combination of vitriol and scholarliness. Perhaps more of the former than the latter. It was his fuel.

"He fancies himself another Hunter S. Thompson," Chris said. "It's like a form of plagiarism, isn't it? But it's worse, because it's more deceitful. He's trying to steal the spirit, not the words, and spirit isn't something you can steal. You either have it or you don't.

"It's embarrassing. Hunter S. Thompson, for all his wackiness—maybe *because* of his wackiness—was a grand stylist. I read a book by this faux Hunter S. Thompson, and it was a crazy story. But there is crazy, and then there is believable crazy. *Credible* crazy. *One Flew over the Cuckoo's Nest* is crazy . . ."

He paused, recognizing the irony of his statement.

"But it is *credible* crazy. It is crazy you can believe. But this poor guy is outlandish, without the talent to pull it off. . . . It reminds me of something you once said about Bob Dylan—and the folk singers who followed him. I forgot your exact words, but the gist was that his followers strived for his profundity, but lacked the talent and intelligence to pull it off. Look at Donovan. *Jesus.* Their ambition exceeded their talent, so they ended up as second-rate—or third-rate—Dylans."

Whatever I said about Dylan, I am sure I did not say it as eloquently as Chris did. He continued, his vitriol growing as he gained momentum, although it was hard to gain momentum when you started at full throttle. His final word on the subject: Dreadful.

The mobile classroom was coming to an end. We arrived at a Chinese buffet in Northwest San Antonio. We talked about other topics during dinner—mainly comics and mythology—and then I dropped him off at his apartment.

"Thanks, Dad," he said.

"Thank *you.*"

CHAPTER 34

In a Foreign Country

ROMANCE WAS A foreign country for Chris, a landscape with strange customs, strange rituals, strange signals. Signals. Chris had trouble reading social signals, anyway, but when it came to romance, his tenuous understanding of code-deciphering collapsed.

Chris met Julie at a ComicCon—Comic Convention—at Texas A&M. They were both sophomores, both enamored of the world depicted in comics—a world where good triumphed over evil, where ambiguity and nuance were no-shows. A simpler world, a world unlike their own.

Chris and Julie may have loved that world, but they had different ways of coping in *this* world. I did not know much about Julie, just what Chris told me, and that info, relayed by a young man in love, seemed dreamily, ethereally positive. But was it accurate?

One day, they set up a date, their first, and Chris was so excited that he called me about it, his voice full of so much passion and urgency that I pictured him standing next to me. I should have been uplifted by his enthusiasm, but it scared me. Would his expectations be dashed? Would they crash into a dark, ugly wall of reality?

Julie never showed up, never explained her absence. They were supposed to meet at the Student Union, but there was no Julie. *Maybe she is outside*, Chris thought. But the more time passed, the more remote that possibility seemed, even to Chris, the eternal optimist. He waited for fifteen, twenty, thirty minutes. He stared at the clock on the wall, as if it were his agent of deliverance. Deliverance never came.

As expansive as Chris could be about subjects he loved—comics, opera, horror stories—he could be equally tight-lipped about subjects that troubled him, including his failed romantic overtures. He did not talk about his disastrous interlude with Julie, and I did not press him. But I could guess what he was going through, what he wanted out of life. He wanted to escape—not escape life, but escape himself. He wanted to dissolve, become invisible, his problems disappearing as he disappeared. But Chris did not disappear. He remained where he was, and so did his problems. And, somehow, he soldiered on.

Chris survived A&M, just as he survived Del Valle. That is how we came to view the phases of his life—in terms of whether he survived them. It was both a low bar and a high bar, low because we should measure success in terms of achievement, high because, for Chris, success meant overcoming obstacles most people never face.

He spoke fondly of some classmates, many of whom, perhaps, registered him as blips on their internal radar, including the young woman who seemed puzzled by a question an English professor asked her. What did you get out of reading *My Ántonia*, the novel by Willa Cather? he asked her. "I learned that Nebraska turns strong women into strong men," she responded.

It took Chris five years to graduate. Not because he was intellectually lethargic—Chris never suffered from that malady—but because he switched majors his junior year, from journalism to

English, and the move forced him to enroll in courses he should have taken before. The extra year of servitude did not bother him. Chris seemed in no hurry to dive into the next phase of his life, mainly because he had no idea what the next phase of his life would be. And he did not seem to care.

After graduating from A&M, he returned to El Paso, where he remained cloistered in his room for weeks, months, his diploma as useless as scratch paper. Antonia was distraught. I was working at the *San Antonio Express-News* by then, so I was little, if any, help. What help could I have provided, anyway, what source of solace or enlightenment? Chris was an enigma, a puzzle beyond our ability to solve.

Loitering in the house for almost a year, Chris finally got a job as a security guard at a warehouse in Northeast El Paso. He worked the late-night shift, so Antonia rarely saw him, but one afternoon, she found an empty bottle of Olde English in his room, a solitary vessel joined by what looked like a cellarful in subsequent days— four one day, six the next, eight the day after that . . . Antonia was worried—worry that multiplied as the bottles did.

Then, two years after graduating from Texas A&M, another Julie appeared, and the drinking stopped. Another Julie? I minimized both women, the original Julie and the new Julie, reducing them to a type, because I feared more heartbreak for Chris.

If it was hard for me, his father, to maintain a positive attitude about Chris, imagine how hard it must have been for anyone else, including any potential partner. This one was another version of Julie. Chris met her online, their paths converging through a mutual love of comic books. They exchanged telephone numbers and email addresses, and their passion for comic books became a passion for each other. She wanted to meet Chris.

She lived in a small town near Orlando, Florida. So Mickey and Goofy were her neighbors. Did that mean her hold on reality was tenuous, shaped by the dream factory next door? A foolish thought, but rooted in another world, another time, I wondered how a relationship could blossom from the bowels of a computer.

No matter. Blossom it did. Eager to meet Chris, she booked a flight to El Paso. Antonia was apprehensive. Where would she stay? And, if she stayed with them, would she sleep in the same room with Chris?

I thought about Julie again, the A&M student. Unable to secure a role with the Cadets, Chris tried a less regimented means of connecting—romance. It should have been easier—no push-ups, no wind sprints, no taking orders. But the tradeoff was predictable. He swapped physical hardship for emotional hardship, a landscape that was more uncertain and, thus, more treacherous.

On uncertain ground when it came to romance, Chris proceeded in the only way he knew how: he flailed. Whatever charm he may have possessed, he did not know to employ it in the service of love. He just knew he had to try.

Chris never had a girlfriend, either in high school or college. It was not for lack of effort. He was remarkably bold, given the barriers life had erected around him. Romance is hard enough for any kid, male or female, but it was worse for Chris, the challenge magnified by his inability to read the social signals apparent to most individuals. He was either too aggressive or too timid, too . . . or too . . .

Whatever the obstacles, she was coming. I was working in San Antonio at the time, and Antonia asked me if I would mind driving over, a 1,120-mile round trip, to help her "cope" with the situation. I said "sure." The girlfriend arrived on a Friday evening, and she was quiet and pleasant, not the kind of person who forced you to "cope" with her foibles. First impressions.

They hit it off, *seemed* to hit it off, their shyness melting in the warmth of their affection for each other. They spoke quietly, tenderly, to each other, their words just above or just below a whisper, depending on your proximity to them. And, yes, they slept in the same room. Then she left, but her presence hovered in the air—and in the heart of our lovestruck son. I wondered if Julie, the original Julie, would rear her ugly head again.

Now here we were, two years later. Summer of 2010. Chris had moved to Florida, and we were visiting the two of them, Chris and his girlfriend. It was a calm evening, a cool breeze blowing from the Gulf. *Aaahhh*. We were miles from the Gulf, but you could smell the fresh, emerald water in the air—the scent of burgeoning life. The stars twinkled above us, along a narrow swath of sky, so bright and accessible that they looked like sequins pasted on a low ceiling.

Up until then, there was little reason to feel positive. It had been a rough week. Negativity floated in the air, like a horde of pathogens, dense but unseen.

I had my misgivings, but I was brimming with joy compared to Antonia and Katy. The evidence was on their side. The "new Julie" treated Chris like a stranger, someone she might walk past in the mall. They rarely spoke to each other, except for snatches of conversation here and there. It was surreal.

Chris seemed lost in the whirlwind of our visit, and she did nothing to help. He would ask her questions, and she would answer curtly, treating him as if he were an interloper, not someone who had been living with her for about a year. When he asked her a question, she would stare at him, a gaze that said, "Now what?" It got worse.

We stayed at a motel, Antonia, Katy, and me, and when she invited us to lunch one day, we seemed like strangers, all of us, the tension overwhelming. Chris was quiet through most of the lunch, memories of grade school haunting this twenty-eight-year-old man. We wanted to leave as soon as possible, but what would we be leaving Chris *to*?

Chris had moved to Florida in 2009, driving the 1,700 miles in his Honda Accord. He made the trip with great joy and optimism, but something happened between the romantic interlude of Texas and the cold reality of Florida. The pathogens started to emerge.

I ignored them, picturing a happy wedding in the hazy future. I saw guests serving their own champagne, which flowed from one of those fountains where the bubbly spilled from tier to tier—a golden waterfall. I may have had too much to drink, or not enough, it was hard to tell. It was just a vision, after all. The ambiguity mirrored my conflicted emotions about the wedding, happy but concerned—concerned about how long the happiness would last, for Chris and everyone who loved him.

It was a dark time, but there was one bright moment, as shimmering as it was unexpected. We were sitting on the patio one evening, the three of us, and she joined us. A love song was playing on the radio. Chris embraced her and, pivoting to gain the proper leverage, twirled her until she seemed about to fall, and then he stopped, holding her like a knight lifting his maiden from the ground, limp and delicate. They looked at each other, Chris holding her by the waist, she suspended inches above the patio floor. And, then, Chris kissed her, a kiss that seemed to last as long as the evening. A beautiful moment. But how long would it really last?

I thought about fate, about the crossroads we face throughout our lives, how a convergence of circumstances can affect two young people. They were born hundreds of miles apart, in different cities and cultures, each traveling a long road to meet each other in the flesh. What did they find? And what would they find in the future? Joy and euphoria? Or hurt and disappointment? It seemed like the latter, at least for Chris.

It is not cynical to describe relationships as minefields. Almost 50 percent of marriages end in divorce in the US. Antonia and I were part of the dispiriting statistics, our marriage dissolving after my move to San Antonio. We remained great friends, but the relationship had imploded. I was not the same person after my mother died, my spirit fading as her life faded.

Antonia and I had been divorced for three years, but we seemed to have a better relationship than Chris and his girlfriend. He looked like a stranger in her home, as if he had stumbled into the wrong house. Chris gazed at her longingly, full of love, but his gaze was met with indifference, if not iciness. She treated him like a prop, not a partner. He breezed through rehearsals for his high school drama productions, but this was real life, and he could not freelance, as he did when he scrawled "Helter Seltzer" on his T-shirt for the staging of *One Flew over the Cuckoo's Nest* at Cathedral High School. She would talk to him without looking at him, walk past him without acknowledging him. It was hard to watch. Already quiet and unobtrusive, Chris seemed more invisible than ever. We saw it as a harbinger.

All of that seemed irrelevant now. He had made his decision, moved to Florida, and yet he could move back. He could fight the pathogens, find a new life back home if he wanted to.

We would have to wait and see. Chris was not compulsive, usually accepting his fate, good or bad, with remarkable equanimity. But was this fate irrevocable, something he had to endure longer than he wanted to? Or could he defy his penchant for tolerating treatment he did not deserve? If he moved back, the decision could be empowering, a move that told him he could direct his own future, regardless of the path that fate seemed to lay out for him. But was he capable of doing that?

CHAPTER 35

He Named Me Malala

AUGUST 18, 2016

IT FELT LIKE a homecoming.

The best thing about returning home is to find that home is the same, that nothing has changed. Nothing had changed at the Wonderland Mall. The food court was still bustling, chefs cooking, customers eating. And the atmosphere was the same, too, with the same warm, dingy glow bathing the shoppers and diners. And Bird. Bird was there, too, pecking at the floor with an almost robotic precision. *Aaahhh.*

The next movie in our lineup was showing at The Bijou. A happy coincidence. It was good to be back.

Another thing remained the same. Two things, really. Chris was late, and I brought a book with me.

When a book title itself is a reading experience, brief but rich, you yearn to dive into the words beyond the title. Who could resist the title *Do Androids Dream of Electric Sheep?* The poetry was irresistible. I had never read Philip K. Dick, had never read much science fiction, period. But there was that title. Irresistible.

The best thing about *Do Androids Dream of Electric Sheep?* is that the title represents a portal into an even deeper, richer reading experience. The prose is worthy of the best noir, gritty but lyrical, with an urgency that compels you from sentence to sentence. There is a surprise on every page, the atmosphere so surreal that each development is neither expected nor unexpected.

"Hey, Dad."

"Hey, Chris."

He was delighted at my book selection, having read it himself years before.

"It's the book *Blade Runner* is based on," he said.

Chris wanted life to proceed in a linear fashion, but he did not *think* in a linear fashion. A comment about A did not necessarily lead to a comment about B. With his synapses leapfrogging from topic to topic, he could reroute any conversation, making hairpin turns on his rhetorical journey. This was one of those moments. I was talking about science fiction, and he started talking about classical music. So I asked him why he liked the music. It was soothing, he said, a lambent light of serenity.

"It relaxes me," he said. "When I'm weary or frustrated, I hear the music, and there's something about the chords that soothes my frayed nerves. It *unfrays* them. *Unfrays*. Is that a word? Well, it should be, because that's what it does for me."

I was surprised by his enthusiasm. He was, after all, raised on blues, soul, country, and rock 'n' roll. I thought Beethoven was someone who should roll over. And the same went for Tchaikovsky.

If I could float into his apartment, if I could spy on him from above, what would I see? Would I see him lounging on his sofa, next to the radio on his end table, his eyes closed, his eyelids fluttering to every chord of genius emanating from the pianos or violins or harpsichords? Would I see his feet rising and falling ever so gently, not tapping or stomping because, after all, this was not rock 'n' roll? This was something more sublime. Would I see a smile crease his lips, savoring melodies that were as light and fragrant as a flower? And, finally, would I see him lost in the rich, sweet galaxy of the music? Chris listened to classical music on NPR, and I asked him who his favorite composer was.

"Oh, man, it would be easy to say Mozart or Beethoven, both of whom are amazing. I also find myself enjoying Prokofiev. He had very bombastic compositions, the kind that could lead troops into battle. But he was very diverse. His compositions could also be very calming, very soothing. . . . But I would have to say that Schubert is my favorite composer—for reasons that have nothing to do with his music, which was also amazing."

Chris pronounced Schubert *Shoo-bear*, the way I imagined an Austrian would pronounce it, while I, a plebeian compared to my son, pronounced it *Shoo-bert*.

"I like Schubert because he was very shy and introverted, and he tried to express his confidence through his music," he said. "He threw himself into the music, and if he wasn't sitting at his piano, he didn't know what to do with himself. I can understand his pain. Whenever he was introduced to someone, he would kind of look down his nose at him and ask, 'So what do you do?' It was a front. He wasn't really that tough and confident, and I can relate to that. . . . And, of course, he made wonderful contributions to the music."

I told Chris that Paul McCartney based "Blackbird," the lovely civil rights ballad on *The White Album*, on a Bach composition.

"Really?" Chris said. "That's interesting . . . Wait a minute, wait a minute . . . I can hear the Bach composition in my mind. I can't remember the title, but I can definitely hear it. Yes, it's 'Blackbird.' And it makes sense. McCartney has written oratorios, which are his modern takes on opera and classical music."

He became so animated that we both forgot about dinner. It was time for the movie, *He Named Me Malala*, a documentary. I picked it for the same reason I picked all the other non-Thursday-night movies: I thought it would inspire Chris. Malala Yousafzai was reaching legendary status, and I wanted to show Chris that a legend, a true legend, is not one who goes undefeated, but one who, having tasted defeat, rises again and again. This was the essence of Malala.

Malala is a child, with big brown eyes that seem to gaze into a future that only she can see. But not her future. *Our* future. For despite her youth, she possesses a preternatural wisdom, a deep empathy, and while most people her age are focused on themselves, she is focused on the world.

The movie portrays a girl with an indomitable spirit, buttressed by courage and integrity. A child herself, she supported the education of other children, *female* children—a taboo in Pakistan, her homeland. The Taliban issued a death threat against her. The threat was not empty; a Taliban gunman shot her in the head in 2012. She was fifteen.

Malala is recovering from the assassination attempt when the movie opens, but the pain never leads to rancor, the scars confined to her head. The attack refuels her ardor, her determination, to support the education of women in Pakistan. She spreads a message of love and peace.

Malala won the Nobel Peace Prize in 2014, an event chronicled in the documentary. You sit in the theater, viewing the announcement, and like a crazed soccer fan, you want to cheer and pump your fists. This is the grandest victory of all—good over evil.

"Hey, Dad?

"Yeah?"

"You know what I liked the most about Malala?"

"What?"

"Well, she's this extraordinary girl, right? She's bright and committed and courageous. And she possesses the best kind of integrity, the kind that remains unwavering in the face of almost certain peril . . . And yet . . .

" . . . And yet . . . At the same time that she is extraordinary, she is also ordinary—perfectly ordinary. She is asked if she likes boys, and her little brother makes fun of her, and you can see her face turn scarlet with embarrassment. For a Nobel Prize winner, she is adorable."

I paused, not sure how to respond.

"I guess great people emerge despite their 'normalcy'—or *because* of their 'normalcy,'" I said, finally. "But we are all normal, really."

"Yeah . . . Thanks, Dad," he said, stepping out of the car.

CHAPTER 36
Julie Reappears

OUR MOST PROFOUND misgivings were realized.

Julie seemed to reappear, the student who stood Chris up at Texas A&M. She reappeared in the guise of his girlfriend in Florida. It was inevitable. The only question was the ETA. It did not happen suddenly—these things rarely do—but when it *did* happen, it grabbed Chris by the throat, as unforgiving as a firing squad.

She taught elementary school, and Chris worked part-time supervising special needs children during their recess periods. They lived in a three-bedroom tract home in a modest neighborhood. It seemed like the suburban ideal for young couples, but . . . Chris should have seen it coming, seen the signals, the icy stares, the constant judgments, the . . . But, no, Chris never saw it coming. It was not part of his makeup to detect trouble, and once he detected it, to avoid it. And, so, it blindsided him.

The relationship collapsed almost immediately, morphing from a shaky proposition to a seismic catastrophe. He started drinking again, finding solace in a bottle because he could not find it anywhere else. The problems we noticed during our visit did not just resurface; they grew. He misread cues and signals, and she reacted with frustration and resentment, ignoring him for long stretches. Then she kicked him out of the house, forcing him to sleep in the backseat of his Honda Accord.

When he started drinking, his girlfriend would text us—Antonia in El Paso, me in San Antonio—photos of the empty bottles. Olde English. It was distressing, and not only because Chris was drinking. We felt, perhaps unjustly—it is unfair to judge a situation when you are not there to witness it firsthand—that his girlfriend was not trying to help him, but to malign him. How productive was it to send photographic evidence of his drinking? And to two individuals thousands of miles away? Why not try to deal with the problem there, where it was occurring?

Yes, we had to know, and, yes, we *wanted* to know. But she knew, too, and she was doing nothing beyond texting us the photos. And kicking him out of the house. It seemed strangely, well, combative. *Your son is a drunk, so there.*

I called Chris, asked him how he was doing. He said, "Fine." Chris was always fine, always OK. No matter what turbulence roiled his soul, the weather report was always bright, always sunny. And always, or almost always, malarkey.

We had to learn the details from her. Chris is a terrific talker—erudite, witty, and informative. But what makes him a terrific talker also makes him a terrible talker. He grandstands, filibusters, explores a topic until there is nothing left to explore. And, then, he explores some more. You get used it, seeing charm in the constant digressions. But these talkathons, these wild, verbal journeys, arise only when there is something he wants to discuss. If the subject is the turbulence in his soul, the mute button turns on.

Chris was *not* fine, and I knew it. He called me one day. I asked him if he wanted to come to San Antonio, for a few days, maybe, a kind of retreat for the soul. Silence. Then more silence. Tick, tick, tick. The silence unnerved me, made me wish he had never called me. And, then, Chris broke the silence.

"Sure, Dad, sure," he said, finally. "I would love to."

OK.

Now what?

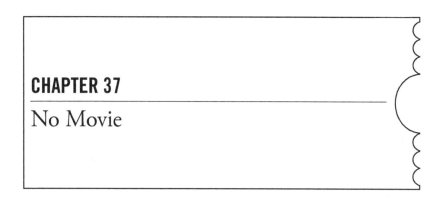

CHAPTER 37

No Movie

SEPTEMBER 8, 2016

IT SEEMS COUNTERINTUITIVE, but it is easy to remember something that was supposed to happen but never did.

If you miss your graduation or wedding, you remember the occasion as if you had gone through it in the first place. Maybe more so, because the ache of loss is as deep as the triumph of achievement would have been. Maybe deeper. So it was with me and my Thursday nights. The free movies were gone, and sometimes, the Thursday nights were gone, too, because Chris had other options, other commitments.

Another Thursday night by myself, confined in my crummy, one-bedroom apartment. I could have gone out by myself, I suppose, but my outing would have been disheartening, tinged by the melancholy of knowing I could have been with Chris. So I stayed at home, saddened by my solitary status, but buoyed by the fact that there was no solitary status for Chris. He had made some friends.

Friends. He met them at the various shops at the Wonderland Mall, a delightful turn of events, so delightful that it relieved my pang for those Thursday nights. I still missed the movies and, more importantly, Chris, but whatever joy I missed Chris obtained. It was a good trade-off. *Friends*. And so I would remember these lonely nights.

Alone in my apartment, I pondered the question I pondered every time Chris was off with his friends. What to do? I could read. I could mope. I could watch TV. I turned on MSNBC. Big mistake. As the presidential campaign heated up, Donald Trump became a fixture on TV, assaulting both our language and our decency. He looked like a buffoon, his orange hair as stiff as a board. He turned every campaign rally into a Klan rally, spewing hate and vitriol with alarming enthusiasm. It was easy to blame his supporters, the people who seemed to fuel his anger. But the truth was the opposite; *his* anger fueled *them*. He used them, and while they allowed themselves to be used and exploited, they seemed lost in the miasma of his charisma.

I resented the blather on both sides of the aisle. The worst offender was Chris Matthews, host of *Hardball* on MSNBC, his voice so loud and shrill that he seemed to have a microphone lodged in his throat. And he rarely let his guests answer his questions, launching into soliloquies that would have made the great Shakespearean heroes seem taciturn. Matthews would have interrupted Jesus during the Sermon on the Mount. He was ousted a few years later for making an offensive remark about a woman that was picked up on a "hot mic." I would not miss him, but in the meantime, his blather was distressing. Chris, the *other* Chris, where are you when I need you?

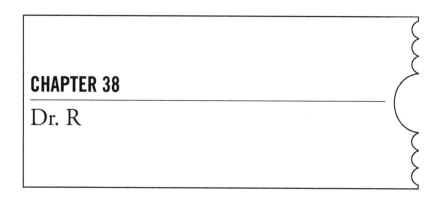

CHAPTER 38
Dr. R

WHEN IT COMES to everything but books, CDs, and DVDs (which barely even existed anymore, having been rendered redundant by all the pay networks), I am a miserable consumer. Books, CDs, and DVDs are easy. I know what I like, and I know what is worthy of my approval. I once read a glowing review of a book by an author I admired, so I went to my neighborhood Barnes & Noble, intending to buy it. But, no, I thumbed through the book, a ritual I followed no matter how much praise the book had garnered from the critics. And I came across this sentence: "He rambled in a disjointed way." Disjointed? How else would one ramble? I thought. I reshelved the book.

So books, CDs, and DVDs—no problem. Everything else? Problem. How would I know which car to buy? Which DVD *player*? Even which shampoo? The marketplace was a maze, and the result was inevitable. I got lost.

Imagine my distress, then, when the product I sought was a counselor. If Chris was drinking, it was clear that we, Antonia and I, had to do what his girlfriend would not—help Chris, not excoriate him. But what could we do? An inept consumer, I looked for a counselor, not for Chris, but for me. I wanted to seek advice on how to help my son before he arrived in San Antonio.

The decision would be crucial. It was not like selecting a toothpaste or a mouthwash. This would be a life-altering choice. Two lives, really. Mine and . . . I was afraid to utter his name, afraid to say . . . *Chris* . . . So much depended on my decision. The hardest choices are the ones you do not want to make, and I did not want to make this one.

I did what most people would do in such situations: I Googled *counselors*. Reviewing name after mind-numbing name, I checked the credentials of the counselors—their degrees, their specialties, their comments. Checked and re-rechecked dozens of names and qualifications. It took me two days. Which one to choose?

And then, as often happens when you feel the most helpless and impotent, it came to me—an epiphany. *Roxanna Ramirez*. It was a hunch, just a hunch. The name had a pleasing alliteration, and based on her résumé, she seemed accomplished and formidable. A doctoral degree from Baylor University, and years of experience as the director of counseling for the Schertz Independent School District, a community just north of San Antonio. All those kids, all those troubled kids. What an enormous challenge it must have been for her—and what a learning opportunity.

There was one other factor. Not all the counselors had provided photos on the internet sites, but Roxanna Ramirez did. And she had a kind face.

I left her a voice mail one morning, and she responded two days later. We set up an appointment for the following week. I wondered if I was going crazy—or if I was being overpowered by wishful thinking—but her voice seemed gentle but firm, and I could swear she sounded as kind as she appeared to be in her photo.

It was Friday, the afternoon of our appointment. I headed north on US 281, the freeway as clogged as my mind. I gripped the steering wheel, and anxiety gripped me.

I waited in the lobby, nervous about meeting a person I had known only through a photo and a brief description on the internet. Was my hunch about Roxanna Ramirez right? I wondered. Was it even wise to act on a hunch? Five minutes passed. I fidgeted, the book I had brought with me resting on my lap, unopened— *Freedom Summer* by Bruce Watson. Drumming the cover with my fingers, I waited another minute, then another. I had been there only seven minutes, but it seemed like an hour.

She stepped into the lobby, opening a door that led down a hallway. I walked into the office, and the first thing I noticed were the walls, plastered with photographs and artwork by young Picassos, one of which depicted what I presumed to be Roxanna Ramirez—a stick-figure Roxanna Ramirez drawn by a child. It was dedicated to "Dr. Rocksanna." I relaxed. The picture was an indication of how her clients, young and old, felt about her, and how she felt about them.

Roxanna Ramirez—AKA Rocksanna—was standing by her desk to the left of the door. Fascinated by her office décor, I did not look at her immediately, but when I did, I was struck by her face, as kind in person as it had been on the internet. Kindness is not a facial feature, but you could see it in her eyes, her body language, the tilt of her head.

Dr. Ramirez had short brown hair, with a wave that slanted across her forehead, and brown, doe-like eyes that reminded me of a young Paul McCartney—a good omen, I thought. She wore blue jeans and a white, long-sleeved shirt. And boots. Brown boots.

Another hunch. It was easy to think of her, even on first glance, as "Rocksanna," a young woman who touched her clients. First impressions are perilous, but I sensed the compassion behind the degrees and job experiences. Résumés are just that, pieces of paper. But here was a young woman, I thought, whose qualifications were buttressed by a humanity that transcended diplomas and testimonials.

We shook hands. I sat on the couch, and she settled in an easy chair, an electronic notepad resting on her lap. She asked me about Chris, about the concern I had expressed in my voice mail to her. Trying to compress a lifetime of worry into a few sentences, I started at the beginning, telling her that Chris always seemed *different*—isolated and aloof, even as a baby. The isolation—and our worries about it—increased as he grew older, his shyness and timidity hindering his relationships with both classmates and teachers. The shyness morphed into awkwardness, the awkwardness into an inability to navigate his way through adulthood. Chris was thirty-one going on thirteen; as he grew older, he kept lamenting, I told her, that being an adult "sucked."

Dr. Ramirez listened attentively, never interrupting unless I had reached a dead end in my efforts to explain Chris. She prodded, gently but firmly, for more details. I told her about his problems with his girlfriend, how she had kicked him out of the house, forcing him to live in his 1995 Honda Accord. The backseat, I said, had become his bed. I pictured him back there, in the fetal position, both physically and emotionally. Antonia, worried that he was depressed, conjured an image neither one of us wanted to confront—Chris as suicide victim. When I called Dr. Ramirez, I felt as if I were dialing 911.

I finished talking, and Dr. Ramirez looked at me, gripping the electronic notepad on her lap. It was as if all the information, all the knowledge and expertise, contained in that notepad had seeped into her mind—years of study distilled into a bright, articulate professional. She spoke with authority and clarity.

"Chris," she said simply, "has Asperger's syndrome."

And then, relying on all that knowledge and expertise and, yes, compassion, she explained Asperger's syndrome to me. It was part of the autism spectrum, she said, a condition so insidious that many people, including counselors, failed to recognize it. That explained why Antonia and I were so befuddled about his . . . his . . . *behavior*. He was so smart, and he seemed so functional, but he was a tick off socially, and the gap between him and his loved ones became a chasm.

Before I left her office, Dr. Ramirez offered me two books from her shelf, both about Asperger's syndrome, *Be Different* and *Raising Cubby*, and both by John Elder Robison. I devoured them, fascinated but disturbed. Every word was a cruel revelation.

"There's no cure for Asperger's," she said.

This was the harshest epiphany: *There is no cure for Asperger's syndrome*. The words echoed in my ears long after they were uttered. They took the air out of me, left me in a state of bewilderment. How could there be no cure? Even cancer has a cure, at least in some cases. But Asperger's? Please, Dr. R, give me something to cling to, I said to myself. Give me a thread of hope. She did.

"There's no cure, but you can deal with it, try to minimize its negative impact," she said.

In an episode of *Boston Legal*, the hit television series that aired from 2004 to 2008, a lawyer is discovered to have Asperger's syndrome. An unusual but likeable man, he purrs when anxiety grips him, often during trials, the soft thrumming breaking the courtroom decorum. "Asperger's syndrome," a colleague says. "That sounds like something you cure with an ointment." If only.

No cure, Dr. R said. It made sense. How can you cure something you can barely diagnose? The condition is too vague, too nebulous, but those with the condition can mitigate their pain through counseling, she said. Early diagnosis is the key.

That left Chris out. And, yet, better to diagnose it at a later age than to keep living in its miserable embrace. *If* you can diagnose it. Diagnosing Asperger's is a huge task. Picture a heavy fog. You sense the objects in front of you, beyond the murky shadows, but they remain dull and shapeless—as amorphous as bloodstains. How do you negotiate a roadblock when the roadblock is virtually invisible?

The condition is named after Hans Asperger, an Austrian physician who conducted his seminal studies in the 1940s. Asperger was a pioneer, and as with many pioneers, his work was so groundbreaking that it took decades for the rest of the world to catch up. The American Psychiatric Association did not recognize the syndrome until 1994—recognition that no longer exists.

Asperger worked with children who, while bright, exhibited the symptoms we now associate with the syndrome. The youngsters displayed poor communications skills, including a lack of empathy with their peers. And they lived in a different world, as if their environment were a tidy little box that few outsiders could open.

So what is the harm in creating your own box, your own space? We all carve out our little havens, our little sanctuaries, right? The difference is that those with Asperger's are obsessed with their worlds, sometimes annoyingly so, and they do not understand when others are not equally obsessed.

They can be remarkably passionate and eloquent, but passion and eloquence have a shelf life, and when it comes to conversations, they pontificate long after the expiration date. They can go on almost endlessly, as Chris did about opera or comic books or limburger cheese, their sentences interrupted by clauses, as if their talks were prepared speeches, complete with colons, semicolons, and, sometimes, periods. This makes bonding with them difficult.

"Some people with Autism Spectrum Disorder have the desire to fit in or want to make friends, while most do not desire to make friends," Dr. Ramirez told me. "They prefer to be in their own world and with their own interests and where they can control their environment."

She may not have realized it, but that described Chris. His experiences could have jumped out of a textbook on Asperger's. As a child, he was obsessed with books. I remembered the day he read *The Strange Case of Dr. Jekyll and Mr. Hyde*, which evolved, in my mind, into *The Strange Case of Christopher Seltzer*. Chris started reading "adult" books when he was eight, long before his classmates could negotiate those complicated sentences. He used words that were longer than stretch limousines. We—Antonia and I— were amazed. What we did not realize, at least initially, is that his intelligence seldom erased the gap between himself and his peers; it widened it.

Another obstacle to diagnosing the condition was the fact that, by 2015, Asperger's syndrome would no longer be recognized by the Diagnostic and Statistical Manual, published by the American Psychiatric Association. It fell under the category of "autism spectrum disorder (ASD)," as it always did—the difference being that it was no longer known as a separate condition. Recognized or not, those who suffer from the condition—or who know someone who does—would tell you that it does exist.

If you have a friend or loved one with Asperger's, you know. Those with the condition can be witty, articulate, and cheerful—on the outside. But what lurks on the inside can be debilitating. Chris was proof.

Sometimes, it seemed, the key to dealing with the condition did not rest with those afflicted by it—at least not entirely. It rested with those who came into contact with them—parents, friends, teachers, even strangers. It was all about compassion and understanding and love.

"No matter what, people with ASD should be treated with respect and never discriminated against," Dr. Ramirez said. "Education about ASD can help others have an understanding and compassion for those on the spectrum."

Dr. Ramirez, whose clients called her Dr. R, asked me about my background, about my mother and father. I gave her a brief description, condensing a vast biography into a short story. My mother fled the Mexican Revolution in 1916, moving from Chihuahua to El Paso, where she would meet my father in the late 1940s. They got married in 1950, and soon afterwards my father, a short story writer, adapted her maiden name as his pseudonym. He dismissed immigration authorities to become a Mexican. It was then that Amado Muro was born.

When I talked about my father, I turned into a human hype machine. But this was no PR malarkey. I was sincere, making the old man sound like the Shakespeare of the Southwest. And I meant it. He was a walking paradox. An Anglo who wrote as a Mexican. A poet who wrote prose. A short story writer whose tales were epic. A man I did not want to be *like*. A man I wanted to *be*. It was a heavy burden, one that would prove too much for me.

A man born into wealth and privilege, my father could have felt entitled, better than anyone else. But no. What others might have seen as a virtue he saw as a stain. He did not deserve what was bequeathed to him; he did not *earn* it. And so he set about earning both respect and self-respect.

Dr. R was intrigued, offering a diagnosis of the man I was praising. Chester Seltzer, she said, may have had Asperger's himself. The symptoms were there—the outsider obsessed with a culture different from his own, his integrity girding him against the barbs that came his way. Chris, she concluded, may have inherited his condition from the grandfather he had never met.

Sitting in the cozy office, listening to Dr. R, I thought about my father. He was a strange man, noble but eccentric, with just enough eccentricity to overshadow the nobility, at least in the eyes of most people. Including my mother. The old man was a challenge, every notion and attitude, every concept and viewpoint, an assault against "normality." He wrote about homeless men, and he lived the life they lived, riding freights, hitting flophouses, selling plasma. The old man would invite these hobos to our house, and sometimes, fighting their shame and embarrassment, they would accept. One day, unaware of the latest invitation, my mother found one of these men in the bathtub, trying to wash weeks of dirt and grime off his homeless body. The tub water was black. My mother screamed.

Remembering his work habits, I pictured my father writing on the sofa, stern and sullen, his brow furrowed in concentration, as if there were a fence, a wall, keeping the sentences out of his brain, his imagination. Keeping them all out. And then, inevitably, there would be a breach. A sentence would climb the fence, scale the wall. And then another and another. A great escape! Sentences rushing pell-mell from his brain to his pen. The old man would smile. But only slightly, the crease on his lips so tight that you had to look hard to spot it. I looked hard, and I kept looking. And, as I looked, he would sit there, the yellow legal pad on his lap, until there were enough breaches to make a short story.

I always wanted to be like my father, and write like him, but I never made it. Maybe I knew, deep down, what a difficult task it would be. . . . But Chris, maybe Chris had no choice. . . . Did the old man pre-figure Chris? Were his eccentricities early versions of the obstacles Chris would face trying to connect with other human beings? Was my father Chris 1.0? And, if so, should I condemn him for the problems he handed down to Chris? Or extol him for the good qualities he gave him?

After speaking to Dr. Ramirez, I left her office feeling both crestfallen and uplifted—crestfallen because I knew what plagued Chris, uplifted because I knew what plagued Chris. The irony was stunning, but it was there. Dr. Ramirez had lifted the fog—or, at least, *part* of the fog—and I could see the path ahead more clearly than ever before.

Ignorance may be bliss, but it is not empowering. Dr. R gave me enough information to fill the archives in my mind, and I found comfort in all the knowledge, all the data. It was encouraging. The more you know—no matter how horrible the implications of that enlightenment—the more equipped you are to combat the obstacles in your way. Does that sound weird? There are people, I know, who feel the opposite, secure in their cocoon of ignorance. I understood. It was like facing an asteroid field, a bombardment of data that could leave you feeling helpless. But it was ignorance that scared me—the dark tunnel that led to more fear and anxiety.

CHAPTER 39

The Jungle Book

OCTOBER 27, 2016

I HAD FOND memories of *The Jungle Book*. We had taken Chris to see the Disney movie in New Jersey, a re-release, and whenever Chris pranced around the house in his underwear, he reminded me of Mowgli, his body lean and lithe, his skin smooth and brown. The boy in the suburbs transformed into the boy in the jungle—a sight that could have jump-started an ailing heart.

It was a sunny afternoon, the sky a warm, blue gauze. I drove up to the theater, the Northwest Cineplex, which did not spark the same sense of anticipation as driving up to The Bijou; The Bijou was special, the cineplex was just another theater. Then something greeted me that heightened my excitement.

I had brought my book with me, *My Father's Paradise* by Ariel Sabar, but Chris made the book superfluous. I glanced toward the box office, and there was Chris, on time—a first. I left the book on the passenger seat, where it would remain, unopened and unread, for two glorious hours. Thanks, Chris.

"Remember how you used to run around in your red underwear in Jersey?" I asked him as we strolled into the theater. "You were so skinny, your legs and arms so long."

"I *do* remember," he said. "You started calling me Mowgli."

"You turned the house into a jungle," I said, laughing.

We talked about Rudyard Kipling, the author of the original stories. He was an imperialist, an ugly philosophy born of the time and place, perhaps, but no less offensive for the soil in which it germinated. We discussed writers who were racist—or allegedly racist. Jack London, Charles Dickens, and William Faulkner, who wrote a story for *Harper's Magazine* that seemed to whitewash the murder of Emmett Till in 1955.

"Thank God for Mark Twain," I said.

"Yes!" Chris responded.

We both agreed that *The Jungle Book* was touched with elements of imperialism, with some critics viewing Mowgli as an emperor and the animals as his minions (although Mowgli is a child of color). This interpretation may have grown, not from the book itself, but from other works by Kipling, including his poem "The White Man's Burden." The views of a racist, after all, make all his books suspect, no matter how innocent they may seem.

The current movie, a remake of the animated film brought to us by the magic of CGI (computer generated images), may not have been innocent, but it was like a lot of adventure movies, impossible to resist—tender one minute, thrilling the next. And the voices of the computer-animated animals. My God. Bill Murray, Christopher Walken, Scarlet Johansson. They were sublime.

"Christopher Walken was great," Chris said afterwards. "He's one of those people whose voice is a personality unto itself. He was the perfect actor to characterize King Louie."

I reminded him, again, of that scene in *Pulp Fiction*, the one where Walken visits a youngster whose father died in a POW camp during the Vietnam War. He tells the boy about the gold watch he retrieved from a bizarre hiding place. The boy stares at Walken, eyes blank, mouth agape. What should have been a poignant moment evaporates into absurdity.

"Ha, that's right," Chris said, laughing. "He was so deadpan as he recounted this ridiculous story."

Afterwards, I wondered, was the movie *The Jungle Book* that good? Or did seeing it with Chris make it *seem* that good? Did having two Mowglis in the theater—one on the screen, the other in the seat next to me—enhance my moviegoing experience? I knew the answer. Chris had nothing to do with the production of the movie, but he was like a bonus director, a bonus screenwriter, a bonus cast of stars, making everything more vibrant, more sumptuous, more enjoyable.

"Thanks, Dad."

"Thank *you*."

CHAPTER 40

Learning from Dr. R

WHEN I RETURNED home after my visit with Dr. R, I was apprehensive, blindsided by conflicting emotions—dread and exhilaration. The apartment was dark, quiet, deserted—a setting that matched my mood. I felt lonely, as lonely as I had ever felt. And yet . . .

Dr. R unlocked a vault of information, much of it dark and ominous, but I was undeterred. I visited her every week, and I kept seeking more and more data, as if embracing the dark would summon the light. The internet yielded article after article, paper after paper, and I read each greedily. Alternately depressing and uplifting, they offered something I craved—a solid foundation of knowledge that enhanced my understanding of the problems my son—and I—faced.

I cannot say that the fog lifted, the fog of Asperger's. It was too dense to dissipate. But I began to appreciate what Chris was going through.

We are all outsiders, every one of us. Billions and billions of people. Misfits all. Some conform; some rebel. But deep down—in that part of our souls we cannot bear to reveal—we are all lonely and alienated. Some more than others. How we deal with this emotional displacement is what distinguishes us. Even the staunchest introvert wants to belong, wants to gain favor with some*one*, some *thing*. My father was an outsider, a liberal in a conservative family, an Anglo who yearned to be a Mexican. I was an outsider, too, shy and lonely, although I was not as courageous or principled as my father. And Chris, well, Chris was the biggest outsider of all.

Society operates under an unwritten code. Call them social clues—clues you can see, clues you can sense. Eyes are windows. Facial expressions are roadmaps. And words are exclamation points that amplify all the other signals. But, when you cannot read the signals, the code is unbreakable, and the music everyone else hears becomes a discordant symphony for those with Asperger's.

Some researchers have isolated the problem to our mental circuitry, the jumbled pathways that lead the autistic through strange corridors, activating emotions that are inappropriate or, worse, unseemly. Individuals on the spectrum lack the crystal clarity that most of us take for granted. The road signs lead them to dead-ends, to worlds undefined by any map.

Human brains have more than 100 billion nerve cells, or neurons, which relay messages with blinding speed. Imagine if those pathways are clogged, blocked, or broken. Imagine the disconnects that may result—laughing at a funeral, belching at a church service.

During my research, I came across a theory called the "competence-deviance" hypothesis. The more respect you command in your field, the more people excuse your quirky behavior. We see this among rock stars and university professors, their genius fortifying them against criticism. But when you lack a résumé, a history of expertise and achievement, your eccentricity is offensive, something to deride. People on the spectrum face this all the time; they are weird, strange, *different*.

Other studies indicate this *difference*, this *alienation*, should be viewed as a positive. The evidence, according to researchers, grows every day: Some of the smartest, most creative people in the world have—or *have* had—traits of autism: Albert Einstein, Dan Aykroyd, Michael Jackson, Isaac Newton, Wolfgang Amadeus Mozart. The list expands as the research expands. Chris—and others like him—are not alone.

Along with the guidance built upon years of research and face-to-face experience, Dr. R recommended books for me, including *Look Me in the Eye*. Written by John Elder Robison, it is a first-person account of the challenges posed by Asperger's—a poignant, sometimes heartbreaking depiction of the struggles faced by these boys and girls, men and women. It is also a plea for recognition, for respect. It reminded me of the sad but triumphant declaration by Sylvia Plath in *The Bell Jar*—"I took a deep breath and listened to the old brag of my heart. I am, I am, I am."

I read *Look Me in the Eye*, and it was just as Dr. R described in her discussions with me: Asperger's was a bitch, although she never used that term (I doubt the word was in her vocabulary). While she described the condition in remarkably vivid terms, her knowledge was based on years of study and counseling. Robison was different. *His* studies were up close and personal. He was on the front lines, his enemies vicious and relentless—enemies, represented by society, that triggered inner strife and turmoil. And so his story rang true.

I thought about Robison, and I thought about Chris. They were different from other people, different in their attitudes and personalities. But there was a pattern to their behavior, a rhythm. You had to expect the unexpected with them, and you had to accept it, recognizing that there was no malice involved, no insensitivity. It was our responsibility to understand. But it is one thing for an individual to reach an epiphany; how do you expand that awareness to the society at large?

When I thought about Chris, I felt like an outsider, diminished, not enhanced, by my "normalcy." I did not feel normal, or what society views as normal. I felt as if there was nothing "wrong" with these individuals, these kids and adults on the autism spectrum. They just exhibited traits that placed them in the minority. If we, the "normal," had been in the minority, I—and people like me—would have been the ones on the spectrum, isolated or, worse, maligned.

I knew one thing. The more I thought about Chris, the more "normal" he seemed. It would be a huge challenge, but as Robert Frost said, "The best way out is always through."

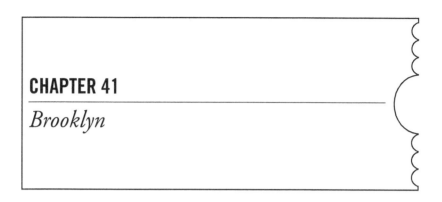

CHAPTER 41
Brooklyn

NOVEMBER 17, 2016

IT WAS GETTING dark, and the sky looked like a giant shadow, soft and blue. The perfect counterpoint to the arrival of the day about ten hours earlier—the bleached pink of dawn. Another day bookended by varying gradations of light. It was 5:30 p.m. Later than our usual meeting time, but since our free movie nights ended, we had more flexibility, unconstricted by the firm Thursday night schedule. I strolled into the mall, holding my book, *Pilgrim at Tinker Creek* by Annie Dillard.

I should have left the book in the car. I walked through the food court, and there was Chris, sitting at a table at the Wonderland Mall. If my jaw had dropped any farther, the janitor would have had to sweep it across the floor. Maybe I should have expected it, considering he was on time for *The Jungle Book*, too.

"Chris!" I exclaimed.

"Dad!" he responded, mimicking my shock.

We both laughed.

"I know, I know," he said, anticipating my next comment. "I'm here early."

"How come?" I asked.

"Well, it was such a nice evening that I thought I would head out early, so I could walk nice and slow," he said.

So shocked that I forgot about checking to see if Bird was around, I sat down, hoping we could resume our conversation of a few weeks ago, about classical music. I asked him who his second favorite composer was, after Schubert, and then, quicker than you could say the "Flight of the Bumblebee," he switched the conversation to science fiction. Of course. It reminded me that Katy thought her brother, in addition to Asperger's, had Attention Deficit Disorder (ADD).

"They call it *science* fiction for a reason," he said. "Isaac Asimov, the greatest science fiction writer of all, teaches you as much about science as you can find in a textbook. But there are no digressions, because all of the data moves the plot forward. That's why I enjoy his books so much."

We went to see Brooklyn. I mean, we went to see the movie *Brooklyn*, not the city Brooklyn, although it seemed if we *had* gone to visit the city, so vivid and enchanting was its depiction in the film. The borough looked as it must have looked in the 1940s, when the movie takes place—tough, lusty, and charming, its streets bustling with an energy that seems almost electric. No, not almost. It *is* electric.

The camera bathes the city in a warm, lambent light—the same light that illuminates the characters. They are fully developed, all of them, some selfless, some selfish, some struggling against their selfishness. The latter include Ellis, the young woman who crosses the Atlantic to pursue a dream, leaving a country that would never leave her—Ireland.

In one lovely scene, Ellis volunteers to serve Christmas dinner at the neighborhood church, a chance for her countrymen to enjoy fellowship in their adopted country. A young Irish immigrant sings a song in Gaelic, and it is so exquisite, so beautiful, that it makes you pine for a "lost" language. It does not matter if you cannot understand the lyrics, the words behind the emotions. It is the *sound* of the words, their rhythm and cadence, that captivate you. Is this why the Irish are such great writers—Joyce, Yeats, Shaw, Wilde, Beckett, Swift, Binchy, O'Faolain, O'Brien, Doyle, O'Farrell . . .? On and on, a galaxy of stars that will shine forever, heirs to a language that touches your soul—music in which the only instrument is the voice. *Aaahhh*, that voice, the voice of the young singer. As the Irish immigrants listen to the song, their eyes well with every note—pain and loss distilled into shiny globules of tears.

For all the drama, pathos, and heartache, Chris and I fixated on one scene afterwards. Ellis is having dinner with the family of the young man who is wooing her. She is Irish, he is Italian—a barrier that proves nonexistent for everyone but the young brother of the wooer. He declares, between slurps of his spaghetti, that the Italians hate the Irish, a comment that causes almost instant indigestion among the rest of the diners. The kid is banished to his room, only to return later, shoved into the dining room by his father. "I'm an idiot," the boy says sheepishly. Everyone laughs.

Whatever animosity the family may have felt toward the Irish dissolves in the presence of this charming young woman. Who could have withstood her charisma, her . . . glow? Not the Italian family.

"Two kinds of people are honest, *unfailingly* honest," I told Chris afterwards. "Drunks and . . ."

"Kids," Chris said, interrupting.

I laughed.

"Yes," I said. "How did you know that's what I was going to say?"

"I was a kid once," he said.

Yes, and Chris was still honest, sometimes brutally so. Did that mean he was still a kid? I resisted answering my own question, knowing that whatever his maturity level, he faced adult-sized problems.

We kept discussing the kid—and what he blurted out. It was a humorous scene with a serious undertone. Forced to apologize, the kid got off easy because of his youth, and because biases tend to melt when you come face-to-face with the people you thought you abhorred. They make prejudice look like what it is—stupid.

It was weird to see, in the wake of our free movie nights, first-run films, but some of them had the look and feel of the classics we used to see on the free movie nights. *Brooklyn* was one of these. We left feeling the movie was destined to become a classic. Maybe, if the free movie nights were resurrected, we would see it again, years and years from now.

"Thanks, Dad."

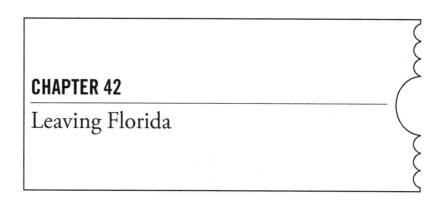

CHAPTER 42

Leaving Florida

JUNE 12, 2012

AIRPORTS ARE ABOUT comings and goings, arrivals and departures. It says so on those television monitors, right? Flight 357 to Kansas City departing at 11:25 p.m. Flight 206 from San Francisco arriving at 5:05 p.m. And, amidst these arrivals and departures, amidst the travelers scurrying from one gate to another, are items you never see on luggage carousels—pasts escaped and futures embraced.

Chris fit both categories. He was fleeing a problem and embracing a dream. The dream? It was simple: a new life.

I picked him up on a Saturday morning. He was waiting outside the San Antonio International Airport, his life for the past three years stuffed into a backpack. A crummy backpack. Ah, if only. If only his last three years could be crammed into that shabby old backpack. After all, it would not be able to hold much sorrow and heartbreak, grief and anguish. But, no, Chris toted those items in another carry-on—his psyche.

Chris was skinny, skinnier than I remembered, his shirt so baggy that it looked like a shawl. Damn. I would have to start feeding him tacos and burritos, Southwestern delicacies he had probably not tasted in months.

Gaunt or not, it was great to see my son who, in my view, arrived in San Antonio on a kind of prison-release program. A few weeks of freedom, perhaps, during which he could relax, regroup, and reconsider his future. He needed it. I could tell. He looked older, his shoulders hunched, his eyes encircled by dark rings of tension and anxiety. Age brought on not by the passage of time, but by the stresses of life. An old man at thirty-two.

I had a one-bedroom apartment, so we alternated between the bed and the couch. It worked out. Chris had been sleeping in his car his last few nights in Florida, so the couch was a luxury.

We settled into a rhythm. I worked, and he stayed at home, recuperating from the emotional turbulence of life in Florida. I bought him a membership at Gold's Gym, and the skinny kid morphed into a powerful adult, his clothes getting tighter every day. No more shirts that looked like shawls.

Chris seemed to walk taller, straighter, his confidence growing along with his muscles. It was a pleasure to see. But it was a ruse, the muscles, the swagger, the confidence—all a ruse. He was physically powerful but emotionally fragile, battered by whatever happened to him in Florida. He would not talk about it, and I felt helpless, witness to an agony I could do nothing to mitigate.

As the weeks progressed, the comfortable rhythm became too comfortable. What I had regarded as a hiatus became a routine. He was not returning to Florida, it became clear, and it was equally clear that he would not try to forge an independent life in San Antonio. He seemed content to keep living with me, with no job and no effort to *get* a job.

Was Chris a freeloader? No, he was my son. But if he was not returning to Florida, he had to take a stand *somewhere*, on his own, taking responsibility for a life that had not gone the way he—or his loved ones—had wanted. Chris had to stand up.

It was a slow, painful process, this standing up, and Chris fought it, fought it fiercely. He started drinking, and I remembered, bitterly, the photos she had texted us. I sat down on the sofa one evening, and I heard a clink. I pulled the sofa from the wall. A bottle fell out. A bottle of Olde English.

"Is that the only one?" I asked Chris.

"Yes," he answered.

I sat back down, and I heard another clink, this one louder. I yanked the sofa again, and I peered behind it. There were nine more bottles, stacked like cords of wood against the wall, all of them Olde English. I grabbed a garbage bag and, without saying a word, hauled them to the dumpster. I wondered how Chris, who lived on welfare funded by his father, could afford to buy ten bottles of Olde English. And I wondered if I could ever trust him again.

The lying disturbed me more than the drinking, particularly because Dr. R had told me that those on the autism spectrum are almost unfailingly honest. Chris looked miserable. I thought about taking him to an AA meeting.

After about two months, I asked him to look for a job, and he said he would, but the job search consisted of sleeping on the couch, all day, every day. One day melded into another and another and . . . The days consisted of nothing more than empty spaces on a calendar. Chris looked like a mummy, wrapped in a blanket, from head to toe, motionless on the sofa. I began to feel what he must have been feeling. Is depression contagious? I wondered. Then I realized it was time . . .

They met, and within minutes, it seemed as if they had known each other for years—Chris and Dr. R. She exhibited the same warmth and amity I had experienced a month before. Initially apprehensive, a tension born of countless punches to the psyche, Chris let down his guard—a response as unexpected as it was sublime. Thank you, Dr. R. I remembered the dread I felt when trying to select the right counselor for Chris. I flung a dart at a dartboard, and the bull's-eye was Dr. R.

Chris talked to Dr. R, and Dr. R listened. But she did not just listen. Chris was not a client to her; he was a human being. And she hung on every word as if the narrative were a campfire tale—an empathy that encouraged him, emboldened him. He talked as I had never heard him talk before. Oh, he could filibuster about opera and comics and limburger cheese. But this was different; this was about a topic usually taboo for him—his inner turmoil. I was amazed. And, then, Dr R went a step further, a step I never would have been bold enough to traverse myself: She asked him about his girlfriend. Silence. Have you noticed that silence can be more shrill, more grating, than the harshest sound? This was that kind of silence. It seemed to last forever. And, then, Chris asked me if I would leave the office. I said, "Of course."

I returned to the lobby, and about fifteen minutes later, Chris called me back in. They did not tell me what they discussed, but Chris seemed relieved, restored. At least temporarily. I knew Chris had endured emotional turmoil in Florida, but I did not want to condemn his girlfriend simply because of my love for Chris, so I was careful about hurling accusations. I remembered something Pete Seeger, the folk icon, said his father told him: "The truth is a rabbit in a bramble patch. One can rarely put one's hand upon it. One can only circle around and point, saying, 'It's somewhere in there.'" The truth about Chris was somewhere in there, among the thick brambles of the Florida grasslands, but when I asked Dr. R, during a later visit, what Chris had told her while I was in the lobby, she maintained the highest professionalism, saying she could not divulge their discussion.

I understood. The discussion was between them—private, sacrosanct. I wanted to know, but I did not want to intrude. I could imagine what Chris told Dr. R, though, and I remembered an email Katy had sent me five months earlier. It was an email to Chris she forwarded to me. She had communicated to Chris after the two of them visited El Paso during the holidays—a visit that concerned her so much that she felt compelled to write Chris afterwards.

Hey, Chris,

I'm sorry about a lot of things, I know our relationship has not been the easiest. I am glad you came this week, and I was very sad to see you leave; mom already told you we cried the whole way back from the airport. We are both still crying about it. I know it was rough growing up with each other, and that the entire family was very tense for a good portion of the time due to different things. I regret this.

I love you very much, Chris, and I am glad to have you as my brother. I hope all of us, you, me, Mom and Dad can spend more time together. I hope you know that you can come back home whenever you feel like it, and that we would be happy to have you back. It does not seem as though you are happy in Florida. I did a lot of watching and listening this past week. I hope you will decide to come back home for a while and weigh your options, and coming back home will always be an option. I also found this, which I hope helps.

http://www.tutoringbycity.com/tutoring_jobs/ tutoring_jobs_osceola_county_fl.htm

... I am glad you liked your bento box (a take-home box of Japanese noodles) and graphic novels; hope you enjoy reading them.

Love, Katy

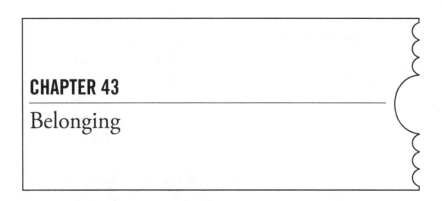

CHAPTER 43
Belonging

DECEMBER 1, 2016

I COULD NEVER get used to my solitary Thursday nights, but it was comforting to know there was a good reason for them. Chris and his friends. He had his own Thursday night dates now, and I was grateful.

His gain was my loss. No, that is not true; his gain was my gain, because when Chris was happy, the dynamics were smoother for everyone. Antonia and I had learned that lesson throughout the years. Chris craved friendship, and when he got it, he was both grateful and greedy, as if he feared the feast would disappear at any moment. I hoped it would last forever.

If it *did*, I would be stuck in my crummy little apartment Thursday after Thursday, which was OK with me. I could watch TV, although the idiot box was becoming just that, with Trump dominating all the cable news shows. Forget that.

I could have read my books, but I would get restless after two pages, wondering what Chris was doing at that moment. He was in a good place, a *safe* place, I knew that. But I wanted details. Who were his friends? What did they talk about? And why did they like him?

The last question was the most important. So why *did* they like him? I wanted to think it was because they saw beyond his quirks, his "different" behavior. They saw someone who wanted to belong—and had a *right* to belong. Did that mean they saw themselves in Chris? If so, the insight was admirable, because we all have a little bit of Chris in us—shy, awkward, uncertain about how to negotiate the easiest social pathways. The problem with some people is that there is a little bit of Chris in them; the problem with Chris was that there was a lot of Chris in him.

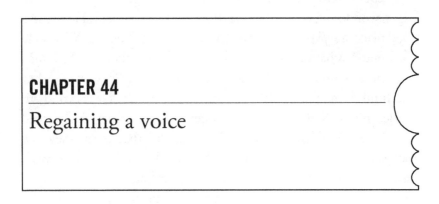

CHAPTER 44

Regaining a voice

JULY–NOVEMBER, 2012

FOLLOWING THE SESSION with Dr. R, I wondered about her private conversation with Chris. . . . His girlfriend seemed to be a constant presence in our lives, despite the thousands of miles that separated us. It could have been oppressive, even debilitating, but I maintained my optimism. I was so encouraged by the session that I fired off an email to Katy—an email that was, in retrospect, remarkably detailed. This was back when Chris, still traumatized by his experiences in Florida, suppressed his rhetorical outbursts. Dr. R, it seemed, was slowly giving him his voice back. I touched on this remarkable occurrence in an email to Katy, who was about to start working toward her MFA in creative writing at UTEP in 2013:

Hi, Katy,

I hope you are well.

I have been having a hard time lately. I assume I will for a while, but that is OK. The counselor is a wonderful person, and she will be great for Chris, I know. She told me, in his presence, that he needs to make a greater effort to converse with me. Just as I ask him questions in an effort to create a dialogue with him—questions that she acknowledged he answers with terse "yesses" or "nos"—he needs to make an effort to dialogue with ME by asking ME questions. So he actually tried when we got home after our last session. Here is what happened:

We were watching an episode of *It's Always Sunny in Philadelphia*. It guest-starred Stephen Collins, by now, like me, an old fart. So Chris and I talked about the episode.

Me: "That guy was in a great rock 'n' roll movie in the late '70s."

Chris: "Really."

Me: "Yeah."

Chris: "What was the name of it."

Me: "Between the Lines."

Chris: "What was it about?"

Me: "An alternative newspaper in Boston."

Chris: "Oh."

He goes back to his computer, so I push the conversation.

Me: "There were some great scenes in this Boston bar. The house band was Southside Johnny and the Asbury Jukes. They never made it REAL big, but they were pals of The Boss, Bruce Springsteen."

Chris: "Oh, yeah, I remember you used to talk about them."

Me: "Well, I am not sure why they never made it big. Their music was the very essence of rock 'n' roll. They poured their hearts into their instruments, and what came out of their horns and guitars and harmonicas was pure and vibrant. I get chills just thinking about them."

Chris: "Cool."

Me: "I wish I still had their stuff. Southside Johnny had one of THE great voices in rock 'n' roll. A kind of Jersey version of Ray Charles. Maybe I will Amazon their CDs."

Chris: "Cool. I would like to hear them."

And that was it. It does not seem earth-shattering, but it was a real breakthrough. I could sense that he was just "making conversation," but I still appreciated it . . . Anyway . . .

I know I get carried away, but I just wanted to let you know . . . These last few weeks have been kind of hard, and that conversation, as short as it was, felt truly liberating . . .

Take care.

Have a GREAT Fourth of July!

Love, Dad

The next step was, if not a job, at least a job prospect. Enter Dr. R—again. She suggested calling the Department of Rehabilitative Services (DARS), which, to my surprise, Chris did, a development I attributed to the persuasive powers of Dr. R. He set up an appointment, and I drove him, and within weeks he had a job.

There was one problem: It was not the kind of job that would seem to suit Chris. He would work for a local cable outfit, going door-to-door to hawk the various packages they offered. What happened next shocked—and delighted—me.

Ignited by the same inner fuel that led him to sign up for the Cadets at A&M, he excelled. Excelled so much that his bosses considered making him a manager. Overjoyed, he told me about his "bright future," flashing a smile that spanned from ear to ear.

The joy would not last. The thought of success was tantalizing, but the pressure to achieve that success, it seemed, was debilitating. He started drinking again, and the company fired him. His mood darkening, he got angry and morose, and one evening we had an argument, over what I cannot remember. I asked him to leave, and he did, sullenly walking out of the apartment without any of his belongings. Then, a few seconds later, I reconsidered my decision, rendered angrily and stupidly. I opened the door, and there he was, sad and forlorn, a Dickensian waif transplanted to San Antonio. After a brief disruption, we were housemates again.

If there had been a self-help group for liars, I would have explored the possibility of hooking up Chris. No such luck. So I turned to Alcoholics Anonymous one Saturday morning in November.

The facility was in a shabby old building in Northwest San Antonio. It is not always true, but exteriors often provide glimpses of what lies inside. This was one of those times. The inside was just as shabby as the outside. It looked like an old VFW hall—worn carpets, pitted walls, wood paneling scarred and bubbled with age.

The meeting was in a large conference room, the ceiling so low that the light bulbs threatened to singe your hair. It was packed. I sat down in one of the last folding chairs available. The testimonials began. If you had seen these men and women at a mall, you would not have thought twice. They seemed ordinary, almost boringly so. But they were afflicted by a disease as cruel as any cancer, and they combated it in the only way they knew how—through a community of similar victims, trying to gain courage through the courage of others.

Could my son feed off that courage? I intended to find out. I was not even sure if Chris was an alcoholic; I only knew that whatever drinking he did was too much, aggravating his already vulnerable condition. I also knew that a community of friends, bonded more by suffering than by a history of companionship, could help him.

Thanksgiving was approaching, and I convinced him to attend Thanksgiving dinner with me at the facility. Convinced him? Well, he did not put up a fight, but his lack of resistance belied his lack of enthusiasm. He groaned his "Young Frankenstein" groan.

They opened two conference rooms for the dinner, each one with the tables arranged in a rectangle. The food was as plentiful as the membership—trays of turkey, dressing, mashed potatoes, creamed asparagus, on and on, enough food to feed an army of alcoholics—and not a drop of liquor with which to wash it down.

I introduced him to some of the members I had met during my previous visit. They were gracious, expressing the hope that they could help him if he decided to come again. One man gave Chris his business card. A middle-aged man with wavy brown hair, he seemed to stand eyeball-to-eyeball with Chris, even though he was about three inches shorter; he kept staring at Chris, his sincerity bulwarked by years of pain he did not want anybody else to suffer.

"I think we can help you, son," he said.

We left, and Chris thanked me, just as he had thanked me after every movie night. I told him to let me know if he wanted to come back, and he said he would. He never did, and I never pressed him, mainly because I never found any more Olde English bottles in the apartment. Their absence did not mean he had stopped drinking; they just meant that I saw the lack of *incriminating* evidence as *exculpatory* evidence. It was my new frame of reference, the positive overwhelming the negative. Was this attitude naïve, even stupid? Perhaps. But I felt that Chris, after years of self-doubt and the doubt of others, deserved to have someone, *anyone*, believe in him.

Where to go from here? My belief in Chris would be tested. The ugly pattern returned—Chris sleeping on the sofa, me staying away from the apartment to escape the oppressiveness. We would go days without speaking to each other, father and son turned into strangers.

We would visit Dr. R every week, sometimes every two weeks, and no matter what burden Chris was carrying at the time, he always left her office renewed, cleansed, fortified. Did it last? Not always. But a moment of hope and joy is something to be savored.

The dynamic—happy Chris one week, melancholy Chris the next—was part of a familiar pattern, dating to his childhood. We dismissed it back then, saying, "Well, that's just Chris. He'll grow out of it." We could not dismiss it anymore, and we did not want to. The one heartening aspect to this problem was that, thanks to Dr. R, we knew the cause: Asperger's syndrome.

If Chris and I could not live together, we would have to live apart. I set him up in his own apartment, about three miles from mine, the same apartment where he would live when we launched our Thursday night dates. He was on jury duty the day his lease started, so I moved his belongings for him—clothes, books, a used bicycle I had bought him. The apartment was on the third floor; I finished just as my lungs—and knees—were about to give out. It was my birthday, sixty years old, September 2014. I went to a bar to celebrate.

The move seemed to rejuvenate both of us. He found a new job as a "stock boy"—do they still call them that?—at a hardware store. Chris would quit that job, only to find a new one, only to quit that one as well. Then he got a *new* new job, this one at a local computer repair shop, and it looked as if this one might be, if not permanent, at least long term. Chris was no computer expert, but the owner knew him, and he guided him through each assignment. You did not want to count your blessings before they arrived, not with Chris, but it was a good sign.

I found an Asperger's support group, housed in the basement of a Northwest San Antonio church. We attended a meeting one Sunday afternoon, Chris and I. The room was clean, almost sterile, white tile and white linoleum everywhere. There were four long tables, joined to form a rectangle. I counted the number of people who showed up: thirty. It was a diverse group, from teen-aged to middle-aged. The only person without Asperger's was the moderator, a woman with a kind demeanor who displayed respect and empathy for everyone in the room. It was like being in a roomful of Christophers.

The moderator opened the meeting, and the visitors introduced themselves, briefly detailing the obstacles they faced as individuals on the spectrum. One teen-aged girl, so shy that she kept her head bowed, tried to speak, but her voice cracked, and her eyes welled. She bowed her head lower, her long, black hair brushing the tabletop. She tried again, but the words, ensnared in her throat, failed to come out, and her brown eyes, already welling, streamed into tears. Her parents hugged her.

"That's all right, honey," the moderator said. "Everyone here understands."

It was time for Chris to introduce himself. He was bold and confident, defiant even, his tone tinged with anger and bitterness. Chris described his social awkwardness, his inability to relate to people, but he focused on the inability of others to relate to *him*.

"I get tired of being on the outside, looking in," he said. "I try to meet everyone's standards of what I should be, but it doesn't work. And, in the meantime, nobody tries to fit *my* standards of what *they* should be. Is that fair?"

Chris kept talking and talking and. . . . It was a filibuster that nobody regarded as a filibuster. The room seemed enthralled.

"Thank you," he said, finishing his introduction.

After the support group, I started attending the weekly meetings of the Autism Society of Central Texas. I took him to some of the meetings, and when he was invited to discuss his condition, he was always articulate and engaging, so compelling that Irma Canfield, the director of the board, asked him to speak at several autism events, including ones sponsored by the Autism Society of Texas, an organization headed by Kathy A. Palomo.

People would come up to Chris afterwards, people with loved ones on the spectrum. They sought him out, craving his input and, yes, wisdom. Chris was, suddenly, an expert on something besides comics and opera and limburger cheese.

I was so impressed with his performances at these events that I called Antonia, telling her how poised Chris was, how passionate and intelligent. I told her Chris should become an advocate for people like himself, people on the spectrum. She agreed, but when I posed that possibility to Chris, he seemed interested but dismissing, as if it seemed like too wild a dream. It did not seem too wild to me.

Antonia and I kept Katy apprised of all these developments. Katy studied the autism spectrum as though it were her college major; she knew more than we did, and she started viewing past behavior through the lens of current research. They loved each other, deep down, Katy and Chris, but during their childhood, their exchanges were tense, even volatile, and whenever Chris yelled at her, she would lock herself in her room, afraid he might explode. Katy was seven years younger, but she seemed more mature, more concerned about her future, the hallmark of adult thought.

There were good times, too, bolstered by photographic evidence—a series of photos Antonia shot in the winter of 2012. Framed and hanging in the den, they show Chris and Katy at their best, strolling in the park across from our home in El Paso. It is snowing, a rare occurrence in El Paso, but their eyes sparkle with warmth, as if defying the cold temperatures. Only transplanted New Jerseyans would take a stroll through the snow in El Paso. They look like a folk duo. Katy is bareheaded; Chris is wearing a beanie, his long hair, unrestrained by his knitted helmet, cascading beyond his shoulders. Who had the longer hair, Chris or Katy? Good question.

Katy cared about Chris, and she was encouraged by the progress he seemed to be experiencing. We were *all* encouraged, but we had learned that encouragement had an evil twin—disappointment. You cannot have shattered dreams without high hopes, so we tried to temper our excitement.

Everything was happening so fast. Or, maybe, it just seems fast in retrospect, but Chris experienced more progress in months than he had in years. The progress was subtle, yes, but it was there, palpable and undeniable. Even he seemed to recognize it. I would ask him how he was doing, and instead of mumbling, "All right," he would say, "Great." *Great.* Even I never said *great.*

It was enough to warm my heart, but there was more and more and more. He found a community of friends at the Dragon's Lair, a comic book shop near his apartment. It was a place where fantasy became reality. There were "gaming rooms" off to the side— long rectangular areas filled with long rectangular tables. He and his friends would meet there on Saturday mornings, playing "war games" for hours and hours and savoring those hours and hours for days and days. They would order pizza throughout the day, and by the end of the last game, the pizza boxes would be stacked as high as Asgard, the dwelling place of the gods in Norse mythology.

Some of his friends were "heathens," Chris told me matter-of-factly one day. Heathens? What the hell were heathens? They belonged between the covers of history books or fantasy books, right? Wait a minute. Chris lived between the covers of history books and fantasy books. We would be eating at a bagel shop near the Lair, and a friend would happen by, and Chris would introduce us. The friend was, invariably, polite and articulate, with a fondness for Chris that was instantly apparent.

One morning, one of his friends walked into the bagel shop, a young man with a clipped way of talking, his sentences beginning and ending with staccato bursts. He was like Chris, obsessed with fantasy and mythology; pleasant but serious, he described the games as if they were lifelines, sessions that were both fun and therapeutic. Afterwards, I thought *that* was no heathen, and then Chris told me, "That was a heathen."

So what *is* a heathen? I asked Chris one day. I am not sure what I was expecting, but what I got was a dissertation. Go figure.

"What's a heathen?" he asked rhetorically. "Well, I suggest you look it up in a dictionary, but my definition is anyone who doesn't follow a mainstream religion. A lot of people regard them as godless, but that's not true. Historically, they believe in different deities from various pantheons. They are said to have started some

Christmas traditions, including the Christmas tree as a symbol of the season.

"In the time of the Vikings, things would grow even in the winter. They would take the tallest tree, chop it down, and haul it back to the village on a sled. Mistletoe was hung from the ceilings to ward off the evil god, Loki. And Odin, the king of the gods in Norse mythology, was seen as a Santa Claus-like figure. He could tell who was naughty and nice."

Heathens. My God, no pun intended, but what a detour Chris had taken, from his days as an altar boy in New Jersey . . . Holy fork in the road. He would even attend heathen events on Christmas, of all days. They were held at a Unitarian sanctuary, the Unitarians known to be progressive and welcoming.

Chris told me about a fellow heathen, an older woman who felt the lonely chill of her outlier status. And what made the alienation more hurtful was that it came from an unlikely source—her granddaughter, who told her she was sad because her grandma, as a heathen, would never make it to heaven. The pearly gates were locked, not by God, but by bias and misunderstanding.

In the dark but delightful claymation film, *The Adventures of Mark Twain,* one of the characters is so desperate to reach heaven that he cannot wait for death to send him on his way. He grabs a jet pack and, spurning the normal route, soars into the stratosphere. The character reaches heaven, but it is the wrong heaven—*Martian* heaven. "Where am I?" he cries out. The Martian version of St. Peter, a bizarre creature sans wings and halo, realizes the gaffe and reconfigures the coordinates, sending the space traveler to Earth heaven.

Chris told his fellow heathen this story. She smiled, and he smiled back. There is a heaven for everyone, their beaming faces told each other.

I calmed down. Viewed coldly and objectively, heathenism is just like Catholicism or Buddhism of Hinduism, a belief system, nothing more. If it seems weird, if it runs counter to your, *my,* belief system, who cares? It may also be wise and instructive to note that some philosophers, including Thomas Paine, viewed *Christianity* as a form of heathenism.

"Putting aside everything that might excite laughter by its absurdity, or detestation by its profaneness, and confining ourselves merely to an examination of the parts, it is impossible to conceive a story more derogatory to the Almighty, more inconsistent with his wisdom, more contradictory to his power than the (Bible story) is," Paine wrote in *The Age of Reason*.

The only thing that matters is whether its practitioners find value in it, whether it helps them cope, whether it makes them better human beings. It helped Chris cope. I could see that. Whether it made him a better human being, well, Chris was already a good human being, heathenism or no. Antonia liked to say that Chris was the kindest person she knew, not because of any philanthropic efforts, but because he seemed to accept his fate with such equanimity.

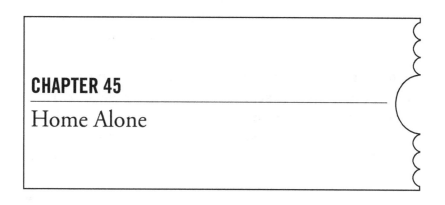

CHAPTER 45

Home Alone

DECEMBER 8, 2016

HOME ALONE. AGAIN. Another Thursday night by myself. It was getting old, this solitude, older than the movies we used to watch together. I was always a homebody, someone who could entertain himself with only two items—a book and a reading lamp. Now, both seemed inadequate. The book failed to enliven me, and the lamp failed to illuminate the book, much less the words on the page.

When I tried to read now, the words blurred on the page, forming blobs that wavered across the squiggly lines. My mind was on Chris. Always on Chris. I knew he was in a better place, but what was that place? *Where* was that place? I knew he had his hangouts, and I knew he had his friends, and I knew that no matter where he was, he was in good company, distracted from the problems that had bombarded him throughout his life.

That knowledge encouraged me, but I still missed him, missed his dissertations about comics and opera and books. I missed his passion, his oratory, as if each thought triggered another and another and another, rhetorical journeys with unexpected destinations. You never knew where Chris was leading you. I missed his enthusiasm, a holdover from his youth. Chris seemed old in so many ways, old and tired, but he seemed young in other ways, important ways, his hunger for knowledge and wisdom as vital as it had ever been. Maybe more so. He learned, and he shared what he learned, whether it was about mythology or religion or cheese. Chris was a professor without a university, and I was his most willing student.

Now, he was in another classroom, another learning lab. The truth is, he acquired as much knowledge as he dispensed. His friends taught him about sharing and trusting and taking chances. He was with them now, I was sure, on this Thursday night, helping him cope with a world which, at one time, seemed beyond his ability to handle. They formed an informal therapy group, men and women who may have been like him, afflicted with conditions that separated them, set them apart from everyone but themselves. And, so, Christopher belonged.

He *belonged.* That awareness, that knowledge that he was part of a community, tempered my loneliness on Thursday nights. I would miss him. I would always miss him. But Chris was in a better place, no matter where that place was.

CHAPTER 46

The Best and the Worst

IT WAS THE best thing I could have done, and it was the worst thing I could have done.

Communicating by email and telephone, I kept Antonia posted about our sessions with Dr. R. I tried to be calm and sober, but it was impossible to contain my enthusiasm, my joy. The details poured out of me—the conversations, the facial expressions, the body language. Dr. R *listened* to Chris, let him rant and rave, with none of the cowed or defensive postures he might have elicited from his family.

Chris felt a freedom he had never experienced before, speaking without the fear of a backlash. The result was amazing: Although he described the slights he experienced, the indignities he suffered, he recounted them without the bitterness that usually colored these recollections. It was a simple but profound change; it meant that, instead of being defined by the pain, he was trying to dissect it, *understand* it. The distinction, I thought, was important; it meant he was becoming more self-aware. He was trying to transcend his condition—a condition he did not even recognize until a few weeks before. Why did people belittle him, look down on him? He was starting to realize that his behavior was governed by a condition neither he nor the experts could understand. There was nothing inherently weird, nothing inherently unlikeable, about him. Dr. R did not just tell him that; she *showed* him that—through her compassion, understanding, and empathy. She said, during a private session with me, that Chris would expound on comic books and opera during their visits, monologues she found "entertaining." Dr. R said Chris was "charming"—the most positive assessment since Coach Leo described him as "cool."

In dozens of emails and phone calls, I told Antonia everything, and she listened with the rapt wonder of someone who cannot believe what she is hearing. "*Ay Gracias a Dios*," she would say. "Oh, thanks be to God." Maybe this is what he needed, she said. Someone who could speak to him candidly but sensitively. Someone without the baggage that weighed his family down. Someone who appreciated him without having to, without the duty or obligation a parent or sibling feels. Someone like Dr. R.

When I spoke to Antonia, I could sense the optimism in her voice, the hope and buoyancy. She cried during one phone conversation, tears of joy, because she sensed, finally, that her positivity was based on something firm, something *real*. "Chris will be all right," she would say during the various stages of his life. It was just a mantra before, words she recited to make herself feel better, to make herself *believe*. No longer. The words dissolved, but the feeling solidified, the feeling that Chris would find his way.

That was the best thing I could do—bolster the belief of a woman who wanted to believe. But it was also the worst thing I could do. I felt that an abundance of faith could be as damaging as an absence of faith, for if the faith goes unrealized, the pain is more crushing, more debilitating, within the believer. The pessimist, after all, expects the worst. Not so the optimist; when the worst happens, the optimist is blindsided. I did not want Antonia to be blindsided.

We had experienced bursts of optimism before, moments when Chris was happy. The joy was contagious. We bathed in its radiant light. If Chris was OK, we were *all* OK. We held onto those moments, hoping they would last forever. But it is easy to be positive when things are going well, when the light absorbs the darkness. The key is to maintain the positivity in the bleak times.

What is worse? To be hopeless? Or to have your hope shattered? Despite my misgivings, I could not hide my optimism. And I did not want to. It had been so long since there was anything to be positive about. Why contain my feelings? I wanted to tell Antonia how positive I felt, how energized about Chris and his future. Was I wrong to do so? If I was, I would deal with the consequences later.

"Tell Chris I love him," she said after one of our telephone conversations.

"I will . . ." I said. " . . . I think he knows, but I'll tell him."

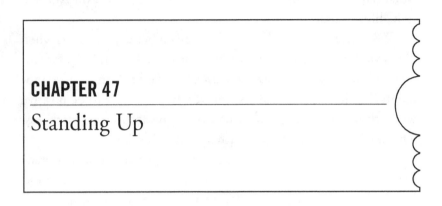

CHAPTER 47

Standing Up

FALL 2013-FALL 2015

OPTIMISM IS A fragile thing, and, the greater your positivity, the easier it is to shatter. Life taught me that dynamic, and Chris had a hand in the lessons. We would meet at the bagel shop on Saturday mornings, just a few yards from the Lair, but the proximity to the fantasy warehouse did not always lift his spirits. He would be morose, answering questions with one-word answers, and I would sit across from him, my body coiling with tension. Why, with the Lair so close, was he acting like this? I wondered.

Maybe he was tired. Maybe he was having a bad day, although the day would have just started when we met at the bagel shop. He never explained, never gave any reasons or excuses. But these moments did not last long, not as long as they used to, and I took comfort in that.

It was easy to dwell on the negative with Chris, but that was my fault as much as his. I had become the human version of the puppy who cowers whenever its owner raises his leg, as if ready to kick the poor dog in the ribs. Calm down, Robert.

One of the best things in the world, I think, is faith; unfortunately, it is also one of the hardest things to achieve. George Bailey, the protagonist of *It's a Wonderful Life*, almost kills himself because he cannot grasp it, cannot hold onto the one thing that might keep him from plunging into the abyss. There were times when I lacked faith, and it pained me.

Chris deserved better; he believed in himself, that was clear. And he deserved for others to believe in him, too. Especially his father. There would be hard times ahead, times when my frustration would make me want to scream and holler. But so what? We all know people who do that to us, friends or loved ones, and they are not all on the spectrum. Chris was a human being, spectrum or no spectrum, and it was unfair to brand him because of a condition he could barely understand. He *had* a condition. What was my excuse?

Then, one day, he seemed to move on from Florida; the move he made geographically he now made emotionally. There was no epiphany, no flashpoint. It just happened, and he seemed relieved. Chris was untethered to the past, at least *part* of the past, and the separation liberated him. He started smiling more often, revealing teeth I had not seen in weeks or months. It seemed like cause for celebration, but some joy is better expressed inwardly, in the heart and soul, so Chris—and I—marked the new beginning without making a toast to it, although I did allow myself a silent, "Here's to you, Chris," whenever I saw him.

I did not expect the sessions with Dr. R to be metanoiac, life-changing, but I hoped they would be life-*defining*. I hoped they would build a foundation on which Chris could view the world—and his place in it. And I knew that Dr. R, by merely listening to him and caring about him, had given him a gift that would sustain him beyond his visits with her.

Besides, I knew, deep down, that this story was not a success story; it was a story, period, with both success and failure thrown in there, as is true with most stories. I *wanted* a success story, wanted it desperately, but I would be satisfied with a story that offered a glimmer of hope. And I saw that with Chris.

He saw Dr. R regularly, sometimes every week, and he emerged from every session with a renewed sense of spirit, his will and courage fortified by someone who understood him. He would even visit her on his own, taking a bus from one end of town to another, because he realized that one hour with Dr. R could last forever. I would tell him what a wonderful person she was, and he would smile, just smile.

It sounds like hyperbole, even in retrospect, but our sessions with Dr. R were as life-changing as a person is likely to experience. She was exceptional, and as with most exceptional individuals, her future seemed to be mapped out early in life, even if she did not realize it. She grew up in Del Rio, one of five girls whose parents were "very supportive." Her mother was a housewife, her father a civil engineer who had served in the army during World War II. Both were Republicans, and the girl grew up with the same conservative bent, although her staunch views would soften as she grew older.

As a student at Sacred Heart Academy, which she attended from first through eighth grades, Roxanna learned to live outside herself, empathizing with girls whose troubles touched her. The classmates sensed her compassion, her kindness. Troubled, sometimes desperate over problems at home and at school, they asked her for advice, and she responded with a wisdom beyond her years. She was becoming, informally, what she would one day be formally—a therapist.

Roxanna played on the basketball team at Del Rio High School, a guard who made up for her lack of height—five-foot-six—with an intensity that bordered on fury. She loved to shoot, but her real passion was passing. Maneuvering through a thicket of arms and legs to find an open teammate, she preferred passing over shooting; an open teammate was a bull's-eye she treasured more than the hoop itself.

Inspired by her ability to counsel her friends, she decided to "help" people for a living, although she did not think of herself as a *counselor* or *therapist*. Not yet. She was in the seventh grade. When she applied for her master's at Baylor about ten years later, she narrowed her focus, concentrating on marriage and family therapy. The decision would be, for her future clients, momentous; two of the beneficiaries were Chris and me.

As the months passed, Chris would see her less and less, his work impeding him from visiting her as often he used to. I was worried, at first, but he did not complain. It was as if the lessons she imparted in her office did not stay in her office; they became part of him, making him whole, allowing him to trust himself and others. He reached out to others, and they became friends, and he began to like himself as much as his friends did. The visits may have dwindled, but the influence Dr. R had on him never did, and it helped him realize that the world was a better place, a *friendlier* place, than he had ever imagined.

Just as Chris saw Dr. R less often, he saw me less often, too. Our dates became infrequent, even rare. When we *did* meet, it was usually for breakfast at the bagel shop, before his gaming sessions on Saturday mornings at the Lair. I did not care. There was a delicious irony to my plight: The loneliness I felt was symptomatic of the loneliness he *no longer* felt. He had his friends, his community, and I was grateful. I pictured him, like Thor raising his hammer to the heavens, proud and triumphant, vanquishing demons as powerful as the villains in his comic books.

My optimism, fragile though it may have been, started to grow. When I looked at Chris, I saw possibilities I had never imagined before. I saw a world that bullied him but could not destroy him. I saw a young man with courage and vision, a vision that included, I hoped, a bright future. I saw Chris.

There were times when, overcome with love and hope for Chris, I would say, "God bless you." And he, heathen through and through, would respond, "Which one?" I would think, good question. And I would answer, "Pick your favorite." And he would smile.

He would smile. There was a time, after his return from Florida, when he rarely smiled, and now, when he did, he was sheepish, almost embarrassed about doing so, as if timid about testing facial muscles that had lain dormant for so long. Was it that simple? No, nothing was ever that simple with Chris. And, yet, he was in a better place than he had been when I saw him standing in front of the airport on that summer day in 2012, skinny and isolated. I hung onto that.

Thank you, Thor. Thank you, Odin. But, most of all, thank you, Antonia. And Katy. And Dr. R. God bless you all.

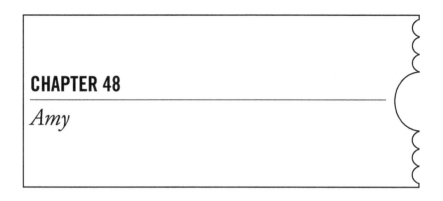

CHAPTER 48
Amy

DECEMBER 16, 2016

THICK, BLACK CLOUDS scudded across the sky, and it started to rain, softly at first, then harder. It was sure to get worse. I rushed to the theater at the Wonderland Mall.

Chris was not with me. Out with friends. Again. I reached the box office at The Bijou, sighing. Well, I thought, at least I would not have to loiter in the lobby, which was both a blessing and a curse—a blessing because I would not have to wait for Chris, a curse because I would not have to wait for Chris. There would be no Chris to wait for.

Disappointed at first, I was glad Chris had another commitment, glad he had found a community of like-minded individuals, bonded by their love of fantasy and romance and make-believe war. Then, too, I had not picked what I referred to as a "Christopher movie"—warm and inspiring, something that would lift his spirits. No, this was an anti-Christopher movie,

Amy, a documentary about the great jazz singer who died of alcohol poisoning in 2011.

I brought my book with me, although I had no intention of reading it in the food court. I was about 610 pages into the 627-page novel, and I just wanted it with me, as though its wit and wisdom could enter my flesh, my bones, my soul. It was *A Prayer for Owen Meany*. The author, John Irving, was a modern-day Charles Dickens, a storyteller so compelling that you finished the book faster than you could say, "The End."

A Prayer for Owen Meany was no different. It tackled faith and love and morality, topics you would expect to find in the great Russian novels. But Irving approached them with a surprisingly light touch—at least, it *appeared* light—making the outrageous seem commonplace and the commonplace outrageous. We call that "life," and Irving depicted it so meticulously and lovingly that you felt all the emotions the characters felt, raw and fierce and beautiful.

And then there was *Amy*, a different animal altogether. You watched the movie, and you fell in love with Amy, not romantically but spiritually. Amy, homely yet beautiful, with wide, catlike eyes, rendered wider and more catlike by all the makeup she applied on her eyes, her cheeks, her lips, until her face looked like a mural, a lovely mural.

Amy was short, thin, and frail. But that *voice*, my God, its power belied the tiny body from which it emerged. How many women—or men—have we known who could transmit such sweetness and pain through their vocal cords? Billie Holiday? Janis Joplin? Etta James? Nina Simone? The list is short.

Amy is a collection of home videos, a scene here, a scene there, each one coalescing into a montage of searing, ugly pain—pain so intense it was hard to watch. Her father was a monster. There was no other word for it. He exploited Amy, viewing her as a paycheck, not a human being. The ogre pushed her beyond her ability to endure, and the result was inevitable: She did *not* endure. The documentary ended with her death, a crushing loss, not only because she was a transcendent artist but because she was a lovely human being.

In one tender, poignant scene, Amy sings a duet with Tony Bennett, their two voices blending into one, warm and rich and incandescent. Amy was, despite her prodigious talent, shy and insecure, and Bennett was kind and nurturing, everything her father was not. It was a beautiful, but fleeting, moment.

The movie ended, and I walked out of the theater, emotionally exhausted. The rain had stopped, but there were puddles everywhere, many of them topped with a rainbow of scum—reds, blues, and purples that emerged from the mixture of rain water and motor oil. A bird glided by, its wings spread like the outstretched arms of a child running toward a parent. Could that be Bird? I asked myself. Yes, surely it was. *Surely.* There was no Chris, but there was Bird. I smiled.

Where was Chris at this very moment? I wondered. I knew he was with his friends, but what was he *doing* with his friends? Was he engaged with them? Were they engaged with him? If he was, if *they* were, it would be lovely.

As I walked to the car, I clutched my book, *A Prayer for Owen Meany*, its warmth the perfect antidote to *Amy*. It is fashionable to be cynical and nihilistic these days—maybe it always was—but Irving resists the temptation. Irving is a believer, an author who is not afraid to declare his faith in God. (The author has said, and I understand, that he prays in "times of crisis," but times of crisis last longer for some people than for others, and a believer is a believer.) There is not a hint of sentimentality in his stance, because he knows that it does not matter what position you take, whether cynicism or optimism; what matters is the intelligence and passion with which you express that belief. *A Prayer for Owen Meany* is a testament to faith and humanity. And I needed it. Katy always said I was a pessimist. Maybe it was time, after six decades on this earth, to take a different path.

It had been a year since Chris and I saw *It's a Wonderful Life*. We had seen a lot of life on the big screen, and experienced a lot of life in the big world. They say "time flies" or time "stands still," but, really, time is a process. The old years are coated with new years, a fresh coat every twelve months, but the old years are still there, still part of you. There is no escaping that. Chris will never forget Florida, never forget the pain he suffered there and elsewhere. It will remain part of him, part of who he is, forever. But maybe, just maybe, he can live with it. Maybe he can do what Amy Winehouse could not—and what George Bailey could. Maybe he can deal with his anguish and try to transcend it. You can ask no more of a person.

Throughout his childhood, we always said Chris was going through a "phase." And we believed it. Or *wanted* to believe it. An optimist, after all, is just a realist with dreams. Like George Bailey. Maybe *this* phase, this *positive* phase, will last a lifetime. As George Eliot, the author of great novels such as *Middlemarch* and *Silas Marner*, is said to have remarked, "It's never too late to become the person you were meant to be."

AFTERWORD

EVEN WHEN THEY are not writing about themselves, writers are, by their nature, self-absorbed. I write to describe myself and those I love. . . . But I write for an invisible reader, a reader who I hope will understand but, more importantly, accept me. That is why I try to be honest about both my virtues and my flaws, although sometimes, I admit, there seem to be more of the latter. I am not a defense lawyer, so I have not tried to excuse those flaws—or justify them. I merely document them in the service of a larger story. It was, nevertheless, humbling to read the finished manuscript, a series of chapters whose impact I failed to grasp as I was writing them. It is a portrait of a man I barely recognize, a man I wish were better than he was. . . . They were not new to me, these accounts, these descriptions. I had lived them, experienced them, after all. But seeing them on my computer screen made them fresh, even shocking, and so I wondered, Who is this man?

But this book is not about me alone. It is about a family. If the other members of that family come off better than me, I am glad—it is what I intended. . . . My only response is that, sometimes, self-awareness comes with time and distance.

I started to write this manuscript five years ago, and I wanted the words I wrote to be true and pure and solid. I think they were . . . Back then . . . Now, more than five years later, I am not so sure. Years pass, and our notions of reality pass with them. Actions and incidents are just that, actions and incidents. They are nothing without our interpretations of those acts and incidents . . .

And, so, what I have written—and what you have just read—is subject, in real life, to change and revision. A book is supposed to be tidy and orderly, a collection of words with a purpose, an agenda, leading to a unified theme . . . But, no, either my skill as a writer has failed me . . . or life has failed me . . . Either way, I sometimes feel undone . . .

I hoped the final chapter of this book would be both definitive and illuminating. It was neither, not for me. I realized it before, but the last five years pressed the point: The story, subject to events I cannot control, will have a life beyond this book.

Life sucks, as Chris often said, and the ending of this book, which I once thought was hopeful and optimistic, sucks also. . . . More than five years after I finished writing the manuscript of what I hoped to be a bright, hopeful book, the hope and brightness have disappeared. They have been replaced by those twin evils—darkness and despair. Hyperbole? Yes. For sure. But only because what you feel in your heart seems worse—infinitely worse—when you put it into words . . .

And so, yes, without going into any rich detail—I am weary of observing and describing—the optimism I felt at the end of chapter forty-eight was misplaced. . . . And yet if I had the courage—and endurance—to go on, I might write a chapter forty-nine, and I might summon the optimism I did during the original writing of the manuscript.

But I do not have that courage or endurance. What I do have is hope. Why? After almost forty years of sorrow, there is little reason for me—or my family—to entertain the thinnest shred of faith. But I do . . . We do.

Chris is thirty-eight now. I hope I live long enough to see him into old age—or even middle age. The chances of that are dim, I know. I am sixty-seven now, and I am sure I am starting to outlive my "sell by" date. Still . . . it would be the thrill of my life if I made it that far. Chris has struggled since our Thursday nights together. Struggled mightily, as I knew he would. You do not conquer a lifetime of pain because you saw a few crummy movies—well, OK, a few great movies—with your father.

No, my desire to see him through middle age is not because of our weekly dates . . . It is . . . how do I put this . . .? It is because of what I saw during those dates. I saw a young man struggling to show the world what he was, really was, inside. He was a man of uncommon intelligence and sensitivity, and it was not his fault that he could not express those traits—or that the world could not recognize them. We cannot change the world, though, can we? We can only change ourselves. And by doing so, maybe then, and only then, can we start to change the world, incrementally, step by step, inch by inch.

Chris is trying. He lives in El Paso now, having moved there in 2020, after the pandemic struck. The pandemic. There were times when what was happening in the family seemed more hurtful, more catastrophic, than what was happening in the world. That is gross, even offensive, hyperbole, of course. One million Americans have died—our neighbors, our friends, our loved ones—and there is no minimizing the tragedy. But we are all narrow-minded when it comes to our families, and the parallel seemed true at the time.

He lives in an apartment by himself now. He moved to El Paso because I could not continue paying for his apartment in San Antonio. I wanted to, but I could not do it forever, and I told him so. Forever finally caught up to us.

Antonia took him in, and when I retired a year later, she helped me financially, keeping me afloat after all those years of paying for his apartment. It was an act of kindness for which I will always be grateful. But I am grateful for more than that. Much more. As kind as she has been to me, she has been that much kinder to our son. Chris has presented the same challenges he has always presented, and she has faced every one with the same grace, dignity, and intelligence she always has. And it has been a 24-7 enterprise, not a Thursday night gig.

Chris lived with his mother for about a year before gaining government assistance to find his own place. We have experienced rough moments, holidays that turned dour and oppressive quicker than you could say Bah-humbug. But Chris was no Scrooge. If he could not generate the cheer appropriate to the Christmas season, it was not out of malevolence or misanthropy. He was just lost in large social settings, and when family and friends gathered at the dinner table, he negotiated the uncertainty with the wavering steps of a toddler, stumbling when everyone else was standing, fuming when everyone else was smiling.

There were times when he stayed in bed, alone with his thoughts, for hours. Did those thoughts assault him, keep him moored to the mattress? A counselor might know, but we are not counselors. We are parents, the loneliest creatures in the world. We have questions, tons of them, but no answers. And, yet, we know this: Love and concern do not offer solutions. All they do is keep us going. Maybe that is enough.

Antonia is patient, always living by his timeline. If he is upset, she waits till the anger passes. If he stops talking to her, she waits till he regains his voice. If . . . Well, no matter what turbulence arises, she handles it. And, when we discuss these incidents later, she shrugs—not a dismissive shrug, but a shrug that reflects the strength and fortitude good people display when tackling big challenges. She is the mother he deserves, the mother a boy like him needs. Boy? He is an adult now, thirty-eight going on twelve,

fourteen, sixteen. . . . He is getting there, his emotional age gradually reaching his chronological age.

I wonder where she gets the poise, the equanimity, to keep going. She has had her own struggles, as everyone has, but that is her
story to tell. I hope she does tell it, but I will not intrude. Antonia
is a better writer than I am, and I have told her so many times. She
chose a different path, teaching others how to write. It was a selfless
decision, but perhaps, one of these days . . . In the meantime, we
have Chris . . .

He works at an industrial laundry, but he has applied for a part-
time job at the El Paso Humane Society, taking care of the animals.
It would be the ideal job for him. He loves animals. They do not
judge him, berate him, condemn him. Antonia has two dogs, Sam
and Dave, both mixed, both aging. Chris loves the animals, and
they love him. He would take the two dogs on walks every morning, outfitting them with sweaters during the winter (no one in El
Paso is used to the cold). There were no counselors around, no Dr.
Rs, but these walks were therapy sessions for him. So, yes, we are
hoping he lands the job. Our hope has always been stronger than
our doubt.

If he does land the job, we hope it will be a launching pad to a
better life than what he has experienced so far. It is hard to deter-
mine if any phase has been rougher than another—childhood, adolescence or adulthood—but we think he has made progress. The
shell is crude, unpolished, but there is a beautiful human being
inside. There are moments when another Chris emerges, the one
we would like to see more often. He is less sullen now, less petulant,
but to say that is to focus on the negative. He is not really less this
or less that; he is more: He is more cheerful, more engaging, more
willing to join conversations that might have bored him before.

We are the beneficiaries of these changes, as temporary as they
may seem, but the ultimate beneficiary will be Chris himself. As he
reaches out, he is also reaching in, to himself. He is not there, not
yet, but he is in the same area code, and that is all we can ask.

I know I could never express these feelings to Chris, not in words, anyway, but I know, deep in my marrow, that he would be able to hear them, uttered or not. There is an eloquence that goes beyond words, a meaning that kneels on the periphery of sound. We hear what is not said, feel what is not stated. I love Chris, and I love Antonia and Katy, and I want them to know that, and to know, also, that they have allies in this world, people who appreciate them, who believe, with all their might, that whatever problems they face can be as transitory as the nightly weather report.

This was a hard book to write, almost every sentence a painful reminder of what I had experienced years before. We had survived the hardships, all four of us, and now here I was, revisiting them, unearthing events that might have been better left buried. Some of the passages jolted us, and yet there was something therapeutic about them, for each misstep led to a greater understanding of Chris and his condition. There were stumbles, but we kept trudging forward, our eyes fixed on a destination that sometimes seemed unreachable. Maybe Octavio Paz was right. There is no meaning; there is only search for meaning.

Life is so complex, so compelling. But it is also boring, commonplace. Things happen slowly, and sometimes we do not see the change in front of us, the various shades and gradations that make us who we are. The changes rarely arrive in thunderous crescendos, announcing themselves with the drama and power of a Shakespearean actor. No, they come softly and gradually, but they come. Eventually. We are waiting.

ACKNOWLEDGMENTS

THANKS TO ROXANNA Ramirez, Dr. R, who, as I described in the book, is a woman of remarkable intelligence and sensitivity. She made me feel like a friend, not a client, and she did wonders for Chris.

My gratitude also goes out to Irma Canfield and Kathy Palomo, both of whom are dedicated, hardworking advocates for those on the spectrum in Central Texas.

I would like to thank Josh Brodesky, the superb and committed editor of the Editorial Page at the *San Antonio Express-News*. He has afforded me the kindness of providing me an outlet for my writing, through columns and editorials, and I appreciate it greatly. I am the rarest of writers, one who does not like to write. Yet, while I do not enjoy the process, I feel compelled to pursue it. So thank you for allowing me to keep honing my craft, which I hope was evident in the book you have just read. Thank you, also, to two members of his wonderful staff—Cary Clack and Nancy Preyor Johnson. I am also grateful to publisher Mark Medicci, who endorsed the decision to employ me as a freelance writer after I left the *Express-News* in 2018. He has assembled a tremendous Opinion and Commentary staff.

This is my second project with the TCU Press, and as with the first, the staff has been extraordinarily talented and extraordinarily kind. Dan Williams and his group of editors, designers, and proofreaders are as dedicated as they are skilled. Special thanks to Kathy Walton, a masterful editor. She is firm but sensitive, and I am grateful for the guiding hand from this consummate professional. Adept and committed, all these men and women prove how essential university presses are in the world of publishing.

I extend the heartiest thank you to my family. They lived this book, and now they have read it. This is their story, and I hope they see value in it. Few social units are as beleaguered as families, and few are as resilient or as courageous. Chris, Antonia, and Katy have exhibited both traits throughout the years, and they will continue to do so, I am sure. Thank you.

ABOUT THE AUTHOR

A NATIVE OF El Paso, Robert L. Seltzer has worked as a features, sports, and editorial writer at such papers as the *El Paso Times,* the *Houston Chronicle,* the *San Antonio Express-News,* and the *Philadelphia Inquirer.* He is also the award-winning author of *Amado Muro and Me: A Tale of Honesty and Deception.*

CPSIA information can be obtained
at www.ICGtesting.com
Printed in the USA
LVHW101247211022
730997LV00005B/13

9 780875 658247